MOZART'S EARLY OPERAS

MOZART'S EARLY OPERAS

Carolyn Gianturco

B. T. BATSFORD LTD · LONDON

ISBN 0 7134 2240 8

Typeset in 11 on 12 pt Bembo
and printed in Great Britain by
Butler & Tanner Ltd, Frome and London
for the publishers B. T. Batsford Ltd
4 Fitzhardinge Street, London WIH OAH

Contents

Acknowledgements

I FIRST PUBLISHED a study on this same general subject in Italy in 1976, and then a revised second edition in 1978. The opportunity of doing a book in English, which meant being able to reach a wider reading public, has encouraged me to do an entirely different study, hoping thereby to make the book more complete and therefore of more value to those interested both in Mozart and in eighteenth-century opera.

I should like to thank my colleagues at the University of Pisa for granting me a six-month sabbatical so that I could complete the work; I am also grateful to the Music Faculty of Göttingen University and the staff of the Göttingen University Library for their kind hospitality which allowed me to work in the peaceful atmosphere of their respective reading rooms. I must also thank in particular the staffs of Deutsche Staatsbibliothek (East Berlin), Staatsbibliothek Preussische Kulturbesitz (West Berlin), British Library (London), Santa Cecilia Library (Rome) and Windsor Castle Library (Windsor) for their willing assistance to aid my research.

To those who know him, it will come as no surprise to learn that whatever I accomplish is due to my husband's continual encouragement. Of a more specific nature was the invaluable aid I received from Mercedes Viale Ferrero who answered my question-filled letters immediately and in such useful detail; and from H. C. Robbins Landon, Giorgio Pestelli and Luigi F. Tagliavini who generously read my typescript and offered suggestions for the improvement of the book. For their professional spirit of willing co-operation, as well as their known competence, I am most sincerely grateful.

C. G.

List of Illustrations

Illustrations are reproduced by Gracious Permission of Her Majesty Queen Elizabeth II (5) and of the Institutions named below.

Foreword

THE OPERAS which Mozart wrote during the last decade of his life are among the fullest realizations of what one means by *dramma in musica*. They demonstrate most convincingly that their composer knew how to combine drama with music in such a way as to create another art medium, one which was new and unique. The text of the drama, the 'word', can often prove itself limited; music, even if less tangible than verbal expression, is able to provide the word with a stronger emotional context and thus augment and clarify its meaning. A composer of opera must understand words: he must comprehend the intellectual and psychological motives which would encourage the use of particular verbal expressions; he must know which rhythmic, harmonic and melodic means would best render specific emotional reactions; he must be capable of expressing musically the most diverse thoughts and emotions, even simultaneously when there be need. Mozart, in his late operas, was a master musician and at the same time a master dramatist.

Even if he did not write as such at the age of eleven when he composed his first work of a theatrical nature (his work was rather that of an *enfant prodige* imitating contemporary models), he did compose with considerable talent. Studying his early operas (those which precede *Idomeneo*, generally considered his first truly mature theatrical work), one has then the opportunity of observing Mozart's development from skilful imitator to accomplished composer, one who understands and makes use of the dramatic possibilities inherent in music. The boy began early in his operatic career to experiment with harmony, form, rhythm, instrumentation, and lastly with counterpoint to obtain an ever more complete musical dramatic expression. Although he treated every musical tool competently, it was only as Mozart became more skilled in employing these various elements not only as independent techniques but as components of a broader context, that one sees him in possession of all the means necessary to create *dramma in musica*.

Therefore this book, in a certain sense, is directed to those who already know the Mozart of *Nozze di Figaro*, *Così fan tutte*, *Don*

9

Giovanni. Die Zauberflöte (or those who would like to know him) and who are curious to learn what theatrical road the young boy and adolescent travelled before arriving at those masterpieces: which efforts preceded them, for what occasions were they written, in which styles were they composed, and how did these earlier works prepare the gifted youngster to become an esteemed opera composer?

Examination of the first twelve works composed by Mozart for the theatre also naturally affords one the opportunity of taking a closer look at the eighteenth-century musical theatre in general, one which was quite different from that not only of today but of the later romantic period with which most opera audiences are more familiar. Moreover, it allows a rather complete insight into the earlier period since in his first years Mozart wrote in various Italian and German genres. This means to find in these works texts not only in German, his own native language, but also in Italian and Latin; to read serious and classical plots together with comic ones; to come upon music often difficult to sing but also melodies so simple they appear almost popular or folk.

From 11 years of age, when he wrote his first operatic work, until 24, when he received the commission for *Idomeneo*, Mozart composed one and part of a second German Singspiel, a comedy in Latin, two Italian *opere buffe*, five Italian *opere serie* and an act of a sacred drama in German in the same serious style, plus incidental music for a spoken German play. These, then, were his first theatrical experiences and in them one finds the usual eighteenth-century conventions both for drama and for music; however, at the same time, there is always Mozart and his individual way of responding to tradition and of behaving within convention which generally results in something more than the arid expression of a stylized genre one might be led to expect. Mozart's early operas are, not surprisingly, a fascinating subject for study.

C.G.
Göttingen, 1981

CHAPTER ONE

Introduction

WOLFGANG AMADEUS MOZART took his first musical ideas from his father, Leopold, a Bavarian born in Augsburg who had come to Salzburg in 1737 to attend the Benedictine University, interrupting his studies probably because of financial difficulty in September 1739.[1] In 1740 he became Groom of the Chamber and musician to the Cathedral Canon and Consistory President, Johann Baptist, Prince of Thurn-Valsassina and Taxis, to whom he dedicated his first trio sonatas. Through the good offices of his employer, Leopold's music was performed in 1742 in the play *Antiquitas personata sive Historia ad Natalem Domini* put on to mark the end of the university academic year. Then in 1743 he obtained the position of fourth violinist at the court, first under Archbishop Leopold Anton von Firmian and then under his successor Sigismund von Schrattenbach in 1753, also taking up the post of Violin Master for the Chapel Choirboys the following year. In 1747 he married Anna Maria Pertl of St Gilgen, whose father's name of Wolfgang was passed on to her son born on 27 January 1756, the only surviving boy of seven children.[2]

Moving ahead in his career, first as Court Composer in 1757[3] and then as second violinist in 1758, Leopold also took charge of his children's musical education. His only daughter Nannerl, as her mother was also affectionately called, at eight-and-a-half was already a competent performer when Wolfgang, four years of age, was allowed to study the harpsichord 'seriously'. Shortly thereafter he also began to compose music but not knowing yet how to write, his father put down on paper for him his first simple efforts. In 1762, together with his sister, he was taken to perform in various cities, including the important centres of Munich and Vienna where the two young but accomplished harpsichordists enchanted the aristocrats at court.[4]

At seven years of age the violin was added to the boy's musical studies, a logical step for a child whose father not only played the instrument but was so interested in the teaching of it that he had written an excellent and most popular violin study, *Versuch einer gründlichen Violinschule*, which had been published in 1756[5] just a few

months after Wolfgang's birth. In 1763, after Leopold had obtained the
more favourable position of Vice-Kapellmeister at court, the whole
family left Salzburg for a concert *tournée* which was to last until
November 1766 and which included a long stay in Paris (November
1763 to April 1764)[6] and an even longer one in London (April 1764 to
July 1765).[7]

During his visit to Paris, the *Avant-Coureur* acclaimed:

> His [Leopold's] son who is seven [actually eight] is a real prodigy. He
> has all the talent and all the science of a maître de chapelle. Not only
> does he perform in a surprising manner the works of the most
> celebrated masters of Europe, but he himself composes them. He
> improvises for hours on end letting himself follow the inspiration of
> his genius; he combines the most precious ideas with a most pro-
> found knowledge of harmony.[8]

Besides appearing before the French aristocracy, Wolfgang published
his first collections of keyboard sonatas there, his opus 1 and 2 dedicated
to French gentlewomen; opus 3 came out in London and was dedicated
to Queen Charlotte in gratitude for a royal invitation.[9] In fact, while in
England Wolfgang played at court on three occasions, and Leopold
briefly related to his friend Lorenz Hagenauer in Salzburg on 28 May
1764 that: 'the King placed before him [Wolfgang] not only pieces by
Wagenseil, but by [J. C.] Bach, Abel and Handel, and he played
everything straight away at sight'.[10]

The interest manifested on the Continent in young Wolfgang not
really as a musician but rather more as an object of curiosity (that is, in
his precocious ability not only to play but to sight-read and improvise)
prevailed everywhere he went. This was certainly the aspect insisted
upon by his father and encouraged in announcements to the public
concerts that the children gave in London. A typical notice of the sort
of performance arranged for him appeared in the *Public Advertiser* of 9
May 1764. For a 'Grand Concert of Vocal and Instrumental MUSIC',
it read:

> The Vocal Parts by the Signoras Sartori, Cremonini and Signor
> Maziotti. First Violin, and a Concerto, by Sig. Giardini. Concerto
> and solo on the Violoncello, by Sig. Graziani. Concerto on the
> German Flute by Sig. Florio. Concerto on the Harpsichord by Master
> Mozart, who is a real Prodigy of Nature; he is but Seven Years of
> Age, plays any thing at first Sight, and composes amazingly well. He
> has had the Honour of exhibiting before their Majesties greatly to
> their Satisfaction. The Whole to conclude with a Full Piece.[11]

This particular performance, to be held on 17 May in John Hickford's large and charming concert room built at the back of his residence in Brewer Street, had to be postponed, once because the necessary orchestral players could not be had from the Opera House,[12] and a second time because Wolfgang was unwell. In the end the concert was given without him and, instead, his first public concert in London was held in the Great Room in Spring-Gardens (21 Dean Street, Soho) on Tuesday, 5 June. As originally intended, the programme was with his sister and others. The children caused somewhat of a sensation by playing four-hand music (probably the Sonata K. 19d), still a novelty although Johann Christian Bach had already written several, indeed perhaps playing one together with Wolfgang while the boy sat on his lap.[13]

It is also in London (where he composed his first symphonies as well),[14] that we find an early 'critic's' notice of young Wolfgang as a dramatic music composer. During summer of 1765, the nine-year-old boy played for Daines Barrington (1727-1800), an 'English lawyer and musical scientist,'[15] who wished to examine him and determine the extent of his genius. Barrington first asked Wolfgang to do some five-part score reading, which task the boy executed admirably as Barrington described in great detail in the *Philosophical Transactions* of 1780,[16] pointing out to his non-musician colleagues exactly why he should have been so surprised at a young boy being able to read several lines of music simultaneously. Wolfgang was also invited to sight-sing, this time together with his father who did not pass the test as well as his son. Now Barrington, knowing that the famous Florentine castrato Giovanni Manzuoli (1725-1782), who was singing in London at the time,[17] had taken quite a fancy to the boy and was actually giving him singing lessons,[18] and that Wolfgang admired him for his singing, proposed the following test of skill:

> I said to the boy, that I should be glad to hear an extemporary *Love Song*, such as his friend Manzoli might choose in an opera. The boy on this (who continued to sit at his harpsichord) looked back with much archness, and immediately began five or six lines of a jargon recitative proper to introduce a love song.
>
> He then played a symphony which might correspond with an air composed to the single word, *Affetto*.
>
> It had a first and second part, which, together with the symphonies, was of the length that opera songs generally last: if this extemporary composition was not amazingly capital, yet it was really above mediocrity, and shewed most extraordinary readiness of invention.
>
> Finding that he was in humour, and as it were inspired, I then desired him to compose a *Song of Rage*, such as might be proper for the opera stage.

The boy again looked back with much archness, and began five or six lines of a jargon recitative proper to precede a *Song of Anger*. This lasted, about the same time with the *Song of Love*; and in the middle of it he had worked himself up to such a pitch, that he beat his harpsichord like a person possessed, rising sometimes in his chair. The word he pitched upon for this second extemporary composition was, *Perfido*.[19]

As is evident from the *vignette*, Wolfgang was neither surprised nor confused by Barrington's request. At nine years of age he understood the expressions 'Love Song' and 'Song of Rage' and knew what elements one would need to render them; he knew by himself, because the English gentleman did not elaborate, that operatic convention dictated that each aria be preceded by a recitative which would explain, in a musical style different from that of the aria, the specific dramatic situation; Wolfgang knew by himself, too, that it would be well to have an instrumental section, a symphony in other words, introduce the aria after the recitative. All this at nine years he understood, and moreover improvised with 'most extraordinary readiness of invention'.

Behind this demonstration of talent there were certainly many evenings spent at the theatre[20] with his father-teacher, and many days with the same dedicated to the study of all sorts of musical scores. The question that of course comes to mind is: what were the operatic scores that Wolfgang studied like? What sort of opera theatre and opera music was there when Wolfgang arrived on the scene? What style of music in general appealed to his contemporaries?

In 1746 the French philosopher Noel-Antoine Pluche described the playing of the most celebrated violinist of Paris, Jean Pierre Guignon, as being *baroque*, as being designed to show off the performer's ability and to surprise his audience.[21] His accusation that Guignon's playing was not singing, effortless and natural was applied by critics to most music of the previous century and to that period's approach to composition and performance. It was not that, instead, a restrained type of music or style was now desired. Quite the contrary, as one understands from C. P. E. Bach's *Versuch über die wahre Art das Clavier zu spielen* of 1753–62. He stated there that music was an art of the emotions and must appeal to the heart; in order to perform well one must be concerned with the music and not just with one's fingers: one must 'play from the soul, not like a trained bird!'[22] Charles Burney remembered Bach playing as he preached, saying that he 'grew so animated and *possessed*, that he not only played, but looked like one inspired. His eyes were fixed, his under lip fell, and drops of effervescence distilled from his countenance.'[23]

In addition to C. P. E. Bach's affirmation of the importance of expressing feeling in music, one could also cite, among many others, Stefano Arteaga's assumption of several years later that, of course, music was 'to depict and to move the passions'.[24] But perhaps the most valuable source to quote, since it was the one closest to Wolfgang and most influential on him in his formative years, is Leopold. In his *Gründliche Violinschule* he, too, asserted that 'one must play with true feeling'.[25] In greater detail, he continued that when learning new music,

> one must search for the character, the tempo and the kind of emotion that the piece requires. ... Finally, when practising one must take pains to find and express correctly the affect which the composer wanted to have brought out.[26]

It was not sentiment that the eighteenth century was reacting to, as these examples clearly show, but rather the Baroque manner of expressing it. The novelty and great revolution in music, clarified and then codified during the course of the late sixteenth and entire seventeenth centuries, was that music could indeed express feelings. Moreover, that it *should*, that that was its main function. Zarlino's oft-quoted remarks on pleasure and delight and edification of the soul being music's purpose, were rejected by the new age that believed music, instead, to be a force for expressing passions and, by so doing, to be a force with which to change the listener's emotional state. The first fruits of the Florentine Camerata were simply the realization of ideas which had been discussed and attempted in various ways for several years. Rhetoric and what one could do with it had occupied literary men for much of the sixteenth century; now that very same verbal rhetoric was translated into musical terms. The communicative force once thought to be the exclusive domain of language was sought also in music, and the speaker's skill to persuade, to delight, to move to tears, to surprise, became the singer's art. The all-powerful poet and his understanding and competent assistant, or so the composer was first considered, joined their talents and *dramma in musica* was born.

The first years of the seventeenth century were concerned with establishing genres and forms with the *new music*, always with the aim of involving the audience emotionally in the performance. Certainly the first operas, those by Monteverdi for example, were very sincere attempts to communicate the drama in its entirety through a balance of the visual and aural arts. But as the means became more sure the goals were exaggerated. Spectacular visual effects, including not only scenery and costumes but marvellous glimpses of Hell, or of Gods moving about on clouds, or of the roaring sea, began to dominate performances. Singers also tried to capture more attention and to 'move' the audience (one feels mainly to applause) by acquiring greater vocal skills which enabled them to embellish ever more the composer's score. The

librettist, too, was caught in the trap and tried to ensnare his audience
by unusual or death-at-any-moment situations, mistaken identity,
more comic scenes, surprising endings. Of course, an opera filled with
only surprises hardly surprises; it certainly no longer conveys or arouses
sincere passions.[27]

Clearly there was need for reform and between them the librettists
Apostolo Zeno (1668–c. 1715) and Pietro Metastasio (1698–1782) managed to effect one. Their new genre as it finally evolved was an attempt
to return to the seriousness of the first operas, and they did this by
removing all comedy and by insisting that the libretti be written in
Italian poetry of an elegant nature as would befit the noble personages
of noble heart that they depicted on stage. Plots were generally derived
from classical history and, in the classical theatrical tradition, tragedy
was never seen on stage; what was more, good always triumphed in the
end. To realize musically this stylized drama, which in effect it became,
the late Baroque composer used an orchestra which consisted mainly of
strings but which soon included occasional wind instruments, accompanied by basso continuo. He alternated his style between lyrical
expressions of passion, known as arias, and more conversational, less
rhythmically-regular sections filled with repeated notes, called recitative: recitative kept the drama going by introducing new developments
into the plot, aria interrupted it as the singer paused to express his
feelings about the particular situation. At Mozart's time the *opera seria*,
as the Metastasian play was called, was three acts of regular alternation
between recitative and aria, with most of the 20 or so arias designed to
show off the singer's particular skills in an outpouring of embellishments
known as *fioriture*.

Eighteenth-century Europe was still dominated by Italian opera,
which is what has been described here. Some local national varieties
were attempted, most successfully in France where the classical tragedy
such as Lully employed was preferred and where comparable musical
stylization took hold early on, but in the main opera was an Italian
invention, and Italian composers and librettists filled requests for its
creation everywhere.

At the same time, a refusal of the *baroque* was beginning to be
evident: the too-surprising and the overly-studied was no longer universally desired. Sentiment, yes, but a refined, more elegant, less anguished sentiment was now preferred. The intent was that it should be
more real and more 'natural'. Complicated compositional techniques,
such as the contrived counterpoint of J. S. Bach, were to be eliminated
and only a single 'expressive' melody allowed to dominate. But
whereas Baroque aesthetic and musical theory determined that each
section of a piece be based on a single and definite motive, which was
the musical translation of a particular passion or 'affection', the new era

motive but the whole flow of music could
~ent, and that various sentiments could be pre-
~musical section. All was to be written in a clear
~nderstood context. As a result, one wanted not
~ a time but several complementing ones and, as
~truments gradually permitted, the orchestra be-
came a ~~~~~~~~~~~~~nsemble, it too recognized as capable of expressing sentiment.

This, in brief, was the situation into which Wolfgang was born and
the changing preferences in which he participated. Certainly he had
opportunity to hear the conservative Baroque style as well as the new
Rococo music not only in Salzburg but even more so on his travels. For
example, his long sojourn in London, from April 1764 to July 1765,
enabled him to hear much music and not just by English composers.[28]
Instrumental music of the Mannheim school was popular and often
compositions by Karl and Johann Stamitz, Richter, Cannabich, etc.
were played at public concerts.[29] One knows from Leopold[30] that
Wolfgang, at least in his performance for the King, was asked to play
keyboard music by Wagenseil, J. C. Bach, Abel and Handel. Of course,
Handel's music, especially the oratorios, continued to be popular in
England long after his death, although Wolfgang does not seem to have
been particularly interested in it until much later when Baron van
Swieten, in 1782, gave him compositions by Handel and J. S. Bach to
study.[31] Besides operatic works the Mozarts could have studied in
manuscript, there were also those performed during their stay in London. The operas they could have heard were several:[32] *Enea e Lavinia*
by Felice de Giardini, the composer known personally to the Mozarts
who had been engaged to perform in their public concert, presented on
5 May 1764 just after the family arrived in London; *Adriano in Siria* by
J. C. Bach given the next season, in January 1765, not successfully
although its arias were often nevertheless sung afterwards in concert;
Demofoonte by Mattia Vento performed on 2 March 1765; *Il Re pastore*,
a most popular Metastasian libretto which Wolfgang himself would
set, this time composed by Giardini and performed on 7 March 1765;
next was *Olimpiade* on 27 April 1765 by Thomas Arne whose success
in *Comus* and *Alfred* was not to be matched here as Burney reported: 'The common play house and ballad passages, which oc-
curred in almost every air in his opera, made the audience wonder how
they got there';[33] 'this failure by a man of real genius'[34] was followed
on 14 May by the pasticcio *Solimano* which closed the 1765 season.

However, the major influence on Wolfgang in London came
through the music and personality of Johann Christian Bach. As
Charles Terry has written: 'Mozart came to England a child, superbly
gifted, precocious, but unformed. He left it, after more than a year's

sojourn, equipped at every point in the technique of his art.
his development was due to contact with the older composer
Queen's master musician, Bach was in charge of the Mozart child
visit to court. He must have been taken by the boy if he allowed him
sit on his lap as they played the harpsichord together;[36] and certainly
Wolfgang was charmed by the older musician, as he confessed to his
father some years later on 27 August 1778 when the two met unexpectedly in Mannheim: 'You can easily imagine his [Bach's] joy and my joy
at seeing one another again. Perhaps his joy is not so sincere, but one
must admit that he is an honest man and treats people fairly. I love him
(as you may know) with all my heart, and have respect for him.'[37] At
the age of 15 Wolfgang rewrote three of Bach's *Klavier* sonatas as
concertos (K. 107); and as Leopold was to mention in a letter to his wife
of 16 December 1774, Bach's keyboard music remained in his
children's repertory.[38] However, it was also in the domain of opera
that Bach influenced Wolfgang.

Johann Christian Bach, known as the 'London Bach' but also referred
to as the 'Milan' or the 'Italian Bach', lost his father at 15 and was then
taught by his brother Carl Philipp Emanuel. In 1754 or 1756 he decided
to be on his own and left for Milan where Count Agostino Litta made
him his private music master and enabled him to study with Padre
Martini, as Wolfgang was to do himself a few years later. There he
came under the spell of the symphonies of Giovanni Battista Sammartini as well as of Neapolitan opera, and began to write similar works.
After his conversion to Catholicism, he became organist at the Milan
Cathedral. But then in 1762 he was called to London as Music Master
to Queen Sophie Charlotte, the German princess who had become wife
to George III; he also founded a successful series of public concerts in
partnership with Carl Friedrich Abel and took charge of the Royal
Opera, composing many works himself in the Italian style. Therefore,
through Bach young Wolfgang was to become acquainted with the
foremost Italian operatic style of the period and 'Bach's elegance, melodic purity, inclination to subordinate dramatic expression to sheer
beauty of phrase, were characteristics he imparted to his young disciple,
who added the qualities of his own flaming genius.'[39] Even from
Bach's supposedly unsuccessful *Adriano in Siria*, which Wolfgang could
have seen, as well as from many other operas he could have studied in
score, the young composer could have absorbed Bach's characteristics,
noting his telling alternation of *forte* and *piano*, the great rhythmic
variety of Bach's lines (in opposition to the use of a repeated motive
typical of earlier music), his new employment of the woodwinds as
participants equal to the violins in developing orchestral material, and
his tendency to use imitation, either between voices or voices and
instruments, but in an obvious and uncomplicated manner to increase

textual interest. 'Music of an elegant charm',[40] one sees in it the beginnings of Mozart's own style, 'though his genius raised his own art to a plane above it.'[41]

In addition to absorbing musical style, young Mozart had to familiarize himself with operatic genres and forms. His examiner Daines Barrington expected him to know, for example, the terms symphony, recitative, *Song of Love* and *Song of Rage* or *Anger*, which the boy did. However, these latter songs were only two of the several kinds of arias the eighteenth century recognized. One visitor to Italy, the English painter John Brown, a very knowledgeable musician, wrote home describing many aspects of Italian opera, including its various arias, and his account[42] is well worth reporting as proof of the sort of information Wolfgang was gathering on his travels and which he would soon be translating into music:

The Airs are divided, by the Italians, into certain classes; these classes are originally founded on real distinctions, drawn from the nature of the various affections of the mind; but musicians, who, like other artists, are seldom philosophers, have distinguished them by names relative to the practice of their own profession. The principal are the following:

Aria cantabile: by pre-eminence so called, as if it alone were Song: And, indeed, it is the only kind of song which gives the singer an opportunity of displaying at once, and in the highest degree, all his powers, of whatever description they be. The proper subjects for this Air are sentiments of tenderness.

Aria di portamento: a denomination expressive of the carriage (as they thus call it), of the voice. This kind of Air is chiefly composed of long notes, such as the singer can dwell on, and have, thereby, an opportunity of more effectually displaying the beauties, and calling forth the powers of his voice; for the beauty of sound itself, and of voice in particular, as being the finest of all sounds, is held, by the Italians, to be one of the chief sources of the pleasure we derive from music. The subjects proper for this Air are sentiments of dignity.

Aria di mezzo carattere: Your Lordship can be at no loss to understand this term; though I know no words in our language by which I could properly translate it. It is a species of Air, which, though expressive neither of the dignity of this last, nor of the pathos of the former, is, however, serious and pleasing.

Aria parlante: speaking Air, is that which, from the nature of its subject, admits neither of long notes in the composition, nor of many ornaments in the execution. The rapidity of the motion of this Air is proportioned to the violence of the passion which is expressed by it. This species of Air goes sometimes by the name of *aria di nota e parola*, and likewise of *aria agitata*; but these are rather sub-divisions of the species, and relate to the different degrees of violence of the passion expressed.

Aria di bravura, aria di agilità: is that which is composed *chiefly*, indeed, too often, *merely* to indulge the singer in the display of certain powers in the execution, particularly extraordinary agility or compass of voice. Though this kind of air may be sometimes introduced with some effect, and without any great violation of propriety, yet, in general, the means are here confounded with the end.

Rondo: is a term of French origin, unknown, I believe, till of late to the Italian musicians. It relates merely to a certain peculiarity in the construction of the song, in which the composer, after having properly established the subject, carries it through a variety of tones, every now and then returning to the principal strain or part, and always concluding with it.

Cavatina: is an expression which likewise relates to the form alone, meaning an Air of one part, without repetition.

These classes of arias, Brown continued, were related 'to the nature of the passions, and their effect on utterance and expression',[43] a clear seconding of seventeenth-century aesthetic musical theory; moreover he believed Italian composers were not guided by any system in observing their distinctions but when writing 'have been merely influenced by feeling'.[44] He then gave a list of possible subjects for each type of aria, citing suitable passages from Metastasio as relevant examples of the classes.[45]

Wolfgang had much to learn, obviously, but he was apparently well on his way to understanding opera if he could musically enter into Barrington's imaginary 'love' and 'rage' situation at only nine years of age and so well that he seemed 'like a person possessed'. Soon after he began to set down what he had absorbed on paper and 15 Italian arias are from this period.[46] All of these various musical experiences were to prepare him for his first major work in theatrical style, *Die Schuldigkeit des ersten Gebotes*, which he was asked to compose in collaboration with two other Salzburg composers soon after he arrived home.

Chapter One: Notes

1. For a list of documents relating to Wolfgang's parents see Otto Schneider and Anton Algatzy, *Mozart-Handbuch* (Vienna, 1962): p. 3 for his father, p. 8 for his mother; for a fuller discussion of the parents and their families see Erich Schenk, 'Mozarts Salzburger Vorfahren', *Mozart-Jahrbuch* III (Augsburg, 1929), pp. 83–93, and the same author's *Mozart and his Times* (referred to from now on as *Mozart*),

translated by Richard and Clara Winston (London, 1960), p. 1 ff. See also the series of essays edited by Ludwig Wegele on *Leopold Mozart* (Augsburg, 1969).

2. His full baptismal name was Joannes (after his paternal grandfather) Chrysostomus Wolfgangus Theophilus (or Amadeus).

3. Salzburg had no regular court composer as such. However, three especially capable instrumentalists of the orchestra were given the title and were expected to furnish music as necessary: see Schenk, *Mozart*, p. 15. Otto Jahn in his *Life of Mozart* trans. by Pauline D. Townsend (London, 1882), I, p. 9 does not speak in especially glowing terms of Leopold's music: 'But there is no originality or inventive power either in the compositions as a whole, or in isolated passages.' He is more enthusiastic when referring particularly to the sacred music which Jahn believed gave Leopold 'a right to an honourable place among contemporary composers, but to no higher rank'.

4. For notices of these early travels see Otto Erich Deutsch, *Mozart. Die Dokumente seines Lebens* (Kassel, 1961), referred to from now on as *Dokumente*, p. 16 ff.

5. Schneider and Algatzy, pp. 5-6.

6. See *Dokumente*, pp. 27-33.

7. *Ibid.*, pp. 33-47.

8. 5 March 1764: *ibid.*, pp. 30-31.

9. *Ibid.*, pp. 30, 33, 39.

10. Wilhelm A. Bauer and Otto E. Deutsch, *Mozart, Briefe und Aufzeichnungen* (Kassel, 1962-75), to be referred to from now on as *Briefe*, I, p. 151. Further on in the same letter (p. 152) Leopold recounts that Wolfgang also played through a trio by J. C. Bach. See also *Dokumente*, pp. 33, 35 and 38.

11. *Ibid.*, p. 34. Carlo Graziani was also a composer as was Felice de Giardini whose opera *Enea e Lavinia* was in the repertory of the Haymarket Theatre. The singers came from the Opera House; the flautist's full name was Pietro Grassi Florio.

12. As Stanley Sadie in 'Concert Life in Eighteenth Century England', *Proceedings of the Royal Musical Association* 85 (1958-9), p. 17 makes clear: 'All concerts were orchestral, often with one or two solo singers, and occasionally with a chorus; there was no such thing as a harpsichord recital, a chamber-music concert or a song recital'.

13. For an interesting history of music in London see Robert Elkin, *The Old Concert Rooms of London* (London, 1955), from which the above information is taken (pp. 42, 44, 48-49, 60-61). The account of Bach and Mozart playing together is related by Charles Sanford Terry in *John Christian Bach* (London, 1929), p. 80, although Terry does not specifically mention a sonata.

14. His very first, K. 16, was scored for two violin parts, viola, bass, two oboes and two horns as were six others from the same period (K. 16a, 17, 18, 19, 19a, 19b).

15. As Mrs Walter Carr describes him in *Grove's Dictionary of Music and Musicians*, 5th ed. (London, 1954), I, p. 458.

16. *Philosophical Transactions* LX (1771), pp. 54-64; repeated in Barrington's *Miscellanies of Various Subjects* (London, 1781), p. 279 ff. The whole account is given in *Dokumente*, pp. 86-91.

17. As Leopold wrote to his friend Lorenz Hagenauer in Salzburg on 8 February 1765: 'No one will make more money this winter than Manzoli [sic] and a few others'. See *Briefe*, I, p. 178.

18. Jahn, I, p. 41.

19. *Dokumente*, p. 89.

20. The Italian Opera House opened in London on 24 November 1764 and, as Jahn, idem. states, it 'had no small influence on Wolfgang's genius'.

21. Noel-Antoine Pluche, *Spectacle de la nature* VII (Paris, 1770), p. 129, quoted in Claude Palisca, *Baroque Music* (Englewood Cliffs, 1968), p. 2.

22. *Essay on the true Art of Playing Keyboard Instruments* translated by William J. Mitchell (London, 1949), p. 150.

23. Charles Burney, *The Present State of Music in Germany, The Netherlands and United Provinces* (London, 1773), referred to henceforth as *Germany*, II, p. 269.

24. Stefano [Esteban de] Arteaga, *Le Rivoluzioni del Teatro Musicale Italiano* 2nd. ed. (Venice, 1785), II, p. 19.

25. The edition of Augsburg, 1770, p. 258.

26. *Ibid.*, p. 260.

27. For a more detailed survey of pre-Mozartian opera see Michael Robinson, *Opera before Mozart* (London, 1966).

28. A. Hyatt King, 'Musik in England su Lebzeiten Mozarts', *Mozart-Jahrbuch 1953* (Salzburg, 1954), pp. 122–127 gives an overall picture of the musical scene in England.

29. *Idem.*

30. His letter of 28 May 1764, *op. cit.*

31. See Wolfgang's letter to his sister of 20 April 1782: *Briefe*, III, pp. 202–203. For a discussion of similarities between Handel and later-Mozart see Karl Gustav Fellerer, 'Mozart und Händel', *Mozart-Jahrbuch 1953, op. cit.*, pp. 47–55.

32. The following list is taken from Charles Burney, *General History of Music* ed. Frank Walker (London, 1935), to be referred to from now on as *General History*, II, pp. 867–869. In addition to these works one must add 'the opera songs and symphonies of [Giovanni Battista] Lampugnani' which Leopold later said he had 'heard so much of' when in London: see his letter to his wife of 5 January 1771 in *Briefe*, I, p. 414.

33. *General History*, II, pp. 868–869.

34. *Ibid.*, p. 869.

35. Terry, p. 80.

36. Bach even directed the Mozarts to lodgings in Cecil Court, St Martin's Lane. See Terry, p. 79.

37. *Briefe*, II, p. 458.

38. In a letter from Munich: *Briefe*, I, p. 507; see also his letter of 21 December, *ibid.*, p. 508.

39. Terry, p. 80.

40. *Idem.*

41. *Idem.*

42. John Brown, *Letters upon the Poetry and Music of the Italian Opera* (Edinburgh, 1789), pp. 35–40.

43. *Ibid.*, p. 41.

44. *Ibid.*, pp. 41–42. This would be in contradiction to German Baroque theory (but perhaps not practice) of the affections where every passion was believed to have a corresponding and exact musical translation.

45. *Ibid.*, p. 44 ff.

46. According to Leopold, some were written in London and others in the Haag: see Ludwig Ritter von Köchel, *Chronologisch-thematisches Verzeichnis sämtlicher Tonwerke*

Wolfgang Amadeus Mozarts 6th ed. (Wiesbaden, 1964) to be referred to henceforth as Köchel 6, p. 32 ff; Wolfgang also did a recitative and aria for tenor when he was back in Salzburg (Köchel 6, p. 47), the *Licenza* K. 33 i/36 mentioned in the next chapter.

CHAPTER TWO

Die Schuldigkeit des ersten Gebotes[1]

DURING LENT, when secular plays and therefore operas were not permitted, it was common in the seventeenth and eighteenth centuries to employ a similar musical style in sacred dramas and, after his return to Salzburg in November of 1766, Wolfgang was to collaborate on just such a work for the following Lenten season. He was, since his London experience, completely absorbed with the idea of composing an opera and even thought of writing one to be performed by the local Salzburg children, going so far as to draw up a list of names for the cast.[2] He had also composed an opera-style tenor recitative and aria, 'Or che il dover ... Tali e cotanti sono', in Salzburg which was used as a *post scriptum*, or, as it was more properly termed, a *Licenza*, intended to celebrate the anniversary of Archbishop von Schrattenbach's consecration on 21 December 1766. A travelling company of Italian performers had been invited to present Goldoni's comedy *Il cavaliere di spirito* at court, together with the musical intermezzo *Li tre gobbi rivali*. As custom dictated, a local poet wrote a laudatory text in honour of the Archbishop which was then tacked onto the festivities, and the Wunderkind, home not quite a month, was invited to display his internationally acclaimed talent by setting it to music.[3] His *Licenza* (K. 33i/36) obviously pleased the court since it was after this piece that he was invited, at the age of 11, to compose an entire act for the coming Lenten production, namely to write Act I of *Die Schuldigkeit des ersten Gebotes*.

The other two acts of the play were to be set to music by more mature composers: Act II was assigned to the Viennese-trained Johann Michael Haydn (1737–1806), brother of the more famous Franz Joseph, who had come to the Salzburg court in 1762 as a performer (he was an excellent violinist and organist) and as substitute Konzertmeister for the oft-travelling Leopold, and whom Leopold respected (in spite of Haydn's drinking) and admired especially for his church music, and of whom, in fact, he felt obliged to write, 'Herr Haydn is a man whose musical merits you will not deny';[4] Act III was composed by Anton Cajetan Adlgasser (1727-1777), a native of Salzburg who had studied first with Eberlin and then in Italy and whose abilities eventually obtained for him the post of court organist which allowed him to compose much sacred music, including oratorios. The libretto was the work of Ignaz Anton Weiser (1701-1785), a Salzburger acquaintance of the Mozarts.[5] Weiser was not a professional poet at all but simply a businessman and politician who enjoyed writing. He had inherited a textile concern from his father which he continued with profit;[6] and in 1749 he also went into politics, first as a member of the City Council and then, in 1772, as Mayor. However, in 1775 he lost the position in an argument with the same Archbishop who would cause so much trouble for Wolfgang, Hieronymous Colloredo, over the cost of renovating city buildings. Weiser was also the half-brother of Leopold's landlady, Frau Maria Theresia Hagenauer,[7] and grandfather of Wolfgang's later friend in Prague, Josefa Duschek.

All of these close connections between composers and librettist prove that the oratorio was a very local affair. Young Wolfgang's success abroad had been noted and accepted at home, and not just by the reigning Archbishop whose court was supporting the performance.[8] In fact, recognition at home and pride not only in the boy but in the whole family is clear from the diary kept by a Salzburg Benedictine, Father Beda Hübner, whose tone is one of admiration as he recounts what one may assume was the general opinion of Wolfgang's accomplishments:

> 29 November 1766. I cannot avoid also noting that today the world famous Herr Leopold Mozart, the local Vice-Kapellmeister, with his family, and two children, a boy of ten and a girl of 13, has arrived to the solace and joy of the whole city. It can well be that I have already elsewhere given an account of the Mozart family, especially since in the past two or three years nothing was written more often about in the newspapers than the wonderful art of the Mozart children. Both children, the boy as well as the girl, play the instrument, or harpsichord; the little girl plays more artistically and is more than equal to her little brother, but the boy plays much more cleverly, and with well-chosen ideas, and with the loveliest of touch, so that all, even excellent organists, are astounded that it be humanly possible for such a boy at six to have been such an artist, and possess an art able to surprise the whole musical world. This Mozart family has been away from Salzburg almost four whole years by now and has travelled over most parts of Europe.[9]

To this favourable judgment on his performing ability was soon to be added an appreciation for Wolfgang's skill as composer.

It cannot have been easy for the Mozart family to adjust to the routine of Salzburg life after having 'travelled over most parts of Europe'. True, it was not exactly the most refined and elegant of societies, as one realizes from the disparaging description of one local:

> The country gentlemen hunt and go to church; those next below them go to church and hunt; the next lower rank eat, drink and pray; and the lowest of all pray, drink and eat. The two latter classes conduct their love affairs in public, and the two former in private; all alike live in sensual indulgence.[10]

Several years later Wolfgang was to complain bitterly about his colleagues, too:

> One of my chief reasons for detesting Salzburg is the impossibility of associating, as an honest man, with the coarse, stupid, dissolute musicians belonging to the court; one is quite ashamed of them and it is they who bring music generally into disfavour.[11]

But in 1766, perhaps the only one qualified to criticize the society or court was Leopold, as Wolfgang and Nannerl were still too young to be aware of such niceties, and Frau Mozart was a simple woman who probably would not have noticed any lack of sophistication on the part of her neighbours.[12] Moreover, all were grateful to Archbishop von Schrattenbach for having allowed Leopold to travel and to come back to a home and job, as well as to the enlightened promise of a moderate pension which the Archbishop provided to all artists in his employ,[13] a reward not to be taken lightly in the eighteenth century. Rather than any real discontent at this point with Salzburg, the family, and certainly Wolfgang, may simply have missed the attention constantly paid to the child performers, as well as the continual excitement of new places and new people. However, as they had to return home, the prospect of Wolfgang's composing his first work of any length in the theatrical style must have given pleasure to the whole family. It also provided an excellent opportunity for him to be judged at court and for Leopold thus to prove that his extended absence on his children's behalf had been merited.

One of numerous such States still in existence in the eighteenth century, Salzburg, although situated between Austria and Bavaria, did not belong to the Empire but was under the control of the Catholic Church. Originally a Roman trading post, it was regained from the Huns but destroyed in 477, and the site was deserted until 696–700 when St Rupert of Worms founded an abbey and monastery there. Soon after, in 739, St Boniface made it a bishopric, and in the succeeding years, as the Germans expanded to the east, the city became increasingly important. In 798 it was made an archbishopric and, richly en-

dowed and favoured with valuable immunities, it continued throughout the Middle Ages to be the centre of an active ecclesiastical province.
Greater honour came in 1278 when Rudolf of Hapsburg recognised the
Archbishop of Salzburg as a Prince of the Empire who from then on
was to serve as political, as well as spiritual,· leader. His position was,
naturally, not hereditary, but otherwise gave every semblance of being
comparable to that of other European Heads of State. The capital of his
principality was also impressive: spanning both sides of the Salzach
River in a narrow valley at the foothills of the Alps, the city was
protected by the Mönchberg (Monk's Hill) on the southwest and on
the north by its fortress, the Hohensalzburg built in 1077 by Archbishop Gebhard, and the Kapuzinerberg (Capuchin Hill). The Archbishop's Palace, or Residenz, although originally built in the twelfth
century, was continually enlarged, and by Mozart's time was an impressive series of buildings arranged around three courtyards and decorated mainly in the Italian style. Apart from the Fortress, the twelfth-
century Church of St Peter, the thirteenth-century Franciscan Church,
and some Renaissance patrician houses, most of Salzburg's architecture
was Baroque and Rococo. Due to its architecture and atmosphere as
well as Salzburg's close ties with the Vatican, the province was often
called 'the German Rome'. Once financially able to support an elaborate court, during Archbishop Sigismund von Schrattenbach's rule
(1753-1771) Salzburg suffered an economic decline; but in spite of this,
his support of music continued although, due to his own conservatism
and piety, he was most favourable towards sacred music. One realizes,
then, that Wolfgang's sacred opera would have had von Schrattenbach's full attention not only because of the novelty of the youth of its
composer but due to its subject.

Die Schuldigkeit des ersten Gebotes was presented in the Rittersaal, or
Knight's Hall, of the Salzburg palace, which was the anteroom to the
state apartments and the Archbishop's residential quarters. Decorated
with scenes from the life of Alexander the Great, the Rittersaal is a
good-sized room, more wide than deep, but certainly not enormous
and not at all reminiscent of a theatre. Although Weiser included stage
directions in his libretto one wonders if, during Lent, and given the
conditions for performing the work, a complete theatrical interpretation would have been possible. Perhaps only modified staging was
attempted, such as costumed singers posed in front of a single set.
Certainly scenery in itself could not have been objected to as often
rather elaborate settings were used during Lent, as reminders of the
penitential season, even inside Roman churches. In any event, Archbishop von Schrattenbach, while severely pious and although he im-
posed stringent moral standards on his court, such as making men and
women sit apart at the university comedies,[14] was an active patron of

music and theatre and it is just possible that he considered a sacred drama edifying for the audience and so allowed more than a concert version of Weiser's play. While Father Hübner's diary is unfortunately not specific as to the sort of performance *Die Schuldigkeit des ersten Gebotes* received, it does tell us that Wolfgang's act was performed on Thursday, 12 March 1767; Hadyn's act was given the following week on 19 March; and the one by Adlgasser still another week later on 26 March.[15]

The theme of Weiser's play as given in his libretto was:

The Obligation of the First and Greatest Commandment, Mark 12, v. 30: Thou shall love the Lord thy God with all thy heart, and with all thy mind, and with all thy soul, and with all thy strength.

The various characters, together with their vocal parts and the names of the first performers, all court musicians, were the following:

DER CHRIST, An indifferent but then zealous Christian (tenor)—Joseph Meissner

DER CHRISTGEIST, The Christian Spirit (tenor)—Anton Franz Spitzeder

DER WELTGEIST, The Worldly Spirit (soprano)—Maria Anna Fesemayer

DIE GÖTTLICHE BARMHERZIGKEIT, Divine Mercy (soprano)—Maria Magdalena Lipp

DIE GÖTTLICHE GERECHTIGKEIT, Divine Justice (soprano)—Maria Anna Braunhofer[16]

The above-mentioned intimacy of the Salzburg musical environment, which also hints at its provincialism to be lamented years later by Wolfgang, may be seen even in the marriages which later took place among the musicians: Maria Anna Fesemayer was to marry Adlgasser; and Maria Magdalena Lipp, daughter of the Cathedral second organist who had been sent by the Archbishop to study singing in Italy, was to become the wife of Michael Haydn.

The libretto explained that the intent of the drama was 'not only to delight the mind but to elevate the soul' and continued, no doubt to the conservative and world-shunning Archbishop's hearty approval, that 'there is no more dangerous state for the soul than lukewarmness in the work of salvation'. It then went on to outline the plot in only somewhat more detail.

In the first part the intellect and judgment of the indifferent Christian are moved by the loving and indefatigable zeal of the Christian Spirit, with the assistance of Divine Mercy and Justice. In the second part, Divine Justice is victorious, the will is ready to fight; and finally in the third and last part is completely freed from fear and hesitation.[17]

In the act composed by Wolfgang, his part of the above summary is realized in the following manner.

In 'an open space in a garden, with a little wood', the Christian Spirit approaches Divine Mercy and Divine Justice asking if they might be able to be more clement and helpful to those men who are not aware of their obligation to obey the First Commandment. He would like that the fear of the Day of Judgment be more firmly impressed in such mortals; Justice and Mercy, while noting that they may not force anyone to be good due to man's Free Will, agree to help the Christian Spirit illuminate humanity. Next we see a sleeping Christian who, hearing an inner voice which asks him to give an account of his past, awakes. Now the Worldly Spirit appears to him and tries to quiet his fears, arguing that the pleasures of life were made by nature expressly to please man. When the Worldly Spirit departs to get food, drink and entertainment with which to convince the Christian of their goodness, the Christian Spirit, disguised as a doctor, presents himself and assures the Christian that he himself can allay all his own fears, and this by taking care of his soul and putting himself in the position of enjoying life in the serenity of virtue. The Christian decides instead to prove the way of life of the Worldly Spirit and the act concludes with a trio by the Christian Spirit, Divine Justice and Divine Mercy who all renew their vow to try and recuperate lost souls.

The play reflects the expected characteristics of the contemporary sacred drama, and Wolfgang was to treat it accordingly and set it in the style of *opera seria*. Dramatically, the work is a continuance of the academic moralizing to be found in early sacred dialogues and many seventeenth-century oratorios.[18] It is not an action-filled piece; rather it is a static intellectual discussion of the eternal good-versus-evil conflict. Each of the several characters is clearly defined as to his position in the struggle and one is confident that no surprises will upset the expected outcome of man overcoming evil. The interest in this type of play is actually not to be found in the plot itself but rather in the language conveying it, although, in this particular instance, 'the verses, richly garnished with Latin texts, have quite the prosaic bombastic character of the period'.[19] Moreover any strength or pseudo-drama can be achieved only through the composer's skill.

As was customary, Wolfgang conceived almost every aria of *Die Schuldigkeit* in a brilliant style, full of *fioriture* (example 1 from No. 6) and in the most usual form of the period, that in two sections with the first repeated, the tripartite da capo aria (only No. 2 'Ein ergrimmter Löwe brüllet' and No. 6 'Schildre einen philosophen' are in another form, the repeated binary).[20] In works intended to be in a 'grand' manner, as was

Example 1

Die Schuldigkeit, the first section of the da capo was generally quite extended, being in fact of two subdivisions itself and much longer than the middle contrasting section of the closed form. Not only does Wolfgang handle the structure competently but, in so doing, he also displays an awareness of the drama unusual for an eleven-year-old boy. One may note this in his orchestrations, which are for a variety of instruments in various combinations chosen to accord with the emotional state expressed in a single aria or accompanied recitative. For example, in No. 2, the above-mentioned 'Ein ergrimmter Löwe brüllet', Divine Mercy describes a forest with a roaring lion and a hunter; and Wolfgang was prompted to use two solo horns and give them brief motives to recall the idea of a hunt.[21] The introduction of a trombone in the accompanied recitative before No. 4 is significant in that the association of the trombone with death, the future life, Judgment – all ideas stated in the text – was traditional.[22] In the accompanied recitative before No. 3 the whole orchestra is used to give emphasis to the words of the Christian Spirit through dramatic chords, scales and rapid arpeggios while he speaks of 'das grässliche Geheul' (the horrible cry) of those who find themselves in Hell; but when the Christian Spirit changes his discourse and begins to speak intently of 'den Eifer, die Beflissenheit, die Wissenschaft des Heils' (the zeal, the devotion, the search for salvation), only the quieter strings accompany his serious words. In No. 3, 'Erwache' (Awake), to convey the tranquillity of the sleeping Christian once again only strings are used.

In these instances Wolfgang chose certain instruments for their quality and their colour and for their capability to evoke the atmosphere of a particular scene. Instrumentation had always been an essential means of communicating drama in music since certain instruments were traditionally associated with specific environments (the trumpet with royalty, drums with military life, etc.) and some were generally considered more adept than others to create desired effects. Throughout Wolfgang's operatic career, as his assurance grows, one will see his choice of instrumentation become increasingly discriminating.

It is interesting to note that the orchestra for which *Die Schuldigkeit* was written, the Salzburg court orchestra, although most competent, as Wolfgang's rather demanding score would suggest, was not especially large, being comprised merely of ten to twelve violins and violas, two to three cellos, two to three bassoons, three French horns, three oboes (two of which players doubled on flute) and one trumpet.[23] However, there were other ensembles at the court (namely a cathedral trumpet band and two other trumpet and drum bands attached to the Chamberlain's office) which were added to the official orchestra at need, and these musicians were expected to be able to play string instruments as well.[24]

Another means used by Wolfgang to emphasize text is his choosing of certain important words and underscoring them with unusual vocal or orchestral treatment. This technique of *word painting* is used from the beginning to the end of the sacred opera. For example, in the first aria for the Christian Spirit the opening text is 'Mit Jammer muss ich schauen unzählig teure Seelen in meines Feindes Klauen den Untergang erwählen' (With lament must I see innumerable dear souls choose ruin in the claws of my enemies): having the voice sustain the word 'Jammer' while the orchestra plays a chromatic but lyrical accompaniment, Wolfgang encourages one to hear the Christian Spirit 'lament'. The second section of the same aria employs dotted rhythms, quicker notes and, very importantly, a less continuous phrase structure to describe the 'ausgebrochnen Flüssen' (the overflowing rivers) of wantonness that carry away thousands of souls. In aria No. 4, 'Hat der Schöpfer dieses Leben' (The Creator has [given] this life), the Worldly Spirit urges the Christian to enjoy life and when he tells him, 'lache' (laugh), Wolfgang puts a florid embellishment on the word, different each time it occurs. Again in the accompanied recitative before No. 5, when the Christian feels 'des matten Herzen Schläge' (weak heart beats), the orchestra plays two-note phrases to represent them, perhaps the first of the innumerable 'heart beats' Wolfgang will describe in his operatic career.

The most salient example of word painting in the sacred opera is in aria No. 5 for the Christian where a particular harmonic passage takes on extra-musical meaning. The text says that fear has entered the heart of the Christian because a voice within him has asked for an accounting of his past: for the opening text 'Jener Donnerworte Kraft' (the power of those resounding words), which refers to the voice he hears, Wolfgang puts 'Jener' on two up-beats which come to fall on the first beat of the next bar for the syllable 'Don-', where, however, he has a dissonant diminished fifth; continuing on, at the third beat the bass moves creating a perfect fourth that the voice finally resolves. But then there is another dissonance at the end of the bar (example 2). This singular

Example 2

CHRIST
(plus Violins
and Violas)
Violoncello,
Contrabass

opening of dissonances on strong beats and of delayed resolutions alerts one immediately to the uneasiness that the Christian feels at hearing the mysterious voice. (The use of the mute by the violins also contributes to the fearful and somewhat eerie atmosphere of the scene.)

Another example of dissonance used for drama is in the same number on the words 'in die Seele dringen', which serves again to underline the sense of the words, in this case 'penetrating the soul' (example 3). The whole aria is full of sevenths and other dissonants which have complicated or retarded resolutions. It is through such independent treatment of the single lines that one is made aware of Wolfgang's already developed melodic and harmonic sense. Even in the second section of the same aria which deals with the echo of the 'Donnerworte' and with its frightening suggestions of what the Day of Judgment will

Example 3

be like ('Ja mit ihrem Widerhall hört mein banges Ohr erklingen annoch den Posaunenschall', Yes, in their echo my anxious ear already hears the last trombone), there are many dissonances.

True, word painting does not delineate a general atmosphere but, by expressing isolated words or particular sensations, it at least underlines dramatic moments; when these moments coincide with the principal emotions of a Number or scene, one is presented with a suggestive indication of the plot. The practice of 'colouring' words was begun in the Renaissance and was used throughout the whole Baroque and Classical periods preceding Mozart, therefore it was not a technique at all unique to him. Regarding its use in these early operas, it is interesting, however, to observe both Wolfgang's familiarity with the convention and the development of his ability to express an isolated idea; one also sees him eventually expanding the isolated depiction to include an even larger dramatic context.

As far as musical texture is concerned, Wolfgang uses a bit of imitation but not actual counterpoint in *Die Schuldigkeit*. His use of sequence, on the other hand, is never banal but always demonstrates a variety of harmony and structure. His noteworthy sense of harmony is revealed more in some single unexpected chord progressions rather than in any larger harmonic plan. For example, the structural outline of the da capo form is generally characterized by the simple and usual tonic-dominant relationship. Wolfgang's awakened sense of organization with regard to form is, instead, occasionally evident, as when he balances a series of da capo arias with an ABAB form towards the beginning and the end of the opera (No. 2 and No. 6), and when he gives to one of the da capo arias an internal ABA structure for the second section (No. 3).

Throughout the whole act Wolfgang's ever-surprising facile melodic writing, a characteristic of all these early works, is clearly evident.

In effect his first composition in theatrical style tried to please the singers by furnishing them with exhibition pieces; but it also shows a certain carefulness on his part in following the plot in order to underline the emotions of the drama. Wolfgang does not attempt consistent characterizations of the protagonists but he does at least express ably what they say at given moments. At 11 he adhered to the conventions of eighteenth-century *opera seria* and given this premise writes well; he does not initiate a new style in *Die Schuldigkeit des ersten Gebotes* but rather writes a competent imitation of an already existing one.

Wolfgang's autograph suggests, moreover, that he did so without difficulty as, even in this early effort, crossings-out are rare and the vocal and orchestral parts seem to have flowed from his pen (sometimes with too much ink!) effortlessly. Occasionally Leopold added a dynamic mark or made an indication clearer but otherwise the boy seems to have needed no help. Certainly the sacred drama was a success since it was repeated, this time on 2 April at the Aula of the Benedictine school, the Gymnasium, which was also to be the patron of Wolfgang's next operatic effort.[25]

Chapter Two: Notes

1. All the music discussed in this study is available in the printed edition of *W. A. Mozarts Werke. Kritisch durchgesehene Gesammtausgabe*. 24 Serien (Leipzig, 1876–1907): Serie V, 'Opern'; and almost always also in that of *W. A. Mozart, Neue Ausgabe sämtlicher Werke* (Kassel, 1955 ff). They will be referred to as *WAM* and *NMA* respectively. *Die Schuldigkeit des estern Gebotes* is to be found in both *WAM*, Serie V, 1, and *NMA*, Serie I, 4, bd. 1 with the modernized title *Gebots*.

   The Köchel numbers used throughout are those of Köchel 6, *op. cit.*, and are indicated simply with the letter 'K'. If these are different from those originally assigned by Köchel in his first edition of 1862, the earlier number is given after the currently assigned one. *Die Schuldigkeit* is listed as K. 35.

2. See Jahn, I, p. 49. Companies of child performers were not unusual and Salzburg was visited by one such group just after the Mozarts returned home (see Alfred Loewenberg, '*Bastian and Bastienne* once more', *Music & Letters* 25 (1944), p. 177 ff). They may have given Wolfgang the idea of composing a work for children.

3. Köchel 6, p. 47, and *Dokumente*, p. 67, according to the Salzburg *Hofdiarien*. In this same period Wolfgang also completed an Offertory for the feast of Saint Benedict for the Benedictine monastery at Seeon. The Mozarts had stopped there on their way back to Salzburg and learning that the monks were without something special to celebrate the occasion Wolfgang provided them with a work for four voices and instruments (K. 34): see Köchel 6, p. 49.

4. Leopold to Wolfgang in a letter of 24 September 1778 in *Briefe*, II, p. 485. Leopold in a letter to his wife of 29 December 1777 complains about both Michael Haydn and his wife, the singer Lipp, drinking too much: *Briefe*, II, p. 212. On 29 June

1778 Leopold wrote that M. Haydn was lazy: *Briefe*, II, p. 381. Whatever the family moral opinion of him, however, Wolfgang used M. Haydn's music for his own study as well as to perform at Baron van Swieten's musical gatherings: see his letter of 12 March 1783 in *Briefe*, III, p. 259.

5. The libretto, to be found in the Salzburg Studienbibliothek and quoted from in *Dokumente*, p. 68, states that the work was: 'In three parts adapted by J. A. W'. The identity of the author proved at first to be a problem but Herbert Klein in 'Unbekannte Mozartiana von 1766/67' *Mozarts Jahrbuch 1957* (Salzburg, 1958), p. 182 makes it clear that in a diary now in the Salzburg Archiv des Stifts, written by a Benedictine of the time, Beda Hübner, the author was affirmed to be Ignaz Anton Weiser. See also *Dokumente, idem*, which cites from the diary. Klein, pp. 171–172, also offers the biographical information presented here on Weiser.

6. At N. 3 of the Alten Markt which presently houses the Sparkasse.

7. According to Charles Osborne, *The Complete Operas of Mozart* (London, 1978), p. 25.

8. Legend had it that von Schrattenbach was not convinced of Wolfgang's abilities and had the boy closeted for a week, during which time he composed *Die Schuldigkeit*.

9. Hübner was in charge of his order's library in Salzburg and was also secretary to the Abbot, actually his uncle, Beda Seeauer. This passage is translated from Hübner's diary as reported in Klein, p. 175.

10. Source unclear but quoted in Jahn, I, p. 336.

11. In a letter from Paris to Leopold of 8 July 1778: *Briefe*, II, p. 395. M. Haydn and Adlgasser were not included in these criticisms.

12. Jahn, I, p. 19 characterized her as being 'far inferior to her husband in civilization'.

13. *Ibid.*, I, p. 235.

14. Schenk, *Mozart*, p. 14. The practice would have been usual at liturgical functions, however.

15. *Dokumente*, pp. 68–69, and its *Addenda und Corrigenda* (Kassel, 1978) by Joseph Heinz Eibl, to be referred to as *Addenda*, p. 11. Wolfgang's autograph for his act of *Die Schuldigkeit* (both Haydn's and Adlgasser's music is lost) is in the Royal Library, Windsor Castle. In 1841 Prince Albert bought it from J. A. André and in 1863 Queen Victoria deposited it in Windsor where C. F. Pohl came across it the following year: see Köchel 6, p. 50, and Jahn, I, p. 53. On the cover of the score, in Leopold's hand and curiously in Italian, one reads: 'ORATORIUM di Wolfgango Mozart composto nel Mese di Marzo 1766', which date would have been impossible as the family was still in the Netherlands and therefore for which one must read '1767'. On the libretto, too, his age is reduced to ten: see *Dokumente*, p. 68. Although Weiser called his drama a *geistliches Singspiel*, the term does not appear on Wolfgang's autograph; it is true, however, that initially any work in German was called a Singspiel: see Chapter XIII on the early history of the genre.

16. Köchel 6, p. 51; Jahn, I, p. 52; and *Dokumente*, pp. 68–69. In the libretto the names of Fesemayer, Braunhofer and Lipp end with '-in' as this syllable denoted feminine sex in Austrian dialect and was widely used even in printed documents of the period. As far as the characters of *Die Schuldigkeit* are concerned, both *WAM* and the Kalmus miniature score (N. 937) are incorrect (that is, they do not correspond to what is given here). As examination of Mozart's autograph proved, the tenor role of 'Christ' is omitted in the printed editions, and the soprano role of 'Der

Weltgeist' is given as though it were for a tenor. The first error is perhaps why most writers, including *Dokumente*, p. 69, believe Joseph Meissner, who sang the role of the Christian, not to have been employed in Wolfgang's act whereas he must have been. Some confusion may have arisen from the fact that the role calls for a tenor and Meissner is generally referred to as a bass; but Schenk, *Mozart*, p. 17 clarifies that Meissner had 'the high pitch of a good tenor and the low pitch of a bass without strain and with fine balance'.

17. The original German text may be read in Köchel 6, *idem* and *Dokumente*, p. 68.

18. See Howard Smither, *History of the Oratorio* (Chapel Hill, 1977) especially vol. I.

19. Jahn, I, p. 53.

20. In all the works discussed in this study, reference is made to 'Numbers' in the musical score. At the time of Mozart composers numbered each musical section which exhibited a closed form. This means that each piece (aria, duet, trio, etc.) received a 'Number'. It is important to remember that these Numbers did not correspond to the scenes since there are scenes which consist entirely of recitative and are therefore without closed forms, as there are scenes which contain more than one closed form. Moreover, each time a character entered or left the stage, and therefore the number of people on stage was altered, it was considered to be another 'scene'. As has been done here, all Numbers will be indicated by 'No.' followed by the number itself.

21. The horn was very popular in England and Wolfgang, after his visit there, often gave the instrument a prominent role. See Jahn, I, p. 40.

22. Association between the trombone and night, and consequently by extension with the world of death, is to be found often in the history of music. One of the first recorded instances is the intermedi presented to celebrate the marriage between Cosimo de Medici with Eleanora of Toledo (1539) where a singer representing La Notte (Night) sang 'Vientene, almo riposo' and was accompanied by four trombones. See Emil Vogel, *Bibliothek der gedruckten weltlichen Vokalmusik Italiens, 1500–1700* (Berlin, 1892), II, p. 382.

23. According to Hermann Abert in his revision of Jahn, *W. A. Mozart* (Leipzig, 1919–1921), I, p. 326; see also Schenk, *Mozart*, p. 15. There were two organs at the court as well.

24. Jahn, I, p. 236 and Schenk, *idem*. The violas and basses (which could have meant bassoons, too, even though not indicated) are normally scored together in the autograph.

25. *Dokumente*, p. 70.

CHAPTER THREE

Apollo et Hyacinthus[1]

BEGINNING IN the fourteenth century, the presentation of plays was an important feature of German academic life. In fact, at universities and gymnasia it was usual for the students to stage a play at the end of every academic year. They might have been tragedies, comedies, or pantomimes, either in Latin (the language necessary to all European men who wanted to be considered 'educated') or in German. In Salzburg these performances took place in a theatre adjacent to the main university aula which had been constructed in 1661 expressly for their presentation[2] and which was furnished with no less than twelve scenes.[3] It was also common for a member of the Archbishop's chapel to write music, often large choruses, for inclusion in the same programme.[4]

Not quite two months after *Die Schuldigkeit*, Wolfgang was asked to compose music for just such a school production. True he was already known to the academic community of Salzburg: in part because the city was a small one where talk of his talent and activities circulated quickly; in part because his father had violin students in the Gymnasium Choir School; and in part because he himself, in 1761 at the age of five, had taken part in the Latin school play *Sigismundus Hungariae Rex*.[5] But certainly, if he were asked so soon after *Die Schuldigkeit* to set another drama to music and this time alone, it must have been because his sacred opera had been received with approval.[6]

Salzburg University and Gymnasium were run by the Benedictines and their Professor of Syntax, a subject taught to third-year Gymnasium students, was Father Rufinus Widl.[7] A Bavarian born in Frauenwörth on the Chiemsee in 1731, Widl began his religious life in the Abbey of Seeon and then, for a year, taught in the philosophy department at Freising from whence he was called to Salzburg in 1763. At the Gymnasium he took a class of students through the various humanity courses until 1767, the year for Syntax, but then from 1768 to 1770 Widl moved to the University where he taught Philosophy. He was called back to Seeon the following year to take up the position of Abbot and died in 1798 while serving as Vicar in Obing nearby Seeon. Widl was, therefore, an educated man who would in 1769 and 1770 also publish books in his own field of philosophy. But in 1767 he wrote a five-act Latin tragedy, *Clementia Croesi*, which was selected to be the main feature in the celebrations at the close of that academic year; he had also written a Latin comedy *Apollo et Hyacinthus*, intending it to be set to music and sung between the acts of his tragedy. It was this libretto which Wolfgang next composed and which on 13 May received 'applausum plurimum'.[8] As Father Beda Hübner wrote in his diary: 'Today after the mid-day meal there was also a comedy at the University written by the Professor of Syntax R[everend] F[ather] Rufinus from Seeon: the music for that comedy was composed by that very famous eleven-year-old youth Wolfgang Mozart, son of Herr Leopold Mozart, Kapellmeister here in Salzburg.'[9]

Seeming to continue the tradition of interspersing the main play with choral music, the three acts of Widl's comedy are named 'Prologus', 'Chorus Primus' and 'Chorus Secundus'[10] and were performed in the following manner: the Prologue of Wolfgang's comedy, which includes an *Intrada* and the set pieces from No. 1 to No. 3 were performed before Act I of the tragedy; the First Chorus, which includes No. 4 through No. 6, between the second and third acts of the tragedy; and the Second Chorus, including No. 7 through No. 9 between the fourth and fifth acts. However, behind these titles one does not find single texts for chorus but rather a continuous tale to be enacted by various protagonists. In short, it was an opera.

The plot which evolved is a bit more complicated than the classical myth of Apollo and Hyacinthus as told by Pausanias in Ovid's *Metamorphoses*. In Widl's comedy, Zephyrus, the Western Wind, loves Melia, the sister of Hyacinthus. When she is to marry Apollo, who was banished by Jupiter and is now under the kind protection of Melia's father Oebalus, the angry Zephyrus kills Hyacinthus and accuses Apollo of the crime. He, in turn, overwhelms Zephyrus with just abuse at his lie and has him carried away by the winds. The truth of the crime is discovered only when Hyacinthus, dying, appears, accuses the Western Wind, and clears Apollo of any guilt. To console the grieving Melia and Oebalus, Apollo has a flower spring from the earth to honour the dead young man. All ends happily with the marriage of Apollo and Melia.[11]

Not surprisingly, the music of this opera is less interesting dramatically than that of *Die Schuldigkeit des ersten Gebotes*. This is not to say that the music as such is not worthy of our attention but that as drama it is less convincing. One can surmise that since the work was to be performed simply as an intermezzo and had such a simple and uneventful plot at that, Wolfgang was not encouraged to do Widl one better and create, through his music, a real drama. Or perhaps he had too little time, too little, that is, for an 11-year-old still new to the opera composer's trade. Probably the real reason was, however, that what was wanted from Wolfgang was not drama as such but simply pleasant music which could also show off the talents of the gifted students who were to sing in the opera, and this he did provide admirably.

In any event the music was not easy and it would seem that by the end of April the student performers were quite involved with rehearsals[12] as there are notices about classes being rearranged 'because of their coming comedy'. The student body at large was also affected by the performance when, beginning on 1 May, they could no longer have daily mass in the usual hall as it had already been transformed into the theatre and the stage prepared. All became very hectic, too, since university scenery had been loaned to a travelling company of Italians performing in Salzburg who returned everything only at the last minute and only after being threatened. Music rehearsals took place even on Sunday, 10 May; then again on 11 and 12 May. But their efforts were fruitful, as were Wolfgang's whose music 'was liked by everyone', as was stated in the Gymnasium records.[13] Whether the boy conducted is not certain although implied by the same chronicler who continued that Mozart 'gave marvellous examples of his musical art on the harpsichord' that same evening.[14]

Having said that *Apollo et Hyacinthus* does not understandably exhibit any further development in Wolfgang's acquisition of musical-dramatic skills, since it is of the same period as *Die Schuldigkeit*, there are nevertheless certain aspects of the writing which can be noted and with interest.[15] While there is a more generally standard use of instruments here than was noted in *Die Schuldigkeit*, one exception is to be found in Zephyrus' aria, 'En! duos conspicis' (So! you are looking at the two) No. 5: Mozart chose to have him accompanied by strings alone and thus have them convey the 'airy' character of the Western Wind. Another exception is in the accompanied recitative between Hyacinthus and Oebalus before No. 7 where the strings are played *con sordini* while Hyacinthus enters dying and says to his father that it was Zephyrus and not Apollo who killed him (example 1). When Oebalus' anger increases as he begins to understand what had happened, and he moves into a true 'rage aria', the mutes are removed and the strings play *Allegro* and now *staccato*. In the duet No. 8 for Melia and Oebalus, 'Natus cadit, atque Deus' (The human disappears, as well as the god), the instrumentation is treated with similar variety: the first violins use mutes to play the melody and the basses (cellos and contrabasses) accompany them *pizzicato*.[16] The writing in all these cases does not quite result in an intensification of the drama, but it does at least show that Wolfgang realized that one should do so and that he was aware of the musical means for creating contrast and for putting a theme in relief, both necessary techniques when writing for the theatre.

Example 1

_cin_the!   na_te!   vi_xit   ex_a_ni_mis ja_cet!

Again as was true in *Die Schuldigkeit*, the predominant form is that which actually retards dramatic action, the sectional da capo form, and it is employed in three solo numbers and in one duet ('Discede, crud-elis!', Go away, cruel one, No. 6). The only instance where the use of the ABA form makes dramatic sense is in No. 1, 'Numen o Latonium', where Wolfgang presents first a chorus accompanied by the entire orchestra of strings, horns and oboes; then a solo section for Oebalus accompanied by strings; and lastly a return of the first chorus. Here the organization is musically satisfying and also permits a continuity of the dramatic and emotional situation. It reminds us of Gluck's ritornello use of the chorus in *Orfeo e Euridice* (1762), not the only instance of such repetition in the history of opera but one with which Wolfgang might have been familiar. More importantly, there are four instances where Wolfgang abandons the ABA form and thus, by doing away with unnecessary repetition, facilitates the moving ahead of the story: aria No. 3 'Jam pastor Apollo' (Already Apollo the shepherd) has only an orchestral ritornello as its da capo and consequently the text follows an AB form; No. 5 cited earlier is in a simpler AA′ form; the already mentioned duet No. 8 is composed without any repetitions as is the closing trio for Melia, Apollo and Oebalus, 'Tandem post turbida' (Finally after troubles, No. 9). One may add that it is only in the ensembles that there is anything suggestive of an imitative texture, the rest of the opera adhering to the usual classical preference for a single melody with unobtrusive accompaniment.

Neither does Wolfgang in *Apollo et Hyacinthus* attempt characteriz-ation through instrumention or thematic material (outside of the ex-ample of Zephyrus cited above). Rather, he suggests the atmosphere or sentiment of the moment.[17] For example in No. 3 his music manages to create a placid pastoral atmosphere when Apollo appears as a shep-herd who cares for his flocks. In No. 4, 'Laetari' (Rejoice), Melia's delight at the prospect of marrying Apollo is immediately announced

by the spirited orchestral introduction (example 2) and then is confirmed by her long 'joyful' phrase on the first word and on 'gaudia'.
Word painting is used to communicate specific feelings also in 'Saepe
terrent Numina' (The Gods often cause terror, No. 2). Here Hyacinthus, singing about the Gods who laugh and play, colours the word
'iocantur' with a long, brilliant *fioritura* (example 3) and his phrase 'Et
amore et tremore' is accompanied by rapid rhythmic ideas in *forte-piano*
contrasts simulating the excitement of 'love and fear' (example 4).
Every time Oebalus sings 'minante' (threateningly) in No. 7, 'Ut navis
in aequore luxuriante' (As a ship in the rolling sea), a decorative phrase

Example 2

Example 3

Example 4

is used to give emphasis to the word. And when he says that anger does not cease to shake him, the strings play tremolos above a chromatically ascending bass.

These isolated examples of Wolfgang's particular interest in the drama in *Apollo et Hyacinthus* are too few to convince us that he tried to write something beyond his efforts in *Die Schuldigkeit*. Not only is there a certain lack of drama (only the duet between Melia and Apollo demonstrates real passion) but there are not even isolated pieces which are singular in this regard, with the exception of those places where he abandoned the da capo form with apparent concession to dramatic continuity.

At the same time we must take note of the performing conditions and realize that all the parts in the opera were taken by male students, some of them still unchanged sopranos and altos. It then becomes easy to conclude that their young ages, the quality of their voices, in a 'clean' execution, would easily have made the opera interesting, beautiful actually, even if not dramatic. Here is a list of the characters in *Apollo et Hyacinthus* with the names of the singers and their class standing as they appeared in the libretto; their surprising ages and voice parts have also been given:[18]

OEBALUS, King of Lacedonia. The distinguished and very learned Mr Mathius Stadler, Scholar of Moral Theology and Law (tenor, 23 years old)

MELIA, Oebalus' daughter. Felix Fuchs, Choirboy, Student of the Grammar Class (soprano, 15 years old)

HYACINTHUS, Oebalus' son. Christian Enzinger, Choirboy, Student of the Rudiments Class (soprano, 12 years old)

APOLLO, Guest of Oebalus. Johann Ernst, Choirboy (alto, 12 years old)

ZEPHYRUS, Intimate friend of Hyacinthus. Joseph Vonterthon, Student of the Syntax Class (alto, 17 years old)

FIRST HIGH PRIEST to Apollo. Joseph Bründl, Student of the Poetry Class (bass, 18 years old)

SECOND HIGH PRIEST to Apollo. Jacob Moser, Student of the Syntax Class (bass, 16 years old)

In any case the composer, being only 11 years old, was the youngest of them all.

Chapter Three: Notes

1. K. 38 in *WAM*, Serie V, 2 and *NMA*, Serie II, 5, bd. 1.

2. *Dokumente*, p. 70.

3. Jahn, I, p. 59.

4. For the pre-Mozartian history of music in Salzburg school productions, see Alfred Orel's introduction to his edition of *Apollo et Hyacinthus* in *NMA*, pp. ix-x.

5. *Dokumente*, p. 16. The text was by Jacob Anton Wimmer whose initials had suggested him at first as the author of *Die Schuldigkeit des ersten Gebotes*; music by J. Ernst Eberlin. On this earlier work see Orel, p. viii.

6. He had also composed the *Grab Musik* (K. 35a/42), a dialogue in cantata form between the Soul and an Angel. Ever widening his experiences, Wolfgang entrusted the role of the Soul to a bass, a voice part he had not included in *Die Schuldigkeit*. Meissner may well have sung it though.

7. Jahn, *idem* says that Syntax was taught to second-year students but Orel, *idem* makes it clear that the subject came after the study of *Poetae* and *Rhetores* and was therefore considered in the third year. The following information on Widl is also taken from Orel, p. ix.

8. From the Gymnasium records as cited by Orel, p. xvi; but *Dokumente*, p. 70 reads instead 'applausum publicum'.

9. Orel, *idem* and *Dokumente*, *idem*.

10. As a matter of fact, the comedy was entitled in this very way on the libretto. *Apollo et Hyacinthus* appears only on a list of Wolfgang's works which his father had made, added there in Nannerl's hand when she was about to sell it in 1799. See Orel, p. ix.

11. In the traditional story there are homosexual implications (the love of Apollo for Hyacinthus and Zephyrus' jealousy) which Widl avoided by inventing a sister for Hyacinthus, Melia (known in classical literature only as one of Apollo's brides). The plot of Widl's *Clementia Croesi* has similarities of plot (e.g. a boy's accidental death and his father's eventual forgiveness of the crime) which made it an interesting companion piece for *Apollo*. See Orel, pp. ix-xv, for a more complete discussion of the plays.

12. The information on preparations for the first performance of *Apollo* are based on Gymnasium records presented by Orel, pp. xv-xvi.

13. *Ibid.*, p. xvi.

14. *Idem.*

15. Since there are mistakes in the Latin of the autograph score (now in the West Berlin Staatsbibliothek Preussischer Kulturbesitz), one wonders if Wolfgang knew the language well enough to enter fully into interpreting the text.

16. This duet apparently pleased Wolfgang as he used the music again for the *Andante* of his *Symphony* K. 43 composed in Olmütz and Vienna in December 1767 even keeping the key the same. See Köchel 6, p. 55, and Roland Tenschert, 'Das Duett Nr. 8 aus Mozarts *Apollo et Hyacinthus* und das Andante aus der Sinfonie K. 43. Vergleichende Studie', *Mozart-Jahrbuch 1958* (Salzburg, 1959), p. 59 ff.

17. As Jahn, I, p. 62, states: 'The young artist asserts his individuality at once whenever he has to express a single emotion, such as he can comprehend and enter into.'

18. The cast is reported in *Dokumente*, p. 71, and Orel, pp. xvi-xvii; the latter also offers the ages of the singers. The autograph score bears the indication in Wolfgang's hand (and in Latin as befitted the occasion): 'di Wolfgango Mozart, producta 13 Maij 1767'. On the last page (f. 81v) one reads 'Finis'.

CHAPTER FOUR

La finta semplice[1]

WHEN ELEANOR OF MANTUA became the third wife of Ferdinand III in 1651, she brought with her to Vienna a love for Italian opera which her husband, himself an amateur composer, encouraged.[2] Ferdinand's son Leopold I was equally interested in music, and during his reign numerous spectacles of all sorts including *feste teatrali*, masquerades and ballets were put on. What was more, in 1665 he commissioned Ludovico Ottavio Burnacini to build the Theater auf der Kortina which opened with the 1668 performance of Pietro Cesti's *Il Pomo d'Oro*, a spectacular production in which a thousand people were involved. Unfortunately the theatre was destroyed, once by the Turkish invasion of 1683 and a second time, in 1699, by fire. Court performances were then held at the Alte Favorita, Laxenburg, Schönbrunn, and the palace art gallery; but finally in 1706 Joseph I commissioned the famous Italian architect Francesco Bibiena to build a grand Opera House[3] which was inaugurated in 1708 with Giovanni Maria Bononcini's *Il Natale di Giunone festeggiato a Samo*. A continual preference for Italians may be seen not only in the court composers and librettists, such as Zeno and Metastasio, but also in the many engineers and scenographers called through the years to Vienna from Italy, among whom were the above-mentioned Francesco Bibiena, his equally famous brother Ferdinando, and his nephews,[4] as well as the Bolognese Antonio Maria Beduzzi.

Always a responsive audience, the aristocracy sometimes participated directly in the opera performances, such as when for Antonio Caldara's *Eurystheo* of 1724 the orchestra was made up entirely of members of the court. By the time of Maria Theresa (1717-1780), several independent theatres had sprung up in Vienna, and these began to favour performances of ballet, making the city one of Europe's capitals not only of opera but also of dance. In 1708 the city council also had a theatre built, the Kärntnerthor Theater, this one to Beduzzi's design. Initially it offered mainly *Volkskomödie* but, reopened in 1763 after a fire had destroyed it, it too became a centre of operatic activity and, as the Hofoperntheater, was dominated by an Italian repertory until well into the nineteenth century. The Burgtheater, although it occasionally

offered prose plays, was from 1741 to 1776 also mainly an opera
theatre. Both the Kärntnerthor and the Burgtheater were essentially
controlled by the ruling monarch.

This happy picture of Viennese musical life, however, needs some
adjusting. In 1740 at the death of Charles VI, when the Hapsburg male
line became extinct and Maria Theresa became Empress, all the theatres
closed and, although they reopened soon after, it was as though the
inner spirit of opera had somehow also waned. The court had already
shown signs of disinterest by its delay in replacing Caldara, a respected
composer of some 78 theatrical productions, when he died in 1736.
Understandably, other more serious questions took their attention,
such as the War of Spanish Succession, the Turkish Wars, and Frederick
the Great's war against Austria fought successfully in 1740-1745 to take
Silesia from her; as a result of these and other conflicts which continued
throughout Maria Theresa's reign, the large empire – comprising Austria, Hungary, Bohemia, etc., not to mention the regions of Lombardy,
Venetia, and Tuscany in Italy – was economically and politically in dire
straits.[5] On the surface Vienna still seemed an important centre for
opera, an opinion encouraged by the arrival there in 1764 of Johann
Adolf Hasse (1699-1783). The Seven Years War (1756-1763) had
caused the King of Saxony to move from Dresden and Hasse to leave
his service after more than 30 years. A German, Hasse had earned his
international reputation as a composer of Italian operas, and his accept-
ance of the position of court composer in Vienna meant not only a
nine-year continuation of his long collaboration with the court poet
Metastasio but that he would now work in close contact with the poet.

At the same time as these two giants of Baroque *opera seria* were
continuing their art, a new and opposing group was seeking to dominate
Viennese music.[6] Christoph Willibald Gluck (1714-1787), after a boy-
hood spent in his native Bohemia, was fortunate in having an
international musical education studying mainly in Milan and London.
Various operatic triumphs, usually settings of Metastasian dramas,
assured his success. Then in 1754 Gluck settled in Vienna and began
composing *opéra comiques*, a less costly type of musical theatre than the
competing *opera seria* and therefore an attractive enterprise in those
times of financial difficulty. Of great assistance to Gluck in his first
attempts at a French style was the General Director of Entertainments
in Vienna, the Genoese count Giacomo Durazzo who was part of a
group of intellectuals which favoured the illuministic movement and
talked about 'expressive truth'.[7] It was he who encouraged Gluck's
collaboration with the librettist Ranieri de' Calzabigi, a partnership
which began with the avantgarde pantomime-ballet *Don Juan ou Le
Festin de pierre* in 1761 and continued with their brilliant operatic success
Orfeo ed Euridice in 1762. Gluck and Calzabigi were in agreement in

their search for a new kind of opera: they sought a genre which would be similar to the French classical tragedy and which was more natural and simple both in plot and music than the Hasse–Metastasio prototype to which they were in opposition. A quiet war was going on in Vienna in those years as Gluck continued to offer *azioni teatrali* with their renewed emphasis on drama. Occasionally he again set a Metastasian libretto; but another Calzabigi collaboration resulted in the successful tragedy *Alceste* performed in 1767 which openly declared the aims of their reform in the preface to the libretto.[8]

Politically and musically this was the unfavourable situation into which Leopold and Wolfgang some what naively stepped on their visit to Vienna in 1768. Having heard at the end of Summer 1767 that Archduchess Maria Caroline was to marry King Ferdinand of Naples, Leopold thought that the celebrations would offer opportunities for his daughter and son to perform. As it was, there was to be either an *opera seria*, *opera buffa*, or play each day, as well as balls and fireworks,[9] and so the family set off hopefully for Vienna on 11 September.[10] Unfortunately a small-pox epidemic sent the children to bed in Olmütz; ready to travel again on 23 December, the family spent Christmas at Brünn with the brother of their Archbishop, Count Franz Anton Schrattenbach; they arrived in Vienna only on 10 January 1768.

At court Maria Theresa, widowed from Francis I in August 1765, was co-regent together with her son Joseph II and 'economy' was their motto. For example, both the Theater am Kärntnerthor and the Burgtheater were rented out and Durazzo had long been dismissed; Maria Theresa did not even go to the theatre and encouraged no great musical expenditure at court.[11] Since the Viennese aristocrats sought to emulate their rulers, many musicians were forced to seek work elsewhere. On 27 February 1772 Metastasio was to describe the situation to his friend Gioachino Pizzi in the following terms:

> But there is not the slightest hint that our sovereigns will have, or more clearly want to have, anything to do with castratos, or composers, or theatrical designers, or poets. The large theatre in the imperial palace in which operas for important people were given at the time of Charles VI has been for many years done away with and made into a salon. There is no longer any female singer or castrato in actual service, apart from some decrepit old one who, in retirement, enjoys imperial generosity as a reward for long years of service. Since she became a widow the Most August Mistress has always rigorously abstained from all spectacles, and our most prudent Cesare [Joseph II], persuaded most reasonably that his first obligation is the continuing of the mourning period, would believe it a big mistake to deplete his treasury by luxurious expenditures.[12]

The Empress was kind enough to see the Mozart children the afternoon of 19 January and greeted them with motherly affection and regret at their illness;[13] however, no commission was forthcoming.

At the same time Leopold was determined that Wolfgang should compose something for the city and had, in fact, already chosen the genre which he believed would best launch his son's career. As he affirmed in a letter to his friend Lorenz Hagenauer in Salzburg, written between 30 January and 3 February: 'Is not the reputation to have written an opera for the Viennese theatre the best way to improve one's standing not only in Germany but also in Italy?'[14] Leopold had reviewed the situation and had concluded that the genre which would have attracted the greatest audience to the theatre and created the most interest in Wolfgang was opera. Not of the Hasse–Metastasian type, though, as he explained in the same letter: 'It is not an opera seria, however, since opere serie are no longer given; and besides the people don't like them . . . there aren't singers here for opera seria.'[15] This was quite true. As Leopold had remarked earlier after a performance of La Partenza, 'The opera by Hasse is lovely, but the singers . . . are nothing special.'[16] Gluck had already had reason to complain about the decline of music in Vienna and the poor quality of the seria singers and had in fact tried to stop further performances of his Alceste because of them.[17] At the same time there were excellent buffo artists about[18] and for these reasons Leopold decided that Wolfgang should compose a comedy for Vienna. Circumstances, as always, were to decide the direction of the boy's creativity.

Even though more accustomed to the goings on of provincial Salzburg, Leopold was sufficiently aware of the affairs and intrigues of the music profession to realize that he could not, point blank, suggest such a work by his inexperienced 12-year-old son to Giuseppe Affligio, 'an unscrupulous adventurer', the 'sole manager of the entire franchise for Viennese spectacles, impresario for all German and French comedians, lord and master of all the singers in Italian opera, seria and buffa, director of the ballet, and king of the unfortunate beasts who were baited in the arena';[19] and so he took fast hold of what was only a casual remark by Joseph II and used it as his entrée into the theatre. As he explained to Hagenauer: 'But to tell the truth, it was the Emperor himself who first gave me the idea of having little Wolfgang write an opera since he twice asked the boy Wolfgang if he would have liked to compose an opera and conduct it himself. He replied, "Certainly, yes." '[20] More tellingly, Leopold went on to confess that this would have been, unfortunately, the extent of court support: 'More than this the Emperor was not able to suggest, as the opera is in Affligio's hands.'[21] Nevertheless, with this weak 'Royal Command', he managed to convince Affligio that an opera by his son would have attracted a large public, including the court led by Joseph II and Maria Theresa.

Somewhat reluctantly the impresario agreed to pay 100 ducats for the opera[22] and gave the boy a libretto originally written by Carlo Goldoni which had already been set to music by Salvatore Perillo and given in Venice in 1764. This was not known in Vienna, though, as the libretto, changed only in part, was passed off entirely as the work of Marco Coltellini,[23] an *abate* from Leghorn, who with Metastasio's encouragement, had left his work as publisher to dedicate himself to writing.[24] He had already had some success, for example with *Ifigenia in Tauride* which he had done for Traetta in 1763 and which Galuppi re-set in 1768; and he would go on to write among other fortunate works *L'infedeltà delusa*, *inter alia* set by Franz Joseph Haydn in 1773, and *Lucinda e Armidoro* for Paisiello in 1777. In 1764 he had become theatrical poet to the court[25] and it was logical that a libretto of his, at least apparently and partly so, be chosen for young Wolfgang. Coltellini's daughter, Celeste, was an excellent, and later famous, mezzosoprano and therefore the writer had enough to recommend him as a poet and man of the theatre as well as of music to have satisfied the Mozarts. Or so it seemed.

At first all went well, Wolfgang set about immediately to compose the opera, and the singers were pleased with their music[26] (Wolfgang rewrote Numbers to be sure of this).[27] A run-through was even done at the home of Baron van Swieten, the music lover who would be helpful again to Wolfgang in later years.[28] But then there was one delay after another, as Leopold wrote on 30 July:

> At first the opera was to have been put on at Easter. But the poet was the first to stop the thing, since, with the pretext of having here and there certain necessary alterations to do, he continued to delay so that by Easter they had received from him only two of the corrected arias. Following this the opera was to be for Pentecost and then for the return of His Majesty from Hungary.[29]

The concerned father was quick to place the guilt for the delay on others, those who, as he saw it, were jealous of the boy, 'among whom Gluck is a dominant figure'.[30] The antagonism increased and a rumour was spread that the boy wasn't ready for such a difficult task, and that when something was composed it was actually his father's work. Leopold put a quick stop to these whispers by having Wolfgang compose an aria on the spot to a Metastasian text chosen at random. The onlookers were quieted.[31] New troubles then arose and, as Leopold wrote: 'Affligio blamed the singers for the delay of the opera and said that they would not have been able nor did they want to sing it. The singers, on the other hand, blamed Affligio and insisted that he not only had said that it would not have been put on, but that he himself told them so.'[32]

Trying to look objectively at the situation one can perhaps suggest that the professional gambler Affligio had reconsidered his decision and decided that an opera by a 12-year-old boy was not a good investment. He was already in financial difficulty at the time due to the lack of box-office success from a French company he had brought to Vienna[33] and he probably did not want to risk another failure. Certainly Wolfgang's lack of experience did not inspire confidence no matter how potentially gifted he was. Actually, while he had many instrumental works to his credit, his vocal compositions to date were very few. In fact the only opportunities he had had of composing for voices with any real musical continuity were *Die Schuldigkeit* and *Apollo*, neither preparatory for the *opera buffa* style. Perhaps there was professional envy and intrigue that upset Leopold's plans, too, although more than likely the generally easy-going Gluck did not actively campaign against the boy; he was probably indifferent to the unknown youngster which, however, in itself might have been sufficiently damaging in the uncertain circumstances.

In any event father and son were made to understand that it would have been better for Wolfgang's reputation if his opera were not put on in Vienna where only an unfriendly claque would have greeted the music. Disappointed, the Mozarts left Vienna but not before Leopold wrote a long letter to Joseph II on 21 September 1768[34] explaining the sequence of events, step by step in great detail, including what Affligio and others had said and the nasty final threat of the impresario that if Leopold really 'wanted to prostitute the boy, he would let the opera be laughed and hissed at'.[35] The letter ended with the complaint, clearly intended at getting an excuse if not a commission but which the Emperor never took to heart, that 'everyone will agree that it was intended only to repress and make unfortunate in the capital of his German native land an innocent creature to whom God gave an extraordinary talent, and at which other nations have marvelled and cheered'.[36] In the end Wolfgang had a few empty words from Joseph II but *La finta semplice*, a 558-page[37] *opera buffa* in three acts written for Vienna, was performed instead on an improvised stage in the Archbishop's Palace in Salzburg on 1 May 1769.[38]

Throughout this whole sad affair, one wonders why Leopold insisted so much: once Wolfgang had completed the score, why did they wait six months to leave? When the problem became evident, why didn't the father realize that they would have lost not only time but money in trying to fight such strong opposition?[39] In a certain sense he was trapped. A comedy had been chosen because Vienna was better equipped to put on this type of opera; at the same time, Salzburg was not. As Leopold wrote of *La finta semplice*: 'But, as it is an opera buffa, and what is more an opera that calls for certain types of comic characters, I must save our reputation here, cost what it will.'[40]

Certainly, the implication in his statement is that *opera buffa* was different from *opera seria*, and in this Leopold was quite correct. First of all, as has already been discussed, *opera seria* was more stylized than *opera buffa*. Its plot, based on mythology or classical history and often making use of allegory, suggested the nature of the music. It was a grand affair seen from the arias that abound in decoration, *fioriture*, intended to show off the singer rather than the character in the drama; and seen from the elaborate scenes and magnificent costumes, intended to show off the richness of the particular court or theatre. Such dramas, where each character came to the front of the stage when it was his turn to sing,[41] were in effect often nothing more than an excuse to dress up the actors and actresses and allow them to exhibit themselves in all sorts of vocal gymnastics. They were made even more complex than the already intertwined and often illogical events outlined in the libretto by the frequent introduction of arias (written either by the composer of the opera or even by someone else) which may not even have been related to the theme of the drama at all but which were simply more occasions for the singers to show off their glorious voices. The opera was 'serious' in its intent, in its musical difficulty, and in its plot which was never frivolous and always managed to let only the noblest of passions be victorious. Moreover, the whole was conveyed in florid, stylized and elegant poetry.

As a contrast to these artifices, short scenes dealing with real life and normal everyday people were often presented between the acts of the serious opera. Vocal exhibitionism was of little importance in these more domestic plots, the real aim being to act. Most of the characters in the stories were set types taken from the ever-popular *commedia dell'arte*: for example, the young and lovely wife married to the old, silly but rich man; her young and handsome lover; Arlecchino who helps his young master conquer the affections of the lovely wife and at the same time flirts with her pretty maid. These humorous situations, first represented as unrelated skits between one act and another of the *opera seria*, were later developed into consecutive acts of a single comedy. At this point they began to be performed apart from the *opera seria* and, presented independently, began also to grow in length and in importance. Pergolesi's *La serva padrona* of 1733 (about which more will be said in the next chapter) is an excellent example of an intermezzo separated from the serious opera with which it was first performed and which achieved international popularity on its own.

Since the situations in an *opera buffa* dealt with familiar contemporary types, and not Gods and Goddesses or Roman heroes, the public expected the actors to resemble real people: they were asked not only to sing but to act convincingly. Writing for such actor-singers, the composer tended to eliminate the florid phrases, the trills, the long-sustained notes of the *virtuosi* of *opera seria* and substitute for them melodies which were simpler and which allowed the text to be understood. Moreover, if a scene required that two or more people be on stage together, the composer of comic opera would not hesitate to have them sing together, whereas in a serious opera solo arias were preferred. And to keep the action going towards the climax of each act, the musical Numbers were often connected in continuous scenes (finales), instead of permitting an aria, necessarily a reflective interruption, to halt the drama. The first real finales were probably composed by Nicola Logroscino and Nicola Piccinni whose *Buona Figliola* (heard by the Mozarts in Vienna)[42] was so enormously well received in Rome in 1761 that the date usually serves to indicate the establishment of *opera buffa* as a distinct genre.

One can understand then why Leopold Mozart was reluctant to leave Vienna, a centre of *opera buffa*, to return to Salzburg, where *opera seria* was performed with greater distinction by court singers, for the first performance of Wolfgang's *La finta semplice*.

As was said, the libretto was originally the work of Goldoni, a master of comedy, and the plot shows many characteristics typical of his work. *La finta semplice*, or *The Pretended Simpleton*, is the story of two brothers: Cassandro, a good-looking man with a dominating personality, and Polidoro, not attractive and even stupid. Both ignore women, Cassandro because he is too proud ever to admit an attraction for someone and Polidoro because he is too timid. They have a sister, their ward Giacinta, a pretty and shy young girl who is in love with Fracasso, a Hungarian officer billeted in their house. Fracasso returns her affections and his servant, Simone, wants to marry her maid, Ninetta; but since the brothers would never consent, Rosina, Fracasso's sister, decides to help them by making both Cassandro and Polidoro fall in love with her. To Polidoro she appears as a woman who must be formally courted with visits and love letters; but since he doesn't know how to write, Ninetta composes the letter for him ... for a price. Rosina makes him believe that she loves him and goes so far as to teach him the proper way for a husband to behave. To Cassandro Rosina appears instead as a simple and ingenuous child (the reason for the title in short) who wants nothing more than to wear his ring. In one scene, she even manages to get Cassandro, who has been encouraged to drink by the soldiers and is now drunk, sit in a corner on the opposite side of the room (the smell of liquor makes her feel ill ...!) and to mime his sentences to her. All of this tires out the poor man since Rosina pretends not to understand his gestures and he cannot understand hers, and so he falls asleep. When he awakes he complains to Fracasso that Rosina has kept his ring. It is soon discovered on his finger (Rosina put it back while he slept) and Fracasso challenges him to a duel for having insulted his sister. Cassandro does not show much courage but at this point the duel is interrupted because it is learned that Giacinta and Ninetta have fled with all the brothers' gold and jewels. He and Polidoro offer the hands of the two women to whomever captures them, and naturally Fracasso and Simone bring back their beloveds. To end the opera happily for all (except Polidoro), Rosina agrees to marry Cassandro.

One can see here quite clearly Goldini's long collaboration with the *commedia dell'arte* companies in Venice: Cassandro and Polidoro are a separation or halving of the traditionally tyrannical but foolish Pantalone; Giacinta is his shy ward; Fracasso is the lover; Ninetta is the traditional maid Serpina; and Simone is the servant Arlecchino. Comedy results from the cleverness and intrigue of one group of characters and the silliness and stupidity of the other, with the situations and personalities made quite clear and painted in broad strokes: this is not a subtle or sophisticated comedy but rather a slapstick farce. One can imagine that the Salzburg singers, versed in the *opera seria* tradition, would probably not have had the experience necessary for the kind of recitation *La finta semplice* required and one can sympathize with Leopold's disappointment.

Wolfgang's score opens with a symphony in the Italian style, in fact his *Sinfonia* K. 45 written earlier on 16 January and now made use of in the opera. Arteaga, in his essay on Italian opera, agreed that a symphony needed to be played before an opera 'to quiet the noisy murmurings of the audience, to attract their attention, and to prepare the soul for silence and repose'. However, as many critics, he argued that its spirit should have been in keeping with the opera, that it should have had the same expressive content as the drama which was to follow.[43] Unfortunately composers generally did not heed the advice and, as noted by Algarotti: 'It [the symphony] is always composed of two allegros and a grave; as loud as can be, it is never varied but proceeds always at the same pace and in the same way.'[44] Adhering to tradition, Wolfgang's symphony to *La finta semplice*, since it was composed earlier, had no intended connection with the sentiments of the opera; moreover, it too was in the three-sectional form most frequently adopted: *molto allegro, andante* and *molto allegro*. Due to rapid modulation, a freer use of dissonance, and a busier orchestra, the symphony has more colour than that of either *Die Schuldigkeit* or *Apollo et Hyacinthus*; also a more developed use of sequence makes it quite tightly organized. The symphony does not have a real ending in the operatic version as the final chords serve to introduce the opening ensemble of the opera. It is a surprising passage and produces a good theatrical effect: at the end of the piece there is an increase of rhythmic intensity and at the moment when one would expect to applaud for the symphony the curtain, instead, goes up; the metre changes from binary (2/4) to triple time (3/4); and the spectacle has begun. Quite ably the young composer has guided his public's attention from the orchestra to the stage.

As was typical of *opera buffa*, almost all the arias of *La finta semplice* are in two parts, either with a single section repeated (AA′), such as No. 6 'Colla bocca e non col core' (With the mouth and not the heart) for Rosina, and No. 22 'Vieni, vieni, o mia Ninetta' (Come, come, oh my Ninetta) for Simone; or with each repeated section subdivided into two contrasting parts (ABA′B′) which generally have a change of metre as well, such as No. 3 'Marito io vorrei, ma senza fatica' (I would like a husband but with no bother) for Giacinta, and No. 18 'Ho sentito a dir di tutte le più belle' (I heard it of all the most beautiful) for Rosina. Certainly whenever there is a change of sentiment in the text Wolfgang reflects this by changing the music, and not only in the binary arias. For example, in one of the two tripartite arias, No. 5 for Fracasso 'Guarda la donna in viso' (Look the woman in the face), the first section of the aria enumerates the enchanting qualities of women which Wolfgang underscores by writing a long *fioritura* on the word 'consolar', an insinuating phrase which ably suggests the idea of a falsely shy woman beckoning a man to her to 'console' him; the second section of the aria, however, recalls that women are unfaithful and ungrateful and here Wolfgang uses instead *staccato* semiquavers in the orchestra to accentuate this new point.

Besides the Numbers which show formal repetition, there are also other non-repetitive ones which are worth noting because they permit dramatic continuity. The duet 'Cospetton, cospettonaccio' (Damn, damnation; No. 19), for example, is a very brisk piece with several passages of orchestral tremolo; dialogue passes rapidly between the two duellers Fracasso and Cassandro, and, avoiding repetition completely, Wolfgang offers us continuous and logical action. In aria No. 20 for Fracasso only the opening part, 'In voi belle è leggiadria' (In you beautiful women there is whimsy), is repeated after which dramatic continuity takes precedence. In the first section of aria No. 17 'Sposa cara, sposa bella' (Dear wife, lovely wife) Polidoro sings a tender placating song to the crying Rosina who has been insulted (or so she says . . .) by Cassandro; then the *Adagio* (indicated *alla breve*) changes into a lighter 3/8 as he tries to send his drunken brother to bed while yet joking affectionately with Rosina to make her forget her wounded feelings; next follows a *Moderato* section in 2/4, with rapid passages in the strings to accompany Polidoro as he scolds Cassandro for having made Rosina unhappy. At this point Wolfgang repeats the whole aria, but it does not seem excessive given Polidoro's excitement; in fact, repetition here serves to underline Polidoro's incapacity to resolve the situation.

One notices Wolfgang's concern for relating structure to drama in yet other ways in *La finta semplice*, even, for example, in the organi-

zation of some recitatives, such as the one sung by Fracasso before aria
No. 3 (example 1). Wolfgang has him repeat the words 'saprò sposarvi

Example 1

a forza' (I will certainly know how to marry you) but in melodic
sequence while the bass rises slowly but insistently in half-steps. Textual
repetition indicates Fracasso's determination but this is emphasized
even more by the insistent type of musical setting Wolfgang has chosen
for it. A similar repetition is used in the recitative before No. 5 where
the melodic sequences coupled with a rising chromatic bass reflect
Cassandro's increasing exasperation with the soldiers who are to be
quartered with them (example 2).

Example 2

Some arias of *La finta semplice* merit attention because they are
further instances of Wolfgang selecting a word or idea to be set in
musical relief. For example, in No. 3 cited above Giacinta lists her
requirements in a husband: he must be a man where she wants him and
when she wants him. She sings 'Insomma io desidero un uomo
d'ingegno ma fatto di legno' (In short I want a man of intelligence but
made of wood). The 'but' is put in relief each time both by a *forte* in the
strings which contrasts with their preceding *piano* and by pauses in the
vocal part (example 3). Wolfgang thus reinforces the contradiction that
follows. Further on in the opera Cassandro sings a brilliant aria which is
full of *forte* and *piano* contrasts (No. 16) and wherein we hear him insist
that 'Ubriacco non son io' (Drunk I am not). The strings play a
weaving accompaniment and often there is an unsteady rhythm, all to
let us know that Cassandro is not telling the truth. In No. 24 'Che
scompiglio' (What confusion) Giacinta sings that she is afraid to run

Example 3

away with Fracasso and says 'tremo tutta di paura' (I'm all atremble
with fear), and the whole orchestra 'trembles' with her.

Delineation of character is more evident in this work than in either
of the two preceding ones already considered and the *personaggi* are
well defined and individual. We can see this, for example, in the arias
'Chi mi vuol bene' (Who loves me; No. 10) and 'Sono in amore' (I am
in love; No. 23) for the servant Ninetta where Wolfgang uses simple
and folk-like music in a *Tempo di Minuetto* which is definitely appropriate to her station in life; in aria No. 2 'Troppa briga a prender
moglie' Simone, the soldier, laments 'To find a wife is too much
trouble' and his music is martial, based on an arpeggiated melody
which contrasts with a repeated rhythmic motive in the violins. In these
three instances the occupation or social position of the character in
question is emphasized by the orchestra as well. Even the *secco* recitatives tend to point up the personality of the character: those for Cassandro, beginning with that before aria No. 5, often contain arpeggios,
scales and other figures in the continuo in order to emphasize his
pompous nature. In the same recitative we can also see how aware
Wolfgang was of timing on stage; in fact he adds flourishes in the
continuo just where a gesture or action might be inserted (example 4).

Example 4

When Wolfgang uses a combination of word painting, particular metre, and instrumentation to express character or situations, which occurs especially in four arias, one is aware of the development of his dramatic sense which has taken place in this period. It would be worthwhile to discuss these examples in some detail to observe the ways in which Wolfgang manages to express atmosphere and sentiment, and to realize that we have here an increasing and a deepening of those procedures which earlier he used in only isolated phrases or sections.

No. 8 'Ella vuole ed io torrei' (She wants and I would take), an aria for Cassandro, opens *Moderato e maestoso*, a suitable tempo for a proud individual who believes he is a grand gentleman, a man of sophistication, intelligent and good-looking. The accompaniment of triplets continues to emphasize both Cassandro's pompous nature and the fact that he becomes 'warm' at every word and look from Rosina: he says that he feels his blood boil in his veins making a 'blo, blo, blo' sound! The minor dominant is introduced when he sings of his lost money and ring, sad thoughts indeed for one accustomed to holding on to every penny. In the next section of the aria he compares himself to a dog saying he will be beaten; for this new idea the tempo changes to *Adagio* and the orchestra illustrates his whining and barking with a characteristic phrase played after each word and during which a comic actor could mime the appropriate gestures. Next there is an immediate return to the opening tempo with well-defined lively melodies full of wide skips making for a brilliant and decisive ending, a certain bid for applause. In this single aria both Cassandro's strength and weakness are revealed. The text alone might have made him appear as someone too silly for Rosina to marry; but the music demonstrates that he is, instead, human and comic in love but yet strong enough to be a credible authoritarian.

Aria No. 9 'Senti l'eco ove t'aggiri sussurar tra fiori e fronde' for Rosina offers a just expression of the text (Hear the echo, wherever you go, murmuring in the flowers and bushes) and renders the idyllic atmosphere not only through lyrical writing but also through effective instrumentation. First of all the oboe is employed intelligently from beginning to end: it seems in fact to be a stand-in for the soprano while it plays *a solo* in the introduction, but then it abdicates momentarily in favour of the voice. Francesco Algarotti wrote that: 'One of the most beloved uses today, sure to get the greatest applause with deafening hand clapping, is the pitting of a voice and an oboe, [or] a voice and a trumpet against one another in an aria; and to have an unending battle between them of various attacks and answers, almost a duel to the last breath.'[45] Wolfgang was obviously aware of the tradition but, rather than employing the singer and instrumentalist in competition here, he has them complement one another to achieve a more expressive interpretation of the text. In fact, he has associated the oboe in a clear way

with Rosina, expressing the girl's thoughts and sentiments the first time
not with words or word painting but through instrumental painting.
Later the oboe returns as an echo of the voice, especially evident in the
passages where Rosina sings appropriately enough of an echo (example
5). Other instruments which collaborate to achieve the right external

Example 5

atmosphere are the English horn and the *Corni di caccia* which imitate
the echo that whispers 'among flowers and bushes'. On Rosina's initial
affirmation 'Senti l'eco ove t'aggiri', the strings begin their whispering
and rustling to suggest the 'murmuring', and the orchestra reflects every
expression of the wandering lover to whom Rosina sings: it cries out
with him (*sforzando* chords) and sighs with him (brief *legato* motives).

Creating a sonorous tribute to the beauty and pain of love is Rosina's
aria No. 15, the most expressive piece in the opera. She sings here to the
'Amoretti' who fly about and wound people, begging them not to send
their darts at her. While Rosina addresses these cupids sustaining a note
for nine and a half beats, the bassoons and violas alternate with motives
that weave about the principal violin melody, thus becoming the
'Amoretti' of whom she sings. On the word 'volando' the violins play
triplets of *staccato* semiquavers in sixths and thus create a sweet 'flying'
sound. Due to Wolfgang's genius, even the wounds of love are beautiful in the minor or diminished intervals he uses. The scene reminds one
of the contained dignity and quiet beauty of the Countess in *Figaro* in
its coincidence not only of atmosphere but of name.

Aria No. 13 for Simone, 'Con certe persone' (With certain people),
demonstrates an interesting rapport between the bass voice and bass
instruments, again at the service of the text. In its opening phrase the
voice remains fixed on one note and the instruments, at first quite close
to it, move away gradually creating dissonances (example 6). The effect
of the resulting harmony is as strong as the determination of Simone to
be firm in the struggle for his Ninetta. When he holds his note in the
midst of changing harmonies he proves his intent. In another moment,
when he shouts 'Madama' to Giancinta, the orchestra replies as if it
were she, in graceful piano phrases. From beginning to end one is made
aware of Simone's strength and also of the gentleness of the woman to
whom he is speaking.

One sees in these examples that an important change has taken place
in Wolfgang's approach to opera: he has begun to think of the orches-

Example 6

tra as an independent entity capable of commenting and explaining, and has thus added another dimension to his ability to interpret *dramma in musica*.

Due to more continually expressive writing, most of the characters of *La finta semplice* are convincing. Ninetta and Simone are presented musically as servants; the simpleton Polidoro is silly; Cassandro is tyrannical but weak in the face of love. At the same time Fracasso and Giacinta are not clearly delineated. In part this is due to their relative unimportance in the plot: they do not appear often, nor do they appear as other than ordinary people, although Wolfgang did his best to increase Fracasso's importance by writing the only tripartite arias in the opera for him (the above-mentioned No. 5 'Guarda la donna in viso', and No. 25 'Nelle guerre d'amore non val sempre il valore', In wars of love valour does not always prevail). This does not mean to say that the music composed for them is inexpressive; it is just not sufficiently telling. On the other hand the person most clearly and best described is Rosina.

The numbers which conclude each of the three acts of *La finta semplice* are typical finales of several sections which exhibit the desired contrasts of metre, structure and sentiment, and which end in a homophonic ensemble. The finale of the third act is particularly noteworthy since it foretells Wolfgang's ability to express various and contrasting sentiments simultaneously through the use of counterpoint. Here his music allows Rosina and Cassandro to swear eternal love while Polidoro gives vent to his anger at the surprising turn of events. There are other details of the finale which also reveal that the drama is beginning to determine what and how Wolfgang writes: for example, he quiets the orchestra for the off-scene words of Ninetta, Giacinta, Fracasso and Simone; and he slows down the brisk movement of the finale with a brief recitative just before the moral of the opera: 'È inutile adesso

di far più lamenti, già queste del sesso son l'arti innocenti e spirto e
bellezza son gran qualità' (It is useless now to lament further, as these arts
of sex are innocent, and spirit and beauty are wonderful qualities). The
interruption intensifies the new entrance of all and thus underscores
their text.

Clearly the ability of Wolfgang to write for the theatre has greatly
developed from the time of *Die Schuldigkeit* and *Apollo and Hyacinthus*.
His application of new dramatic skills is, of course, not consistent; but
he is becoming conscious of new musical techniques with which to
express drama and has experimented with them here with success. The
genre of *opera buffa* furnished him with more opportunity to use his
fantasy than the stylized sacred opera or the Latin comedy. Even if *La
finta semplice* did not launch Wolfgang's career as his father fervently
wished, it was all the same a significant experience for him. The art of
delineating a character was introduced into Wolfgang's work through
the needs of the comic opera.

In listing the *personaggi* and singers of the first performance of *La finta
semplice* I have included the role that the same person sang in *Die
Schuldigkeit*. The difference in the type of character each one was now
expected to portray underlines Leopold's hesitation at having them do
an *opera buffa*. It should also be kept in mind that Meissner, Lipp,
Braunhofer and Spitzeder were soloists at the Cathedral, again not a
recommendation for their *buffa* abilities.[46]

FRACASSO, Hungarian Captain (tenor)—Jos. Meissner (Christian)

ROSINA, Baroness, sister of Fracasso, who pretends to be simple
(soprano)—Maria Magd. Haydn Lipp (Divine Mercy)

GIACINTA, Sister to Don Cassandro and Don Polidoro (soprano)—
Maria Anna Braunhofer (Divine Justice)

NINETTA, Maid (soprano)—M. Anna Fesemayer (Worldly Spirit)

DON POLIDORO, Gentleman, foolish brother of Cassandro (tenor)—
Franz Anton Spitzeder (The Christian Spirit)

DON CASSANDRO, Gentleman, foolish and miserly brother of Polidoro (basso)—Joseph Hornung

SIMOME, Lieutenant to the Captain (bass)—Felix Winter

The programme for the opening made it clear that the composer was
'Signor Wolfgango Mozart in Età di Anni dodici'.[47]

Chapter Four: Notes

1. K. 46a/51 in *WAM*, Series V, 4.
2. The following account of music in Vienna is based on Joseph Gregor, *Geschichte des
   Österreichischen Theaters* (Vienna, 1948), and Otto Rommel, 'Vienna', *Enciclopedio
   dello Spettacolo* (Florence, 1962), IX, col. 1651ff. A brief account in English may
   also be found in 'Vienna', *The Oxford Companion to the Theatre* (Oxford, 1951),

p. 827, edited by Phyllis Hartnoll. See also Otto Michtner, *Das alte Burgtheater als Operbühne* (Vienna, 1970).

3. On what is today the Michaelerplatz.

4. For a brief discussion of the Bibiena family and several illustrations of their work see 'Fernando Galli Bibiena: La Nuova Regola' and 'La Scuola dei Bibiena', pp. 79-86 and pp. 87-96 respectively in *Illusione e pratica teatrale* (Vicenza, 1975) edited by Franco Mancini, Maria Teresa Muraro and Elena Provoledo; illustrations are at the end of the volume.

5. An adequate summary of these events may be read in the *Encyclopaedia Britannica*. Burney gave the same reasons for Vienna's official lessening of interest in music in *Germany*, I, pp. 366-367.

6. The following events are well presented in Giorgio Pestelli, *L'eta di Mozart e di Beethoven* (Turin, 1979), pp. 77-83. See also Paolo Gallarati, *Gluck e Mozart* (Turin, 1975).

7. An expression of Gasparo Angiolini, the Florentine choreographer of Gluck's ballet and author of *Lettere a Monsieur Noverre sopra i balli pantomimi*, (Milan, 1773) and *Riflessioni di Gasparo Angiolini sopra l'uso dei programmi nei balli pantomimi* (London, 1775).

8. Vienna, 1769. The preface is reprinted among other places in Pestelli, pp. 288-290, and in an English translation by Eric Blom in Alfred Einsten's *Gluck* (New York, 1962), pp. 112-114.

9. As Leopold attested from Vienna in a letter to his friend Lorenz Hagenauer on 22 September 1767: *Briefe*, I, p. 238.

10. *Dokumente*, p. 71. The following events up to the family's arrival in Vienna in January 1768 are documented on p. 72. Leopold's letters to his friend, landlord and financial advisor Lorenz Hagenauer and his wife, Maria Theresa, recount their adventures: see *Briefe*, pp. 238-251.

11. As Leopold laments to Hagenauer on 30 January-3 February 1768: *Briefe*, I, p. 255.

12. Mario Fubini, ed. *Pietro Metastasio: Opere* in *La Letteratura italiana* (Milan, 1968), 41, p. 808.

13. *Dokumente*, p. 72; and as Leopold recounted in a letter of 23 January 1768 to Hagenauer: *Briefe*, I, p. 253.

14. *Briefe*, I, p. 258.

15. *Idem*.

16. *Briefe*, I, p. 239: 29 September 1767 to Hagenauer. On that occasion the Mozarts heard the tenor Tibaldi, the castrato Rauzzini from Munich and the prima donna Deiberin.

17. According to Jahn, I, p. 69. In the same letter of 30 January-3 February cited above (p. 258), Leopold says *Alceste* was performed by the *buffo* singers.

18. *Briefe, idem*.

19. Erich Schenk, *Mozart*, pp. 104-105. Affligio had permission to conduct animal-baiting shows which Schenk says (p. 105) was 'the most profitable business in the Viennese amusement industry'. For a more complete account of this eighteenth-century personality mentioned by Casanova in his memoirs and who was similar in his many escapades, see J. G. Prod'Homme, 'Deux collaborateurs italiens de Gluck', *Rivista Musicale Italiana* 23 (1916), pp. 201-218.

20. *Briefe*, I, p. 257, letter of 30 January-3 February 1768.

21. *Idem*.

22. As explained by Leopold in a letter to Emperor Joseph II of 21 September 1768 now in the Glasgow University Library: see *Dokumente*, p. 75, and *Briefe*, I, p. 280.

23. See Emilia Zanetti, 'Coltellini', *Enciclopedia dello Spettacolo*, III, col. 1147-1149. Coltellini was a follower in Calzabigi's reforms.

24. See Metastasio's letter to Coltellini of 7 March 1761 in which he expresses appreciation and encouragement for the young man's work: *Lettere del Signor Abate Pietro Metastasio* (Florence, 1787-89), Tomo IV, pp. 74-76. As a publisher Coltellini had put out among other works Algarotti's *Saggio sopra l'opera in musica* (1763) and the Italian translation of the *Encyclopédie* (1770-1779).

25. In 1772 Coltellini succeeded Metastasio as *Poeta cesareo*.

26. As Leopold wrote to Joseph II in the same letter: *Dokumente, idem*, and *Briefe*, I, p. 279. The singers were named by Leopold in his letter to Hagenauer of 30 January-3 February (*Briefe*, I, p. 258): the men he listed were Caribaldi, Carattoli, Poggi, Laschi and Polini; the women were Bernasconi, Eberhardi and Baglioni.

27. The same letter to the Emperor *op. cit.*: *Dokumente*, p. 76, and *Briefe*, I, pp. 281-282. Kochel 6, p. 68 also states that Fracasso's 'Guarda la donna' (No. 5) and Ninetta's 'Sono in amore' (No. 23) were rewritten while the middle of Fracasso's 'Nelle guerre ... ' (No. 25) was revised.

28. *Dokumente, idem*; *Briefe*, I, p. 281.

29. Again to Hagenauer in Salzburg: *Briefe*, I, p. 270. Leopold's letter to the Emperor says the same thing in other words: *Dokumente*, pp. 75-76 and *Briefe*, I, pp. 280-281.

30. The same letter to Hagenauer, *idem*.

31. *Ibid.*, p. 270 ff.

32. *Ibid.*, pp. 272-273. Leopold's letter to the Emperor again re-words the same events: *Dokumente*, p. 76, and *Briefe*, I, pp. 281-282.

33. Bernard Paumgartner, *Mozart*, revised Italian edition, translated by Carlo Pinelli (Turin, 1978), p. 142.

34. *Op. cit.*: *Dokumente*, pp. 74-77, and *Briefe*, I, pp. 279-283.

35. *Ibid.*, *Dokumente*, p. 77, and *Briefe*, I, pp. 282-283.

36. *Ibid.*, *Dokumente*, p. 77, and *Briefe*, I, p. 283.

37. *Idem*.

38. Jahn, I, p. 98. *Dokumente*, p. 82, gives the programme for the Salzburg performance. Deutsch also says there that, according to the diary of Abbot Bede Seeauer, the possibility that the opera was requested to celebrate the Archbishop's Name Day on 1 May becomes questionable since the prelate seems to have been away at Hallein at the time. Act I of the autograph score disappeared after the war; Acts II and III are in the Staatsbibliothek Preussischer Kulturbesitz in West Berlin.

39. Leopold's Salzburg salaries as Violin Master to the Royal Chapel and as Vice-Kappellmeister were interrupted in March 1768 with the concession that while he could stay away as long as he liked, he would not continue to be paid: see *Dokumente*, p. 73.

40. In the letter to Hagenauer, *op. cit.*, *Briefe*, I, p. 271.

41. On this custom see Pierluigi Petrobelli, 'Lo spazio e l'azione scenica nell' opera seria settecentesca' in *Illusione e Pratica Teatrale*, p. 25 ff., and Sven H. Hansel, 'Stage deportment and scenographic design in the Italian Opera Seria of the Settecento', Report of the Eleventh [IMS] Congress Copenhagen (Copenhagen, 1974), I, p. 415 ff.

42. *Dokumente*, p. 77; Leopold's letter to Joseph II reports that one of the delays in

putting on Wolfgang's opera was that Affligio wanted to have *Buona figliola* performed (*Dokumente*, p. 76, and *Briefe*, I, p. 281).

43. Stefano Arteaga, II, p. 272.
44. Francesco Algarotti, 'Saggio sopra l'opera in Musica' [1755], *Opere del Conte Algarotti*, 2nd ed. (Leghorn, 1764), II, p. 273.
45. *Ibid.*, II, pp. 278-279.
46. Abert-Jahn, I, p. 320.
47. *Dokumente*, p. 82.

CHAPTER FIVE

Bastien und Bastienne[1]

IN 1746 *La serva padrona* by Pergolesi was performed at the Hôtel de Bourgogne, seat of the Italian *commedia dell'arte* in Paris. Originally written in 1733 for presentation between the acts of Pergolesi's own *opera seria Il prigionier superbo* in Naples, the intermezzo received only four performances the first time in Paris, perhaps because the already dead Pergolesi was but little known at the time. However when, six years later in 1752, Eustachio Bambini, Director of Italian Opera at Strassburg, managed to obtain the necessary authorization to put on the same intermezzo with a travelling company of Italian players, but this time at the most important Parisian musical theatre and the respected seat of the *tragédie lyrique* of Lully and Rameau, l'Opéra, the work was an enormous success. Arteaga, who called the composer 'the great Pergolesi', affirmed his music to be 'inimitable ... due to the simplicity of its style coupled with greatness, to its true representation of affection, to its naturalness and vigour of expression, to its exactness and unity of design'.[2]

La serva padrona also touched off the famous *Querelle-des Bouffons*, a literary war involving all the Paris intellectuals, musicians or not, who discussed *ad nauseam* the relative merits of French music and Italian music. In 1753-1754 alone, at least 60 brochures were written taking one side or the other of the question. Strangely, and illogically, most participants compared the existing French *serious* opera with the newer Italian *comic* opera. Hurrying to follow quickly on the heels of the success of *La serva padrona*, the surprised Bambini soon put on other Italian comedies, all also short and with only two or three characters as was typical of the intermezzo. These works by Pergolesi, Rinaldo da Capua, Leo, Jommelli, etc. had an even more positive outcome in that they encouraged the French to create their own 'national' comic opera, in French and following a French style.

An important role in these various results was taken by Jean-Jacques Rousseau who in 1753 also wrote a pamphlet, his being entitled *Lettres sur la Musique Françoise*. Charles Burney noted that, as a direct result of it, there was a revolution in French sentiment and that 'the ouvertures and act tunes of this theatre [the Comédie Française], as of the *Theatre Italien*, are all either German or Italian; they begin to be ashamed of their own music every where but at the serious opera'.[3] Crusader in everything for a 'return to Nature', soon after Pergolesi's *La serva padrona* and in frank imitation of it, Rousseau also wrote a French comedy, *Le Devin du Village*.[4] The simplicity and tunefulness of the work made it an immediate success, even with the unmusical French monarch, as Jelyotte, one of the performers in the little opera, reported to the composer: 'The whole court is enchanted with your work: the King, who, as you know, doesn't like music, sings your airs all day long with the falsest voice in this kingdom, and is asking for a second performance this week.'[5] The opera was translated and presented everywhere, including New York in 1790.

Another sign of its success was the parody of *Le Devin* presented in 1753 by Charles-Simon Favart (1710-1792), Director of the Opéra Comique, under the title: *Les amours de Bastien et Bastienne*. Here Rousseau's formal Arcadian shepherds became simple French country people, and instead of giving an idealized and idyllic vision of country life, they now expressed sentiments more in keeping with their daily life: all very 'natural' and rustic. Madame Favart, who took the leading female role, was the first actress who dared appear on stage in genuine peasant dress and she and her *sabots* caused such a sensation that she was painted specially in the costume.[6] Favart's parody, translated into German by Friedrich Wilhelm Weiskern (1710-1768), son of a Master of Equitation from Saxony and one of the best comedians of the time, had been given in Vienna's Kärntnerthor Theatre with music by Johann Baptist Savio in 1764 and was to be the libretto for Wolfgang's *Bastien und Bastienne*.[7]

Weiskern's version of *Bastien* had been performed by adults but it soon passed into the repertory of the Felix Berner company of professional child performers. As Loewenberg noted, 'All the actors, singers and dancers were children from the age of 5(!) onwards, guided and supported by a few grown-up members, such as the ballet master and the musical director.'[8] In December-February 1766 the troupe visited Salzburg,[9] just after the Mozart family returned home from their Grand Tour, and it is possible that they performed *Bastien und Bastienne* with Savio's music and that Wolfgang not only saw it but began to set the libretto himself. Certainly in Leopold's list of his son's works the Singspiel comes before *La finta semplice*, although it must be admitted that this may have referred to the final version of the *opera buffa* which may not have been settled upon until after *Bastien* had been performed in Vienna. In lieu of more positive information about Wolfgang composing the music while still in Salzburg, one may suppose that it was while the Mozarts were awaiting news of the outcome of *La*

finta semplice that the boy was invited to set to music the play by Franz
Anton Mesmer (1734–1815), a medical scholar living in Vienna.[10]

Mesmer was soon to complete his university studies in medicine and
theology (1771) with a thesis discussing planetary influence on man. He
then went on to experiment with the use of magnetism in medical
treatment and found that he could cure his patients from their nervous
disorders even without a magnet, through a faculty he termed 'animal'
magnetism. Although Mesmer was forced to leave Vienna in 1777
because of disagreements with medical colleagues over his methods, and
again later, after he set up a fashionable practice in Paris, was called
a charlatan by the French Academy of Medicine and Academy of
Sciences, he may well have had a suggestive influence on his patients
and was able to cure them through hypnotism.[11] When he and Wolfgang first met, though, Mesmer's ideas were still not formulated and he
was simply an interested music lover. It was only in 1790 that Wolfgang was able to caricature Mesmer and his magnet so amusingly in
Così fan tutte. Wolfgang's opera *Bastien und Bastienne* was given in
Mesmer's Viennese home in the autumn of 1768.[12]

The story deals with a shepherdess, Bastienne (soprano), who is
unhappy over the loss of her beloved Bastien (tenor), recently attracted
instead to a *dame de Ville*. She asks help from Colas (bass), the local
magician, who assures her that Bastien will return; when he does,
however, she must feign disinterest. Soon after Bastien does come back
ready for a reconciliation; and when Colas tells him Bastienne has
found someone else, he too seeks the magician's aid. Now Colas pretends to conjure up Bastienne who arrives only to recite the part
outlined for her by the magician, although with difficulty when she sees
that Bastien seems likely to leave her for good. This leads them both to
mutual compromise and to the swearing of eternal faithfulness. The
comedy ends with all three praising Colas.[13]

As was true of the new French *opéra comique*, *Bastien und Bastienne*
exhibits an essential difference from all Italian opera, comic as well as
serious. Both in France and in Germany, as well as England, comedies
were not entirely sung. While the closed forms that present the more
expressive and static moments of the drama (the arias, duets, trios, etc.)
were set to music, the recitatives, which convey the various developments of plot and are usually dialogues, were not sung but merely
spoken. In part the Singspiel, or 'song-play', derived from the shows
done in Germany by travelling companies of performers which offered
to the public something different from the foreigner's art, that is from
Italian opera. At the beginning music had a simple and only incidental
role, in the form of songs or dances interpolated in the play, but soon it
acquired greater importance. The strength of these plays *with* music
(and not dramas *in* music) was the language: the public enjoyed the

spectacle more because they were in German. They were also immediate and simple.[14]

Bastien und Bastienne is generally considered to be the first Singspiel of
a reasonable musical-artistic level, and this from a boy of 12. Not only
that, but a boy occupied (as one believes now in the absence of contrasting information) with writing his very first *opera buffa* and caught in a
mesh of confusion and intrigue in the process. Obviously it was completely different from all that Wolfgang had previously composed for
the theatre, both because of the spoken recitatives and, more importantly, because of the traditional simplicity of the German Singspiel and
its particular pastoral character. One notices this latter quality even in
the two purely instrumental sections of *Bastien und Bastienne*, the *Intrada*
and the interlude for Colas' entrance which contribute to the rustic
atmosphere by suggesting the sound of bagpipes. The *Intrada* consists of
only one theme (a foreshadowing of Beethoven's 'Eroica' motive)
presented in various tonalities over a drone which goes on from beginning to end; the interlude is also a single melody and is supported by
only D and A pedals. Both pieces are brilliant and gay. Luckily Wolfgang's abilities to project himself into dramatic situations and to imitate
musical styles, noted in his ready gift for improvisation which always
surprised his concert audiences, served him well when having to set a
new work in a new genre.

Even if the aria melodies of *Bastien und Bastienne* are simple, they are
not banal, as they are enriched by the interesting harmonic colours
chosen by Wolfgang. Since both stylized repetition and vocal decoration would have been too heavy for the popular flavour of the opera,
all motives are treated intentionally quite modestly: they are a bit more
rhythmic in the somewhat excited numbers but are never passionate or
frenetic. And almost all are continuous in form: some are in one section, as No. 1 'Mein liebster Freund hat mich verlassen' (My dear friend
has left me), No. 4 'Befraget mich ein zartes Kind' (A tender child
asked me), and No. 8 'Grossen Dank dir abzustatten' (To give you
many thanks); others are in two sections, such as No. 2 'Ich geh jetzt auf
die Weide' (I go now out to pasture), No. 5 'Wenn mein Bastien einst
im Scherze' (When my Bastien once in jest), and No. 6 'Würd ich auch,
wie manche Buhlerinnen' (Would I, too, as some lovers), implicating
through a change of metre a change of feeling. The only ABA aria is
No. 12 'Er war mir sonst treu und ergeben' (He was moreover true and
faithful to me), but since the last section, even though it repeats the
opening music, has new words, it too produces a good dramatic
effect.[15]

The most singular aria in the Singspiel is 'Diggi, daggi, schurry,
murry', sung by Colas when he uses his 'magic art' to make Bastienne
appear (No. 10). It suggests the spooky and unnatural atmosphere of

magic most marvellously. A relatively static vocal part in the manner of an incantation is accompanied by leaps, semiquavers, and chromatic-note passages in the orchestra; it is through these means that one can imagine every sort of thing, visible and invisible, flying about. If one remembers the love Wolfgang had for games and his lively imagination, one can believe that he enjoyed himself in a particular way when composing this scene; he probably not only wanted to write the music but to perform it![16] Another aria worthy of mention is 'Ich geh jetzt auf die Weide' cited above (No. 2) for Bastienne, where a rather repetitive melodic phrase becomes quite tender due to the careful instrumental accompaniment (example 1). Even the contrast between an undulating line for strings and a vocal part with leaps is effective (example 2).

Example 1

Example 2

In addition to these examples, one must also notice the ensembles[17] which exhibit aspects already observed in *La finta semplice*. In fact these pieces, with the exception of the continuous and non-sectional No. 7 'Auf den Rat' (To the advice), are written in the typical manner of the Italian *opera buffa* finale with various contrasting sections joined together. The duet No. 15 'Geh! Herz von Flandern' (Go! fickle heart), introduced by a sentence of accompanied recitative and twenty bars of *arioso*, and the trio No. 16 'Kinder! seht, nach Sturm und Regen wird ein schöner Tag gebracht' (Children! see, after storm and rain a lovelier

day has come) are not as grandiose as true *opera buffa* finales would be
(the plot and general musical style would not permit that) but nevertheless they exhibit the same characteristics: when the text and with it
the sentiment expressed change, the music too changes in metre, tempo
and colour, the voices enter as quickly or as slowly as they would in
conversation, and the melodies, following the rise and fall of excited
discourse, are all quite natural. Moreover, the two numbers follow one
another directly with no dialogue separating them. The harmony and
the texture of the ensembles are equally simple: in No. 7 and in No. 15
the voices sing separately or together in thirds; the trio finale is also
homophonic.

Wolfgang's ability to write comedy is once again evident in *Bastien
und Bastienne*. All is light and gay, with the sadness of Bastienne treated
with a just amount of tenderness. One laughs at Colas' magic, at the
pretended disdain of Bastienne, at the decision of Bastien not to kill
himself but to run away; and one laughs when all three, including the
magician himself, sing his praises. *Bastien und Bastienne* demonstrates
Wolfgang's ability to absorb the German style just as *La finta semplice*
had demonstrated his first mastery of the Italian style; moreover he was
capable of applying the newly-learned techniques of *opera buffa* directly
to his first Singspiel.

Following the performance in Mesmer's house, there was talk of
repeating the Singspiel in Salzburg but in operatic form, that is with the
recitatives sung. For this eventuality Wolfgang began to compose the
missing parts and, even if it is not certain if the performance ever took
place, the results should at least be mentioned.[18] The interest in *secco*
recitative which Wolfgang had manifested in the contemporary *La
finta semplice* is, not surprisingly, evident also in *Bastien und Bastienne*
where the newly-composed sections manage to be both harmonious
and yet adequately declamatory (example 3, recitative before No. 2).

Example 3

They seem to confirm that Wolfgang considered not only the arias but
the whole opera to be important in developing a plot, an approach
which was not quite typical of the period according to both Algarotti
and Arteaga who, in their essays on Italian opera, noted that in general
recitative was not carefully composed but more or less left to the hit-
and-miss improvisation of the singers, a practice lamented by all
however.[19]

In October–December of 1774 the Berner children's company returned to Salzburg and while it is known that this time they performed
Bastien und Bastienne,[20] it is not certain with whose music: if not with
Savio's, could it have been with Wolfgang's? If so, it might have been
that his sung recitatives were used for this performance.

Chapter Five: Notes

1. K. 46b/50 in *WAM*, Serie II, 3, and *NMA*, Serie II, 5, bd. 3.
2. *Op. cit.*, II, p. 22.
3. *The Present State of Music in France and Italy* to be referred to hereafter as *Italy*
   (London, 1771), p. 45.
4. Jean-Jacques Rousseau, *Confessions*, II, Everyman's Library (New York, 1964), pp.
   34–35.
5. Arthur Pougin, *Jean-Jacques Rousseau musicien* (Paris, 1901), p. 67, but translated by
   John F. Strauss in 'Jean-Jacques Rousseau: Musician', *Musical Quarterly* 64/4 (1978),
   p. 480.
6. Jahn, I, p. 89. The authors of the French parody were Madame Marie-Justine-
   Benoîte Favart, her husband, and Harny de Guerville: see Rudolf Angermüller's
   introduction to his critical edition of *Bastien* in *NMA*, p. vii.
7. The actor Johann H. F. Müller, according to Angermüller, p. ix, had by Wolfgang's
   time added Nos. 11, 12 and 13 to the libretto.
8. Alfred Loewenberg, '*Bastien und Bastienne* once more', *Music & Letters* 25 (1944), p.
   177.
9. *Ibid.*, p. 178.
10. As Angermüller pp. xii–xiii, points out, the only source for this affirmation is Georg
    Nissen (*Mozart*; Leipzig, 1828) and is perhaps dubious.
11. For a summary of Mesmer's brochure *Mémoire sur la Découverte de Magnetisme animal*
    see Friedrich Melchior Grimm, *Correspondance littéraire, philosophique et critque* (Paris,
    1812–14), Part III/2, pp. 456–464; Part III/3, pp. 10–20, gives notice of the French
    commission formed to investigate Mesmer's work.
12. Not in the supposed Garden Theatre which had not yet been built. In Abert's
    revision of Jahn's work, I, p. 137, he proves Jahn, who believed Wolfgang's Mesmer
    was not the magnetizer (I, p. 86), incorrect.
    The autograph of the score has disappeared since World War II. It bore the
    following inscription in Leopold's hand, once again in Italian: 'Bastien, et Bastienne,
    di Wolfgango Mozart, 1768 nel suo 12mo anno.'
    In the same period Wolfgang also composed an Offertory (K. 47b) and a trumpet
    concerto (K. 47c), both of which are lost, as well as a Mass (K. 47a/139) for a
    Viennese orphanage where the children had their own orchestra: see Leopold's
    letter to Hagenauer of 12 November 1768 in *Briefe*, I, p. 285.
13. Jahn, I, pp. 90–91, gives the versions by Rousseau, Favart and Weiskern of the
    opening aria 'Mein liebster Freund hat mich verlassen'. He says that, in general, 'the
    French parody has been most skilfully travestied ... The verses are equally tame
    and clumsy all the way through; and even taking into account the prevailing low
    standard of cultivation and taste, it is difficult to believe that the operetta could have
    been produced at a private home of any importance.'

Savio's music is not extant. Alfred Lowenberg in 'An unknown Edition of the *Bastien und Bastienne* text' (Part II of 'Some stray notes on Mozart'), *Music & Letters* 23 (1942), p. 319 ff, reported a 1774 copy of the Weiskern/Müller libretto to be in the British Library.

14. For a more informative summary of the history of the Singspiel, see Chapter XIII.

15. P. 91 of *NMA* offers other stanzas of text to Nos. 2, 4, 5, 6, 9, 11 and 16 which are found in printed librettos; however, it is not known if they were intended to be sung.

16. Loewenberg, 'An unknown Edition ...', p. 321, noted that the words to 'Diggi, daggi' were not in the libretto he discovered and believed 'that the new song, if not actually a "literary" work by the boy himself, was written at his suggestion by his father or some friend'. It is worth mentioning that Act I of Gluck's well-known *La Rencontre imprévue* also contains an aria with nonsense words, Le Calender's 'Castagno, castagno, Pista fanache'.

17. No. 13 'Geh hin!' (Go away) is not a true duet but rather an aria sung first by Bastien and then repeated immediately by Bastienne.

18. The recitative texts may have been adapted for music (i.e. versified) by Johann Andreas Schachtner, court trumpeter at Salzburg who later would provide Wolfgang with the libretto to *Zaide*: see Köchel 6, p. 71. Also see Angermüller, p. xi, for a summary of the various writers' contributions to Wolfgang's *Bastien*.

19. Arteaga, II, pp. 280-281, and Algarotti, II, p. 291.

20. Loewenberg, 'Bastien ... once more', p. 180.

CHAPTER SIX

Mitridate, Re di Ponto[1]

THE MOZART FAMILY had left Salzburg for Vienna on 11 September 1767 and were not back until 5 January 1769, an absence of almost one and a half years. Long before they were home, though, Leopold was already planning another trip, this time to Italy.[2] They could not get away immediately from Salzburg, however, mainly because affairs as to Leopold's position at court needed to be arranged; the father was also concerned to find something there for Wolfgang. In the meantime more music was composed. On 14 January, just a few days after settling in, Wolfgang finished a *Missa brevis*; and in February another *Licenza* for Frau Haydn.[3] Then there was *La finta semplice* to rehearse and perform on 1 May.[4] Social occasions filled their days, too, such as Adlgasser's third marriage, this time to the soprano Maria Anna Fesemayer who had sung the part of Weltgeist in *Die Schuldigkeit* and Ninetta in *La finta semplice*. Leopold and Wolfgang were both witnesses,[5] a sign of the intimate friendship of those involved. Another old connection was revived when Wolfgang wrote music to celebrate the closing of studies for Rufinus Widl's class,[6] part of which Cassation he was to use again as a March in his next opera.[7]

Leopold was busy, too, writing the Preface to the second edition of his *Violinschule* which he finished on 24 September,[8] and requesting letters of introduction from Hasse to friends in Italy. Hasse's response, two letters to Giovanni Maria Ortes in Venice, are interesting as they reveal his favourable impressions of Leopold and Wolfgang made at the time of *La finta semplice* when they met in Vienna. In fact he wrote to Ortes, 'I limit myself to beg you again to consider them as my friends'.[9] By 14 November Leopold had managed to convince the extremely understanding Archbishop von Schrattenbach to make Wolfgang third Konzertmeister of his chapel, of which Leopold himself was Vice-Kapellmeister;[10] this unpaid position having been obtained, father and son set off for Italy, alone this time, on 13 December 1769, and were not to return until more than a year later on 28 March 1771.[11]

Within a month Wolfgang had given his first concert in Italy for the Accademia Filarmonica in Verona[12] and had his portrait painted by Saverio Dalla Rosa.[13] In all his concerts Wolfgang was of course to play something prepared; but he also demonstrated his abilities to sight-read, improvise, and to compose not only for keyboard but also for violin and voice. The air of a circus act, so evident on his earlier travels, was no doubt Leopold's doing as he desperately wanted all to marvel at his wondrous son's many and precocious talents.

On 2 February 1770 Leopold and Wolfgang were in Milan and heard the dress rehearsal of Piccinni's *Cesare in Egitto*, which Leopold declared 'right good'; another day they heard Jommelli's *Didone abban-donata* (originally of 1741):[14] as Wolfgang had already written to his sister, 'now we always hear operas'.[15] In fact in Milan alone they went six or seven times to the opera.[16] He was interested in everything, the singers, the plot, the dancers, etc., and described all in a lively conversational manner that surely enabled his mother and sister to live his adventures with him.

On 7 February father and son were invited to dine with Count Karl Joseph Firmian, Governor General of Lombardy, who was a nephew of Leopold's first Salzburg Archbishop and whose brother was the present Superintendent and Inspector of Music at Salzburg. Wolfgang also played at Firmian's and among the listeners was the Italian maestro of symphonic music and teacher of J. C. Bach and Gluck, Giovanni Battista Sammartini;[17] when he performed again at Firmian's residence on 18 February, the Este duke Francesco III and his granddaughter Maria Beatrice Ricciarda were present.[18] This meeting prompted his being asked to compose three arias and a recitative to Metastasian texts[19] performed at another musical party Firmian gave for more than 150 guests on 12 March.[20] The favourable impression Wolfgang made at this concert, or Accademia as it was called in Italy, would result in his being commissioned to compose music for Maria Beatrice's wedding to Archduke Ferdinand of Austria in 1771 (the serenata *Ascanio in Alba*); an immediate outcome of his performance, however, was a contract to do an opera for Milan, the as yet unnamed *Mitridate, Re di Ponto*, which would be given beginning on 26 December 1770 at the Teatro Regio Ducale.[21] The gentlemen Firmian had invited to hear the 14-year-old composer were actually in financial control of the theatre which, according to Burney, was organized in the following manner:

> The opera here is carried on by thirty noblemen, who subscribe sixty zechins each, for which every subscriber has a box; the rest of the boxes are let for the year at fifty zechins *la prima fila*, or first row, forty the second, thirty the third, and in proportion for the rest. The chance money only arises from the pit and upper seats, or *piccionaija*.[22]

Singers who would figure in Wolfgang's forthcoming opera were

met on their tour, such as Antonia Bernasconi in Milan[23] and Giuseppe
Cicognani in Milan and again in Bologna;[24] and an old acquaintance
from London, Manzuoli, was visited in Florence where the Mozarts
continued their travels.[25] He told them he had been signed up to do the
Milan opera,[26] news which must have pleased not only the singer who
was very fond of Wolfgang, but the boy as well. It was also rumoured
that either Antonia Maria Girelli Aguilar or Anna De Amicis-Buonsolazzi would sing, too, and Wolfgang hoped that De Amicis and Manzuoli would perform so that, as he wrote home, 'we would be with
two good acquaintances and friends'.[27] In the end none of these singers
performed in *Mitridate*; however Manzuoli and Girelli did the wedding
serenata, and De Amicis performed in Wolfgang's serious opera of a
few years later, *Lucio Silla*.

It is also in Florence that one reads the first public notice of the
proposed opera. The *Gazzetta Toscana* announced on 7 April 1770:
'After a trip to Rome he [Wolfgang] will go to Milan, called there expressly to set to music the opera which is to be put on next Carnival.'[28]
Without doubt father and son were well pleased with the results of
their tour thus far, and were grateful for the friendship and guiding
hand of Count Firmian. Not only had he invited the Mozarts often to
his home, and organized the Accademia where the Milanese nobles had
decided to commission Wolfgang, but the final contract for the opera
was also drawn up in his house. According to its terms Wolfgang was
to be paid 100 *gigliati* and they would be given free lodging.[29] Since the
opera was to be put on in the Christmas period, the recitatives were to
be composed and sent to Milan in October. Wolfgang himself had to
be there by 1 November in order to write the arias, a usual practice
since the music was always designed to suit the particular singers.

As the Florence newspaper foretold, the Mozarts went on next to
Rome, arriving 'under thunder and lightning at the mid-day meal' on
11 April.[30] Here, among other concerts for the Roman aristocracy, 'the
most fastidious judges of music in Italy',[31] Wolfgang also played at the
German College and met there the Salzburg singer Joseph Meiss-ner,
who had sung the part of Christ in *Die Schuldigkeit* and Fracasso in *La
finta semplice*.[32] The visit to Rome was yet another occasion for Wolfgang to display his phenomenal memory by writing down Allegri's
Miserere after hearing a performance of it in the Sistine Chapel. Next
came the long trip by carriage to Naples where they arrived 14
May, but the reward of the sights they saw and the music they heard
made up for their hardship. They were able to attend the rehearsal of
Jommelli's *Armida* at the San Carlo Theatre at the end of May, in which
Anna De Amicis sang,[33] and to meet both Jommelli and Paisiello.[34]
On 26 June, after another terrible carriage trip of 27 hours,[35] the
Mozarts were back in Rome where, on 5 July, the Pope's Secretary of

State, Cardinal Pallavicini, conferred on Wolfgang the Cross of the Golden Spur, an houour which of course pleased him although he personally never used the title of 'Cavaliere'.[36]

Returning to Milan the Mozarts stopped in Bologna where Charles Burney met them by chance, as he recounted on 30 August in his diary.[37] As the Mozarts explained to him, Leopold had hurt his leg so badly when their carriage horse fell on the return trip from Naples, that he could not walk and had to stay in bed for three weeks. As seven more weeks were required before he was ready to travel again, their plans were changed,[38] and instead of more touring Wolfgang renewed contact with Padre Giovanni Battista Martini, whom he had met earlier in his tour, and did many exercises in counterpoint and fugue which he showed to the Italian expert of polyphony. In the meantime work on the new opera also progressed. On 28 July Leopold wrote to his wife: 'Yesterday we received the opera libretto and names of the performers. The opera is called *Mitridate, Re di Ponto*. Such is by a poet from Turin, Sig. Vittorio Amadeo Cigni-Santi and was performed in 1767.'[39]

After naming the singers who were to make up the cast, Leopold commented that they knew some of them personally: 'Bernasconi we know. Herr Sartorini [nickname for Pietro Benedetti] sang for us in Rome. Cicognani is here, and our good friend Ettore is also presently here.'[40] This was essential for, without knowing the capabilities and preferences of the singers, Wolfgang could not begin to compose their music. As was usual, the composer shaped his music to the singers and did not write simply as his inspiration dictated. In any event this would have been foolish as the performers had the final word as to what they would or would not sing.

The summer and autumn months thus went by with Wolfgang hard at work at counterpoint, the *Mitridate* recitatives,[41] and four symphonies in the Italian style.[42] He also sat the difficult exam for entrance to the Accademia Filarmonica of Bologna and, with Padre Martini's help, was accepted, to the delight of the whole family, even though he was younger than their statutes stipulated.[43] But finally father and son left for Milan where they arrived on 18 October to prepare the performance of *Mitridate*.[44] Unfortunately things began in a way which was reminiscent of Vienna and the problems over *La finta semplice*, as Leopold wrote to his wife on 10 November:

The first battle, thank God, we have won and an enemy beaten, who brought all the arias of the prima donna which she is to sing in our opera to the house, and wanted to persuade her to sing no arias by Wolfgang. We saw them all, they are all new arias; however neither she nor we know who has composed them. She, however, refused these evil people.[45]

As Leopold had mentioned earlier to his wife, the libretto for *Mitri-date* had already been set to music in 1767. This was in Turin by Quirino Gasparini (1721-1778), and it was his music which was thrust on Antonia Bernasconi, the *prima donna*, although without Gasparini's knowledge.[46] Since the soprano did not allow herself to be influenced, the experience was a positive one as it permitted the young composer to see another setting of the same music, at least for her arias and duet and possibly, later on, of the whole opera. Actually several formal similarities may be noted between the Mozart and Gasparini versions, but as far as musical and dramatic substance is concerned, Wolfgang's is the better setting.[47]

Things proceeded more tranquilly and the *prima donna* was truly pleased with her part. As Leopold recounted to his wife on 10 November:

> [Bernasconi] is completely overjoyed with Wolfgang's arias for her, written to her desire and wish, as is her maestro Sig. Lampugnani with whom she goes over her part [and] who cannot give enough praise to Wolfgang's arias.[48]

But Leopold saw danger lurking around every corner:

> We have stopped a second storm between yesterday and today; and if one and the other can be avoided, as I hope, all with the help of God will go alright. That an opera then receives general applause in Italy is only a lucky chance which seldom happens because there are many factions. And even a moderate, or a bad, solo dancer has her factions which join in her bravos and shouting.[49]

Time was getting short, too; the *primo uomo*'s arias still had to be composed but he had not yet arrived. Leopold worried on 24 November:

> Wolfgang has his hands full, now that the time is approaching, and he has done only a single first aria for the primo uomo because he is still not here, and double work he does not want; consequently [he] prefers awaiting his presence in order to measure the suit properly on the body.[50]

When all were finally assembled rehearsals began. Wolfgang, as we have seen, was anxious to please and rewrote numbers when asked; in fact seven arias and a duet were rewritten.[51] From Leopold's letters home we know that there was a second recitative rehearsal on 8 December to check that copies were correct, which they were; then a small orchestral rehearsal with only 17 members, again to check parts, on 12 December; next a general rehearsal in the smaller Redoutensaal on 17 December with all 60 orchestral members; and finally, on the 19th, they rehearsed in the theatre as they did again on the 22nd.

Smaller recitative rehearsals continued at the same time with the final dress rehearsal scheduled for Christmas Eve, two days before opening night.[52] Leopold himself, although he admitted he may have been speaking with fatherly pride, said: 'I find that the opera is good and written with much feeling.' He also liked the singers but felt that as to the opera's success 'much is due to luck, as in a lottery'.[53]

Of course his negative attitude was a natural consequence of their bad experience in Vienna as well as worrying events in Milan. He had to fight against rumours here too:

> Before the first rehearsal with the small orchestra people did not miss the opportunity of shouting out before with satyr-like tongues, and so to prophesize, that the music was something immature and wretched. They affirmed that it would be impossible for so young a boy to write, not even a German, but an Italian opera; and that even if they saw he was a great virtuoso, nevertheless it was impossible that he could understand and comprehend enough of the necessary *chiaro ed oscuro* of the theatre.[54]

Luckily though, as had happened in Vienna, these rumours were stopped once Wolfgang's music was heard: 'Everyone from the first evening of the first small rehearsal was astonished and says not another syllable.'[55]

Leopold became more relaxed as the opening approached:

> My consolation is that I see that the performers as well as the orchestra are pleased and I myself, praise God, have ears. During rehearsal I stood way back under the main entrance to hear it properly at a distance. Perhaps my ears were partial! Due to that, we see and hear that our good friends are fun and amusing; and [I] congratulated my son with joy. The opposing ill-wishers are now dumb.[56]

Another favourable sign was that the copyist liked the music, as Leopold boasted:

> The copyist is absolutely delighted, which in Italy is a very good omen; for when the music is a success the copyist sometimes makes more money, by selling and dispatching the arias, than does the Maestro for the work.[57]

Not only those involved in the production praised Wolfgang's music, but the Milanese public happily greeted it with approval. The critic for the *Gazzetta di Milano*, Giuseppe Parini, wrote on 2 January 1771:

> Last Wednesday the Regio Ducal Theatre reopened with the presentation of the drama entitled Mitridate, Re di Ponto, which met with public satisfaction both for the good taste of its decorations and for

the excellence of the Music, and ability of the Actors. Some arias sung by Signora Antonia Bernasconi express passions vividly and touch the heart. The young Maestro di Cappella, who is not more than fifteen years old, studies the beautiful in nature and represents it adorned with the most rare musical graces.[58]

Leopold was more flamboyant in his enthusiasm, which surely was mixed with relief. Just three days after the opening he wrote home:

> God be praised, the first presentation of the opera on the 26th had general applause. And two things which in Milan are never seen, happened: namely, that (again as is customary the first evening) while one never calls 'come out' at the first performance, an aria of the prima donna was repeated; and, secondly, that after almost all the arias, with the exception of some of the arias of the less important roles, an astonishing clapping of hands and shouting of 'Viva il Maestro', 'Viva il Maestrino!' ensued.
>
> On the 27th two arias by the prima donna were repeated. It was Thursday, but already [past midnight] Friday, and one tried therefore to shorten it [the opera] but the duet also had to be repeated. Then the noise began.[59]

On 2 January 1771, when Leopold wrote to Padre Martini recounting the trials and tribulations of the opera as well as its success, he was able to boast:

> The first opera [of the season] in Milan usually has the misfortune, if not of failing, at least of having a small audience, as all the world awaits the second. But for the six performances given so far the theatre has always been very full, and every evening two arias have had to be repeated, with much applause for the most part for the others.[60]

These enthusiastic notices continued and the opera went on to enjoy about 20 performances in all. As was the custom for the composer, and as his contract bound him to do, Wolfgang himself played first harpsichord and conducted for the first three performances.[61] But then he was able to sit in the audience with his father, 'a while here and there, where it pleases us' and 'where everyone wants to speak with the Maestro and see him close at hand'.[62]

The Teatro Regio Ducale had been opened exactly 53 years before Wolfgang's opera on 26 December 1717 with Constantino by Francesco (not to be confused with Quirino) Gasparini. It was modernized in 1752 and again in 1770 in time for Carnival, the traditional Italian opera season, and Mitridate's opening. Burney has given us a good description of the theatre:

The theatre here is very large and splendid; it has five rows of boxes on each side, one hundred in each row; and parallel to these runs a broad gallery, round the house, as an avenue to every row of boxes: each box will contain six persons, who sit at the sides, facing each other. Across the gallery of communication is a complete room to every box, with a fireplace in it, and all conveniences for refreshments and cards. In the fourth row is a *pharo* table, on each side the house, which is used during the performance of the opera. There is in front a very large box, as big as a common London dining-room, set apart for the Duke of Modena, governor of Milan, and the *Principessina* his daughter. . . . In the highest story the people sit in front; and those for whom there are no seats, stand behind in the gallery: all the boxes here are appropriated for the season. . . . Between the acts the company from the pit come up stairs, and walk about the galleries.[63]

Obviously, in this free atmosphere, one was not expected to listen to the music all the time but, besides eating and drinking, one could also gamble at cards. Burney did, as a matter of fact, complain that 'the noise here during the performance was abominable',[64] but Leopold and Wolfgang made no mention of any such disturbance.

From another, less lively, point of view one could describe the Milan theatre as consisting of three parts: the *auditorium* for the spectators; the *palcoscenico*, or stage, for the scenery; and the *proscenio*, located under the proscenium arch and well in front of the stage proper, where the singers came to stand when they sang their arias. As Francesco Algarotti remarked, the *proscenio* extended several feet into the theatre proper: 'By placing the actors in the midst of the audience, there is no danger that they are not marvellously well heard by everyone.'[65] Whenever such access to the stage was possible, singers were advised to enter the proscenium either from just behind the proscenium arch or from in between the first two flats of scenery, which meant that in the eighteenth century it was possible that very little of the stage was used for the actual dramatic action and certainly only the proscenium for singing.[66] Sharing the stage with opera, as Wolfgang had remarked on his first visit to Milan, was ballet,[67] considered an important part of the entertainment at the Ducal Theatre. From its opening, the theatre offered ballets or short pantomimes as intermezzos between the acts of the operas,[68] and this practice still prevailed for Wolfgang's *Mitridate*, as Leopold complained: 'The opera with three ballets lasted six full hours; one should shorten the ballets as they last two full hours.' He was sorry mainly for the people as 'the majority still had to go home to eat'![69]

Vittorio Amadeo Cigni, or Cigna-Santi (1728-1785), the opera's librettist, was a Turinese, a member of that city's Accademia dei

Trasformati and had, as was said, written *Mitridate, Re di Ponto* for the 1767 season of the Turin Teatro Regio which was used with only slight alterations by an unknown poet in Milan. In three acts, his *opera seria* was based on a translation by Giuseppe Parini of Racine's non-historical account of Mitridate.[70] Between Racine and Cigna-Santi, relatives and friends were invented or eliminated to construct a story which had really nothing to do with the ruler of *c.* 135–65 B.C. who had fought courageously and often against Rome but, rather, told of two brothers and their father fighting over one woman.

When notice of Mitridate's death reaches Nymphaeum, his sons Sifare (Xipares) and Farnace (Pharnaces) become rivals for the hand of Mitridate's betrothed and already-declared Queen, Aspasia, and for the throne. Aspasia favours Sifare but while the three of them are discussing the situation, Arbate, the Governor of Nymphaeum, announces that Mitridate is not dead and is on his way home. The brothers agree to abandon their aspirations and the Queen promises not to tell Mitridate of their love for her. However, the ambitious Farnace plots with Marzio (Martius), the Roman Tribune, to have him march his troops against Mitridate. Mitridate eventually arrives and apologizes to Arbate for having been defeated by Pompey; he has with him Farnace's betrothed, Ismene, a Parthian princess, but unfortunately the son is not pleased. Ismene realizes this and laments the situation to Mitridate. Having already learned from Arbate of Aspasia's weakness and Farnace's designs, Mitridate replies that probably his son will soon be dead and that she then could marry Sifare. Of course Ismene replies she is in love only with Farnace. Now Mitridate meets with Aspasia accusing her of infidelity but also arranging for their immediate marriage as he must leave again. He also confronts Farnace with the knowledge of his plot against him. The son admits his guilt but accuses Sifare of also loving Aspasia. The lover, in fact, has already planned to flee but, discovered by Mitridate, is now imprisoned together with Farnace, and all three are condemned to death. An attack by the Romans, however, changes the situation. Farnace, freed by Marzio, manages to burn the Roman fleet and both he and Sifare fight against the enemy. The Romans are conquered, but in the fray Mitridate is mortally wounded. Before dying he unites Sifare and Aspasia and forgives Farnace who is now in love with Ismene.

This complicated plot, based on historical figures but diverging from history, in which honour is tried and danger imminent, a story of nobles of noble or ignoble passions where good triumphs, was a typical example of eighteenth-century *opera seria*. Vastly different in its libretto from a contemporary *opera buffa*,[71] *Mitridate, Re di Ponto* was, being an *opera seria*, also very different musically. The first clue to this is in the cast itself. Whereas an *opera buffa* generally employed only normal male voices, *opera seria* relied on the unusual soprano and contralto voices of the castrated male. These unfortunate but musically splendid creatures had had a long history in Catholic church music where, although the female range was desired, women could take no part. In opera they made their debut early, in Monteverdi's *Orfeo*; and although the church forbade the practice of castration, female roles were taken by these men with high voices since women were not at first permitted on stage or in oratorios.

The British Consul of Naples had told Burney that:

> this practice [of castration] is absolutely forbidden in the Conserva-
> torios, and that the young *Castrati* come from Leccia in Apuglia
> [Lecce in Puglia]; but, before the operation is performed, they are
> brought to a Conservatorio to be tried as to the probability of voice,
> and then are taken home by their parents for this barbarous purpose.
> It is, however, death by the laws to all those who perform the
> operation, and excommunication to every one concerned in it, unless
> it be done, as is often pretended, upon account of some disorders
> which may be supposed to require it, and with the consent of the
> boy. And there are instances of its being done even at the request of
> the boy himself.[72]

Outside Italy castratos were deplored but yet employed, necessarily and with great success, wherever Italian *opera seria* was performed. The castrato was generally possessed of an enormous range (from soprano to tenor and occasionally bass) and even though his voice was more powerful than the female correspondent, it was also very agile.[73] Man-zuoli, Wolfgang's great friend, who has often been mentioned and whom Daines Barrington had the boy imagine as he improvised, was a castrato as were three of the singers of *Mitridate, Re di Ponto*. Apart from occasional arias, such as those Wolfgang had written for one of these, Cicognani, and for another castrato Giuseppe Aprile, when he met the two in March 1770 in Bologna,[74] this was his first notable music for the voice; it was certainly the first opera he had been asked to compose for castratos, which was perhaps why Pietro Benedetti's delay in arriving was so especially worrying as he was the main male soprano in the opera.

For the Turin 1767 production of *Mitridate*, the sets were by the Galliari brothers, Bernardino (1707-1794), Fabrizio (1709-1790), and Giovanni Antonio (1714-1783), famous throughout Europe for their work. The eighteenth century was an important one for the visual, as well as the aural, arts of opera: what should be seen on stage and how to represent it was the subject of heated discussion not only by librettists and composers (and impresarios who claimed to be speaking for the public), but by stage designers who were causing their own theatrical revolution. In 1785 when Stefano Arteaga published the second edition of his study on Italian Opera, the changes wrought by the 'Inventori delle Scene' were still a cause for marvel. Speaking of theatrical perspective, as he called the field, he wrote:

> The art of making very small places seem spacious and grand, the ease and rapidity of quickly changing a scene, the manner of artificially varying the strength of the lights, and above all the invention of the incidental points, or rather, the manner of viewing the scene at an angle, brought the science of illusion to its summit. The great secret of the arts is the presenting of objects in such manner that fantasy does not stop where the senses stop, but that there always remains something for the spectator to imagine which the eye does not see and the ear does not hear. Thus breaking away sometimes from perspectives which set on a central point, which are, so to speak, the end of visual and imaginative capability, was as though to open an immense career for the industrious and restless imagination of those who, from a distance, look on the scenes.

After naming the Bolognese artist Ferdinando Bibiena as responsible for the new conception, Arteaga continued:

> Then perspective was no longer employed to place before the eyes fantastic beings, who have no relation to us, but to represent and refine the real objects of the Universe. And thus drama left the slavery where it had been kept, oppressed by the machinists and the impresarios.[75]

It was this very intent to represent 'the real objects of the Universe' which distinguished the work of the Galliari brothers. Their sets for Gasparini's *Mitridate* combined artistry with reality or, rather, offered reality as the artist intended his spectators to apprehend it.[76] Called to design the scenery of the same libretto in Milan one cannot expect that the Galliaris would have used the same sets they had prepared for Turin. This was not within theatrical fair play, certainly not when the theatres were geographically so close. However, since the practice for a set designer was to present a series of sketches to the theatre from which the ones to be realized were chosen, he could have used the rejected sketches for another opera. The problem here is that the Turin and Milan stages were so different that it would have been impossible for the Galliaris to adapt the Turinese sketches for use in Milan as their whole conception would have made them unsuitable.[77] Unfortunately, no sketches specifically for Milan seem to exist; at the same time one is assured from the reputation of the Galliaris and the importance of the Milan Ducal Theatre that Wolfgang's *Mitridate, Re di Ponto* must have been visually interesting and stimulating.[78] For the boy, it was his

first personal contact with eloquent creators, not of his own art but of
a necessary handmaiden to theatre music, who one feels would
have made him think further and deeper about what opera was meant
to be.

The cast for Wolfgang's *Mitridate, Re di Ponto* was the following:

MITRIDATE, King of Ponto and other kingdoms, betrothed to
  Aspasia—(Guglielmo D'Ettore (tenor)

ASPASIA, betrothed to Mitridate and already declared Queen—
  Antonia Bernasconi (soprano)

SIFARE, son of Mitridate and Stratonica, in love with Aspasia—Pietro
  Benedetti (soprano)

FARNACE, Mitridate's first son and in love with the same—Giuseppe
  Cicognani (contralto)

ISMENE, daughter of the King of Parti, in love with Farnace—Anna
  Francesca Varese (soprano)

MARZIO, Roman Tribune, Farnace's friend—Gaspare Bassano
  (tenor)

ARBATE, Governor of Nymphaium—Pietro Muschietti (soprano)

Following the usual scheme of an *opera seria*, two of the principal
characters of *Mitridate*, Aspasia and Sifare, begin the opera by each
singing an aria. Every act of an *opera seria* generally provided an aria,
or occasionally two, for each singer; however, by the end of the third
and last act, the main characters would still have out-sung the others:
in Wolfgang's opera, Mitridate sang five arias, Sifare, Aspasia, and
Farnace four, Ismene three, Arbate one. The first (and only) aria by
Marzio, 'Se di regnar sei vago' (If you want to rule), is not heard till Act
III (No. 23) but since according to tradition it is in a bravura style as are
all first arias (with the exception of Mitridate's), it provided Bassano
with an effective show piece. Once again in the usual manner of *opera
seria*, the ensembles are few: there is only one duet (which however
greatly pleased the singers)[79] and a five-part finale (actually three-part
music for five singers).

The majority of the arias, intended to be rather forceful exhibition
pieces for the singers, are orchestrated not for strings alone (as had been
the case for six arias in the *opera buffa La finta semplice* and as was true of
six arias in *Mitridate*) but have the added colour and strength of brass
and woodwind instruments. Leopold described the unusually large
Milan orchestra to his wife, saying that the members were divided in
the following manner: 28 violins (14 firsts and 14 seconds), 6 violas
(often asked to play *col basso*), 2 violoncellos, 6 contrabasses, 2 harp-
sichords; then 2 oboes and 2 flutes (and when flutes were not called
for these players doubled on oboe), 2 bassoons (which doubled the
cellos when not specifically scored for), 2 trumpets (or 'clarini') and 4

horns;[80] to this list must be added the timpani called for only in No. 7, the March which accompanies Mitridate's entrance.[81]

One wonders if the audience at *Mitridate* had the same reaction to the orchestra as Burney, who wrote:

> In the opera-house nothing but the instruments can be heard, unless when the *baritoni* or base voices sing, who can contend with them; nothing but noise can be heard through noise; a delicate voice is suffocated: it seems to me as if the orchestra ... played too loud.[82]

Perhaps Wolfgang's cast was a more forceful one than the singers Burney heard. Also, the young composer handled his instruments wisely and often the orchestra provided only a sustained accompaniment, such as in the aria No. 14 'Nel grave tormento' (In serious torment), so as not to disturb the voice at its intricacies. There is also more use of tremolo by the orchestra than in any preceding opera: Wolfgang seems now to realize that in certain situations it is the quality of the sound rather than its loudness which can accentuate emotion. Aria No. 11 for Farnace, 'Va, va, l'error mio palesa' (Go, go, reveal my mistake), is one of these cases.

Another critic of the orchestra at Milan was Arteaga who accused Giovanni Battista Lampugnani of having enlarged the ensemble by adding not only more strings but 'the most noisy instruments' such as horns, bassoons, drums. He felt that 'in some of the arias one hears accompanied in that manner, one would say it was a fight of two enemy armies on a field of battle'.[83] He realized that poetry such as Metastasio's needed the orchestra to depict its images,[84] but things had gone too far: 'In the fray of the harmony, among the many sounds piled one upon the other, among the millions of notes which are needed by the number and variety of parts, who is the singer whose voice can pierce through? Which is the poetry that would not remain confused and overly burdened?'[85] Even though Arteaga considered its size a disadvantage, the Milan orchestra certainly provided an important opportunity for Wolfgang to write for a large and competent group and he took advantage of their co-operation to score well for them in *Mitridate*; he would also take away what the experience taught him and apply his new knowledge to future works.

As usual Wolfgang followed tradition when expressing words and feelings in *Mitridate*. For example, in aria No. 2 'Soffre il mio cor con pace' (My heart suffers with peace), the word *pace* is given special treatment since this is the main idea of the text. His approach to form was also that of his contemporaries who, by the 1770s, were no longer treating the tripartite form in the traditional manner. The da capo aria which had consisted of two contrasting sections (contrasting in character and generally also in time and key signatures) with the opening section repeated in its entirety at the end had, by the time of Wolfgang's *Mitridate*, become outmoded although occasionally still employed. In its stead a rather more complex structure, which one might term *dal segno* rather than da capo and which showed connection with the early bipartite sonata form, was preferred. Here, much in the manner of the classical concerto, an instrumental introduction presented in the tonic the two themes of the following opening vocal section. This first vocal section (A) was therefore bithematic but here *a* was in the tonic and *b* was in the dominant; it was repeated (A'), however now *a'* was modulating and *b'* was in the tonic. The text thus far was that of a single stanza but as it was sung at each theme (*a, b, a', b'*), it was heard four times in succession; in bravura arias *b* and *b'* were characterized by passages of virtuosity. The second vocal section (B), relatively unimportant and in another key (often also in another tempo and metre), was based on a second stanza of text which was generally heard but once although single words might be repeated. At this point there was a return to the opening vocal section, however not from the very beginning (which would have been da capo) but *dal segno* which could have appeared at A' or even at only the last section (*b'*) of A'. (Sometimes, of course, instead of referring to a sign, the section might have been written out in full, but the principle was the same.)

This popular form with its abbreviated repeat was employed several times by Wolfgang in *Mitridate, Re di Ponto*: for example in No. 1, Aspasia's 'Al destin che la minaccia'; No. 2, Sifare's 'Soffre il mio cor con pace'; No. 6, Farnace's 'Venga pur, minacci e frema'; No. 9, Ismene's 'In faccia all'oggetto'; No. 13, Sifare's 'Lungi da te, mio bene'; No. 15, Ismene's 'So quanto a te dispiace', and so forth.

Another common eighteenth-century variant is that wherein the second section B is no longer a separate one, and here analogy is to be made with the later classical sonata. An opening vocal section (A) based on a first stanza of text is still comprised of two themes, *a* in the tonic and *b* in the dominant, but the repeat A' at this point is eliminated; the second stanza, moreover, is now set to music which serves as a transition or development section (B); after which the first stanza returns with a recapitulation in the tonic (A'). Wolfgang also offered examples of this shorter form in *Mitridate*, notably in No. 3, Arbate's 'L'odio nel cor frenate'; No. 4, Aspasia's 'Nel sen mi palpita'; No. 8, Mitridate's entrance aria (termed a *Cavata*) 'Se di lauri il crin adorno'; No. 11, Farnace's 'Va, l'error mio malese'; etc.

Apart from demonstrating Wolfgang's skill with the various and typical *opera seria* aria forms and revealing the marvellous vocal abilities of *Mitridate*'s cast (such as is evident from No. 13, Sifare's 'Lungi da te', Far from you, which showed off Benedetti's wide range and facile agility to great advantage: example 1), these are the least interesting

Example I

numbers in the opera as far as Wolfgang's response to the drama is concerned. More pertinent and relevant to his awareness in this regard are the arias wherein, for a dramatic purpose, he varied one of these schemes, or employed an ABA'B' form, or wrote continuous music. As examples of the first of these less-usual treatments, one may cite No. 5 and No. 16. In the normal (non-sectional) ABA' form, the composer generally gave more attention to the subdivision *a* than to *b*; but in these two cases the second part of the first section (A*b*) receives more emphasis than the first (A*a*). In other words, while there is always a long section which brings back the opening material in these two Numbers it seems to be preceded by a short introduction: A (*a* short, *b* long) BA' (as before). This deviation from traditional practice produces fine musical variety and also better dramatic sense since in these two cases the second phrase of text is more important than the first.

In the first example Wolfgang realized that Sifare's words, 'Parto: nel gran cimento sarò germano e figlio' (I go: in the great battle I will be brother and son) required only simple statement while the following impassioned words, 'Eguale al tuo periglio la sorte mia sarà' (My fate will be equal to your danger) needed a more extended exposition. By contrasting the two phrases and giving the second more emphasis, Wolfgang presents a human being who, although he has decided to do good, is afraid of a danger greater than his noble intentions. Similarly in No. 16 'Sono reo, l'error confesso' (I am guilty, I confess the error), the first part of section A is indicated *Adagio maestoso* and the second *Allegro* allowing Farnace to confess his guilt slowly but then to involve Sifare quickly with the accusation, 'Ma reo di me peggiore il tuo rivale è questo' (But more guilty is this your rival).

Aria No. 12 offers another unconventional disposal of tempos and sections: here the ABA form is substituted by the ABA'B' form, that generally associated with *opera buffa*. When Mitridate speaks to Sifare saying 'Tu, che fedel mi sei' (You who are faithful to me), the tempo is *Adagio*, the music lyrical; but after a phrase of fourteen bars he turns to Aspasia reprimanding her with 'Tu ingrata' (You ungrateful one) and sends her away with music which is completely different in character – *Allegro* with frequent *forte-piano* indications from beginning to end –

creating an excited and angry contrast with the music of the first section. Even without the text the action would have been described with force. Unfortunately, as the sections are repeated (and a Coda added), part of the dramatic efficacy of the aria is inevitably lost, even if the form in itself, unusual as it was in an *opera seria*, would have created some interest for the audience. No. 14 for Aspasia, 'Nel grave tormento' cited above, exhibits the same form (minus the Coda) and an analogous change, due to its text, from *Adagio* to *Allegro*.

Another variant and the one most responsive to the drama is that which is *durchkomponiert*. The duet No. 18 is at least in part an example of such writing. After an initial repeated section, 'Se viver non degg'io' (If I don't have to live), wherein Sifare and Aspasia alternate singing different texts but to the same music, continuous music follows at 'Ah, che tu sol, tu sei, che mi dividi il cor' (Ah, that you alone, you are, who divides my heart), and Wolfgang has them sing first in imitation, the musical expression of unity of thought, and then actually together in thirds (example 2). The ABCD text, therefore, is set in an AABC

Example 2

ASPASIA
SIFARE

mi di vi diil cor

musical structure. Since Wolfgang omitted the second stanza of text (musically the B section) in arias No. 10 and No. 20, 'Quell ribelle e quell'ingrato' (That rebel and ingrate) and 'Vado incontro al fato estremo' (I go to meet my destiny) for Mitridate, they also result in a non-da capo musical setting (AA').

Mentioning Mitridate, another characteristic of his music must be noted. D'Ettore, whom Burney called 'a famous tenor', was not a *cantante d'agilità* and therefore was unable to sing *fioriture*.[86] Instead his large range (c' to c'''') and ability to execute difficult leaps were put into relief by Wolfgang. Of course in 'Quell ribelle' mentioned above, in which Mitridate is decided to oppose those who oppose him, the dramatic force of the text might sensibly preclude vocal decoration; but it is to his credit that the young composer manages in each of Mitridate's arias to have it appear natural and almost indicative of the ruler's authority that his part be free of the passages of semiquaver ornamentation typical of the rest of the opera.

Another aria of the 'unadorned' type is 'Nel sen mi palpita' (In my breast it beats), No. 4 for Aspasia. In an unusually short introduction (especially considering the dimensions typical of *opera seria*) Wolfgang created the necessary atmosphere for the second aria of the Queen, an anguished outcry of her anxiety over Sifare and of their love motivated by the unexpected return of Mitridate (example 3). The aria is accompanied by strings and oboes (plus *ad lib.* flutes) which serve to reflect her agitated state of mind. The setting is, apart from a single brief *fioritura*, syllabic, thus implying, in agreement with John Brown's analysis of such

Example 3

dramatic situations, that the involvement of the character in the drama
'is of a nature too serious and important' for impersonal trills or runs.[87]
The aria is not a long da capo either. Aspasia reveals her feelings and
leaves, since to repeat them too much would only weaken their
dramatic impact, and one can imagine that Bernasconi, with her 'neat
and elegant manner of singing',[88] would have made the aria a success.

Even the recitative in *Mitridate* receives dramatic treatment. Worth
mentioning in this regard is Scene 4 of Act III, beginning 'Lagrime
intempestive' (Untimely tears). It is a mixture of various styles and
probably the most dramatic use of recitative made thus far by Wolfgang; since the recitatives were composed while father and son were
in Bologna, it is of course possible that Padre Martini had a hand in
the composition of this scene, or that he at least supervised its
composition.[89] The scene begins with eight bars of *secco* recitative and
calls for only the usual continuo instruments at first; but when Aspasia
is handed a cup of poison to drink as she has been unfaithful to Mitridate,
strings, oboes (and flutes) and horns are added to the harpsichord and
bassi (which now include bassoon) and an excited *Allegro* section of
accompanied recitative follows. As Aspasia thinks of her beloved Sifare
and realizes she will be united with him in the tomb, she becomes
quieter and after 24 bars the accompanied recitative turns into real aria.
Her *Andante* cavatina 'Pallid' ombre' is directed to the 'Pallid ghosts' of
the Elysian fields whom she asks to watch over her. But at the returning
realization that she must drink the poison, her fears are renewed and
with them the accompanied style of recitative returns (example 4) to

Example 4

allow her to express her several different thoughts in changing tempos of [*Allegro*], *Andante*, *Allegro*. The scene is the first example of Wolfgang deviating from the normal alternating pattern of recitative/aria, recitative/aria and is an excellent one at that.

The tendency to deviate from general practice achieving, at the same time, a better interpretation of the drama is, in fact, the principal characteristic of Wolfgang's work in *Mitridate, Re di Ponto*. In *Die Schuldigkeit des ersten Gebotes* and in *Apollo et Hyacinthus* he was interested in expressing the text (not character) within the established forms of *opera seria*. *Mitridate* is also an *opera seria*, and a successful attempt at the genre with grand tripartite arias knowingly embellished. But while it does contain expected examples of expression based on single words, it above all presents changes of form which permit a more complete realization of the drama and of the characters.

Wolfgang absorbed much from the repertory of *opera buffa* and profited from his own experience when writing *La finta semplice*, since he applied not simply the form but the style of *opera buffa* to *Mitridate*. The lyrical arias No. 13 'Lungi da te' for Sifare (notable also for its unusual and lovely use of solo horn) and, even more so, No. 4 'Nel sen mi palpita' and No. 14 'Nel grave tormento', both for Aspasia, seem to be applications of his graceful *cantabile* style for Rosina of *La finta semplice*; these last were certainly the numbers which struck the critic of the *Gazzetta di Milano* when he wrote that they 'express passions vividly and touch the heart'. It is also in the same aria No. 4 that the oboe is briefly used (example 5) as it was earlier in Rosina's aria No. 9 'Senti l'eco ove t'aggiri'. As has been seen, Wolfgang introduced the ABAB form of *opera buffa* into his *opera seria* and wrote arias similarly without *fioriture*. Even the recitative continues to undergo changes initiated in *opera buffa*: in *La finta semplice* Wolfgang had given shape to some recitatives and had provided a recitative for Cassandro with a more moving accompaniment; now in *Mitridate* he makes use of the different dramatic powers of *secco* recitative, accompanied recitative and aria to build an entire continuous scene.

The form and style of traditional *opera seria* were the basis for Wolfgang's composition in *Mitridate, Re di Ponto*, but he made relatively free use of it, making changes he felt necessary for the drama. And this in his first important *opera seria* and at only 14 years of age.[90] One sees his growing interest in composing for the theatre, in ingeniously applying what he learnt about instrumentation, form and style from preceding operatic experience and, without doubt, from other vocal and instrumental compositions.

Example 5

Chapter Six: Notes

1. K. 74a/87 in *WAM*, Serie V, 5; and *NMA*, Serie II, 5, bd. 4.

2. As he wrote to his friend Hagenauer from Vienna on 11 May 1768: see *Briefe*, I, p. 264.

3. The Mass was K. 61a/65 and the *Licenza* K. 61c/70: see *Dokumente*, pp. 79 and 67; *Addenda*, p. 13; and Köchel 6, pp. 78–81.

4. See Chapter IV here and Jahn, I, p. 98.

5. *Dokumente*, p. 83.

6. He was now Professor of Logic. See Chapter III here on *Apollo et Hyacinthus*.

7. K. 62 and 62a/100: Act I, scene 10, No. 7. The 'Numbers' for *Mitridate* are those of *NMA*.

8. *Dokumente*, p. 84.

9. Letter of 4 October: *ibid.*, p. 85.

10. Guiseppe Francesco Lolli was Kapellmeister and Ferdinand Seidl and Johann Michael Haydn first and second Konzertmeister: see *Dokumente*, pp. 86 and 93, and *Addenda*, p. 14. In all, Leopold served under seven Kapellmeister at Salzburg (for a complete list see Schenk, *Mozart*, pp. 15-16) and while one is certain he would have liked the post for himself, in truth his absences from court made this impossib!e.

11. According to C. Hagenauer's diary cited in *Dokumente*, p. 92. For complete documentation on this and all Wolfgang's trips to Italy, see *Mozart in Italia* edited by Guglielmo Barblan and Andrea Della Corte (Milan, 1956).

12. An account was printed in the *Gazzetta di Mantova* on 12 January 1770: see *Dokumente*, pp. 95-96, and 'Nell'enthusiasmo di Verona' by Raffaello Brenzoni in *Mozart in Italia*, pp. 46-56, which also includes a photograph of the relevant page (Tavola vi).

13. *Dokumente*, pp. 93-94 and Brenzoni.

14. *Dokumente*, p. 100, and *Briefe*, I, p. 311. On their way to Milan, the Mozarts stopped in Mantua (see Erich Schenk, 'La sosta a Mantova', *Mozart in Italia*, pp. 57-63). Their stay in Milan is documented by Guglielmo Barblan, 'A Milano', *idem*, pp. 64-75.

15. From Verona on 7 January: *Briefe*, I, p. 301.

16. Wolfgang to his sister, 3 March: *Briefe*, I, p. 319.

17. *Dokumente*, *idem*.

18. Leopold to his wife, 17 February: *Briefe*, I, p. 315. On the Duke's identity see Barblan's clarification in 'A Milano', pp. 70-71.

19. They were probably 'per pietà, bell' idol mio' K. 73b/78, 'Fra cento affani' K. 73c/88 and 'Per quel paterno anplesso' K.73d/79, and more than likely were for castratos: see Köchel 6, pp. 98-100. Firmian had given Wolfgang a complete edition of Metastasio's works (see *Dokumente*, *idem*). He also wrote letters of presentation for the Mozarts; one was to Count Gian Luca Pallavicini of Bologna who invited 150 nobles to his home to hear Wolfgang and who, in turn, introduced Leopold and Wolfgang to Count Lazzaro Opizio Pallavicini, Secretary of State in Rome: see *Dokumente*, pp. 100-103, and for more details, Luigi F. Tagliavini, 'Primo contatto bolognese' in *Mozart in Italia*, pp. 76-86.

20. Leopold to his wife, 13 March: *Briefe*, I, p. 320; also see *Dokumente*, p. 100 and its *Addenda*, p. 15.

21. *Briefe*, *idem*. Initially Wolfgang was to do the more prestigious second opera of the season and Carlo Monza's *Nitteti* was to have been first (see Leopold's letter home of 30 June 1770 in *Briefe*, I, p. 366) but for some unknown reason the order was reversed (see Leopold's letter of 4 August in *Briefe*, I, p. 377).

22. *Italy*, p. 83. He notes that the gold *zechin* was equal to 9 English shillings.

23. From Leopold's engagement book in *Briefe*, I, p. 322. Bernasconi, daughter of a valet of the Duke of Würtemberg, who had been educated as a singer by her stepfather, Andrea Bernasconi (Kapellmeister at Munich since 1754), had started out as a *buffa* singer and had had great success in Piccinni's *Buona figliola*, where Wolfgang first heard her. She then broadened her repertory to include *opera seria* roles making her debut in Gluck's *Alceste* of 1767. She was probably the intended Ninetta of *La finta semplice*.

24. *Idem* and p. 330; also *Dokumente*, pp. 101-102, and Tagliavini, *ibid.*, p. 82. The Mozarts had heard him sing in Cremona in *Clemenza di Tito* and Wolfgang wrote home that he had 'a lovely voice and a beautiful cantabile': see his letter of 26 January 1770 in *Briefe*, I, p. 310. On the way to Parma, at Lodi, Wolfgang composed his first string quartet K. 73f/80 of three movements; a rondeau was added in 1773 or 1774: see Köchel 6, pp. 100-101.

25. *Addenda*, p. 16; *Briefe*, I, p. 332. On the Mozarts' stay in Florence see Adelmo Damerini, 'Una settimana a Firenze' in *Mozart in Italia*, pp. 87-95.

26. As Wolfgang wrote to Nannerl on 21 April: *Briefe*, I, p. 339.

27. *Idem*.

28. *Dokumente*, p. 105. For a facsimile of the page, see Tavola xv of *Mozart in Italia*.

29. Leopold in a letter to his wife on 24 March: see *Briefe*, I, p. 325. According to Mercedes Viale Ferrero in a private communication, 100 *gigliati* (incorrectly called *cigliati* by the Mozarts) was the normal fee paid to a composer and was roughly equivalent to the price of 300 meals. In short, Wolfgang and Leopold would have been able to eat for at least 75 days on this sum. However, a star singer could have earned anything up to 1,000 *gigliati* for a season (i.e. for two operas). On Manzuoli's fees, see Wolfgang's letter to his sister of 23-24 November 1771 in *Briefe*, I, p. 451.

30. *Addenda*, p. 17. On the Mozarts' visit to Rome and Naples, see Guglielmo Barblan, 'Intermezzo romano-napoletano e la questione della Gabrielli' in *Mozart in Italia*, pp. 96-107.

31. Burney, *Italy*, p. 382.

32. *Dokumente*, p. 109, and *Briefe*, I, p. 345.

33. *Briefe*, *ibid.*, pp. 355 and 358.

34. *Ibid.*, pp. 355 and 362. On Neopolitan influence in Mozart's operas, see Giovanni Carli Ballola, 'Mozart e l'opera seria di Jommelli, De Majo e Traetta', *Analecta musicologica* 18 (1978), pp. 138-147.

35. *Dokumente*, p. 111.

36. *Ibid.*, pp. 111-113. Wolfgang had an audience with the Pope himself on 8 July.

37. *Ibid.*, p. 113. It was at the Mass and Vespers of the Accademia Filarmonica held in S. Giovanni in Monte.

38. Wolfgang in a letter to Thomas Linley in Florence on 10 September 1770: *Briefe*, I, p. 388. On this stay in Bologna, see Luigi F. Tagliavini, 'Accademico filarmonico', in *Mozart in Italia*, pp. 108-122.

39. *Briefe*, I, p. 373.

40. *Ibid.*, I, p. 374.

41. He began the recitatives on 29 September as Leopold wrote to his wife: *Briefe*, I, p. 393.

42. As Wolfgang wrote to Nannerl on 4 August: *Briefe*, I, p. 377. One of these would be K. 73q/84 but it is not certain which the others are as none other has the three-movement form particular to the 'Italian' symphony.

43. Leopold to his wife on 20 October: *Briefe*, I, p. 396, and *Dokumente*, pp. 114-115. It should be remembered that the four-part counterpoint written by Wolfgang was completely rewritten by Padre Martini and only then was the boy accepted for membership by the Accademia Filarmonica. However, on this the letters home are silent. See Tagliavini, *ibid.*, for a detailed account.

44. Leopold to his wife: *Briefe*, I, p. 395. For a detailed account of the Mozarts' stay in

Milan and Wolfgang's work on *Mitridate*, see Guglielmo Barblan, 'Di nuovo a Milano per il battesimo di operista' in *Mozart in Italia*, pp. 123-135.

45. *Briefe*, I, p. 402.

46. As Leopold explained to Padre Martini on 2 January 1771: *Briefe*, I, p. 413. The same leading role in the Turin production had been taken by Antonia Maria Girelli Aguillar who would sing for Wolfgang in *Ascanio in Alba* (according to Luigi F. Tagliavini, 'Quirino Gasparini and Mozart' in *New Looks at Italian Opera*, ed. William W. Austin; Ithaca, N.Y., 1968, p. 164).

47. See Tagliavini, *ibid.*, pp. 151-171, for a comparison of the two settings.

48. *Briefe*, I, p. 402.

49. Leopold to his wife on 17 November: *Briefe*, I, p. 404. This 'second storm' was probably with D'Ettore and must have been serious as Leopold reminded Wolfgang of it some years later when the young man was in Paris: see his letter of 11 May 1778 in *Briefe*, II, p. 353. One sign of Wolfgang's difficulties with D'Ettore is that his entrance aria 'Se di lauri il crin adorno' had to be written four times before the singer was pleased.

50. *Briefe*, I, p. 405.

51. These were: No. 1, Aspasia's 'Al destin che la minaccia'; No. 8, Mitridate's 'Se di lauri il crin adorno'; No. 9, Ismene's 'In faccia all'oggetto'; No. 13, Sifare's 'Lungi da te, mio bene'; No. 14, Aspasia's 'Nel grave tormento'; No. 16, Farnace's 'Son reo, l'error confesso'; No. 18, the duet for Aspasia and Sifare 'Se viver non degg'io'; No. 20, Mitridate's 'Vado incontro al fato estremo'. See Jahn, I, p. 175, Köchel 6, pp. 118-119, and Tagliavini's introduction to his critical edition of *Mitridate* in *NMA*, pp. viii-ix. He reports that the aria sung by Bernasconi in Act III, scene 5, 'Secondi il ciel pietoso', was by an unknown composer. Wolfgang was receiving the usual treatment bestowed upon opera composers, not upon *Wunderkinder*.

52. See his letters of 8, 15 and 22 December in *Briefe*, I, pp. 407, 408 and 409-410 respectively.

53. Letter of 8 December, *op. cit.*

54. Letter of 15 December, *op. cit.*

55. *Idem.*

56. Letter of 22 December, *op. cit.*, p. 410.

57. Letter of 15 December, *op. cit.*

58. *Dokumente*, p. 117.

59. Letter of 29 December: *Briefe*, I, p. 411. The Milan theatre was always closed on Friday.

60. *Briefe*, I, p. 413.

61. Leopold to his wife on 5 January 1771: *Briefe*, I, p. 414; and *Dokumente*, p. 116. Giovanni Battista Lampugnani, mentioned earlier as Bernasconi's maestro, was at the second keyboard; when Wolfgang sat in the audience, he moved to the first harpsichord and Melchiorre Chiesa took over the second keyboard. Leopold marvelled in the same letter that: 'If anyone had told me fifteen or eighteen years ago, when I heard so much of the opera songs and symphonies of Lampugnani in England and Melchior Chiesa in Italy, that these two men would perform your son's music, and take his place at the keyboard to accompany his opera, I should probably have directed such a person to the madhouse as an idiot.'

62. *Briefe, idem.*

63. *Italy*, pp. 81-82.

64. *Idem*, p. 82. He also said (p. 102) that 'the lights at the opera-house here affected my eyes in a very painful manner', which is strange in a day when candles were the source of light. Perhaps some sort of reflectors were employed as well, such as Garrick was known to have used in London, which would have increased the strength of the light somewhat.

65. *Op. cit.*, II, p. 317.

66. See Hansel, *op. cit.*

67. Letter of 26 January 1770: *Briefe, op. cit.*

68. Ettore Capriolo and Graziella Huen de Florentiis, 'Milano', *Enciclopedia dello Spettacolo* (Florence, 1962), VII, col. 552. The Regio Ducale burned in 1776 and a new and larger public theatre, the present La Scala, was built in 1778 to replace it.

69. Letter of 29 December, *op. cit.*, p. 411. Not all theatre-goers felt like Leopold. As a matter of fact, Burney was disappointed that in Naples, for example, ballets could be given only at the royal theatre, San Carlo, which meant that operas performed elsewhere had no ballets: see his *Italy*, p. 310. For the Milan production Francesco Caselli was the choreographer and the 28 members of his company danced *Il Giudizio di Paride*, *Il Triofono della Virtù a fronte d'Amore* and *Dame, e Cavalieri, che applaudono alle Nozze d'Aspasia, e d'Ismene* (this last being connected with the plot of Wolfgang's opera): see the libretto, folios 3v-4, a copy of which is in the East Berlin Deutsche Staatsbibliothek.

70. *Dokumente*, p. 116, and the libretto. Parini was the critic of the *Gazzetta di Milano* quoted above.

71. See, for example, the plot summaries here of *La finta semplice* and *La finta giardiniera*.

72. *Italy*, pp. 302-303.

73. The most complete study of the subject is Angus Heriot, *The Castrati in Opera* (London, 1956). See also Arteaga, I, p. 351 ff for his account of the use of the castrato and then of women on stage.

74. Both singers performed at the Bologna *Accademia* held for Wolfgang: see *Briefe*, I, p. 322; *Dokumente*, pp. 101-102; and Tagliavini, *Mozart in Italia*, p. 82. The latter (in note 3) also cites Rutini's favourable comments on Aprile. Burney, on the other hand (in *Italy*, p. 328), said of Aprile that he had 'rather a weak and uneven voice, but is constantly steady, as to intonation. He has a good person, a good shake, and much taste and expression.' See note 24 here for Wolfgang's reaction to Cicognani's voice.

75. II, pp. 76-77, but actually based on Algarotti, II, p. 303.

76. On the Galliari brothers' work in Turin see Mercedes Viale Ferrero's chapter 'Scenografia' in *Mostra del Barocco Piemontese. Catalogo* (Turin, 1963), I, pp. 1-56. Tagliavini has included four of their sketches for Gasparini's *Mitridate* between pp. 162 and 163 of his article 'Quirino Gasparini and Mozart', *op. cit.*

77. On the Turin theatre see Mercedes Viale Ferrero, 'Die Bühnenausstattung des Teatro Regio di Torino (1667-1740)', *Hamburger Jahrbuch für Musikwissenschaft* bd. 3, *Studien zur Barockoper* (1977), pp. 239-272 which includes a design of the stage on p. 264. Tagliavini does not seem to be aware of the differences between the two stages: see his introduction to *NMA*, p. x. The Galliari sketches for Turin are in the Bologna Pinacoteca Nazionale.

78. The various sets for *Mitridate, Re di Ponto* were complemented in the *Gazzetta di Milano*. Described briefly in the libretto, they were the following:

Act I: Square of Nymphaeum with a view of the port in the distance.

Temple of Venus with Ara lighted, adorned with myrtle and roses.

Sea port, with two fleets anchored at the canals. A view of Nymphaeum on one side.

Act II: Apartments.

Mitridate's camp. To the right and front of the theatre a great Royal Pavilion with seats. Behind are thick woods and armed soldiers, etc.

Act III: Hanging gardens.

Inside the tower connected to the walls of Nymphaeum.

Ground floor entrance hall, connected to the large courtyard in the seat of the Kingdom of Nymphaeum from which in the distance [one sees] the Roman ships burning at sea.

79. Leopold wrote to his wife on 15 December, *op. cit.*, that Benedetti said that if the public did not like his duet with Bernasconi, he would have himself castrated a second time!

80. Leopold declared the members of the orchestra to be 60 although he accounted for only 56: see his letter of 15 December, *op. cit.* The four horns were used together only once by Wolfgang (in the duet No. 18, 'Se viver non degg'io'), and once he scored for three (No. 13, 'Lungi da te'); otherwise he employed them in pairs.

81. This was K. 62 and 62a/100 written for Salzburg. See note 7 here and the related passage in the text.

82. *Italy*, p. 104.

83. *Op. cit.*, II, p. 257.

84. *Ibid.*, p. 263.

85. *Ibid.*, p. 257.

86. *Italy*, p. 133. For a brief comparison between D'Ettore's similar parts in *Mitridate* and in Sacchini's *Scipione*, also of 1770, as well as a musical example from the latter, see Luigi F. Tagliavini, 'L'Opéra italien du jeune Mozart' in *Les influences étrangères dans l'œuvre de W. A. Mozart* (Paris, 1958) pp. 146–149.

87. *Op. cit.*, p. 60.

88. Burney, *General History*, II, p. 886. By 1778, though, he felt that her voice 'was feeble and in decay'.

89. See Leopold's letter from Bologna to his wife on 24 March 1770: *Briefe*, I, pp. 325–327.

90. The autograph of the score is lost (see Köchel 6, p. 119 on its history), apart from some sketches and first versions of arias (included by Tagliavini in the *NMA*); however copies supervised by Wolfgang exist (see Tagliavini's introduction to his edition). An eighteenth-century copy made by the contrabassist Domenico Dragonetti now in the British Library lacks the recitatives. It also contains the aria 'D'un padre l'affetto' probably not by Mozart.

CHAPTER SEVEN

Ascanio in Alba[1]

WHILE PERFORMANCES of *Mitridate* were going ahead happily, Wolfgang was honoured by being made a member of the Accademia Filharmonica of Verona.[2] Leopold and Wolfgang were not idle either. There was more musical entertaining, for example at the home of Count Karl Joseph Firmian, the gentleman who had been so instrumental in obtaining the Milanese contracts for Wolfgang. There were also more trips, this time to Turin, which had an active court theatre but where no contract was obtained, and to Venice.[3] Apparently Leopold expected the Venetian nobility to make more of a fuss over his son and seemed to Hasse's friend Giovanni Ortes 'a bit piqued' by their behaviour; Wolfgang, on the other hand, had a couldn't-care-less attitude to their indifference of which both Ortes and Hasse approved.[4] His was certainly the wiser, especially since what both father and son really desired, a commission for an opera, did eventually come forth. On 17 August 1771, when they were home in Salzburg where they had arrived on 28 March after an absence of $15\frac{1}{2}$ months, a contract arrived for Wolfgang to write an 'heroic opera' as the second opera for Carnival 1773 at the San Benedetto Theatre in Venice.[5] As events turned out, the opera never came to fruition.[6] In the more immediate future, however, there were two other works for Milan. As Leopold wrote to Count Gian Luca Pallavicini in Bologna, stretching the sequence of events a bit in order to excuse himself for not writing:

> Hardly had we arrived home when I had a letter from the management of the Theatre in Milan in which it was agreed that my son write an opera for Carnival 1773 [the contract was actually received March 1771], and shortly after he was told to be in Milan at the beginning of the next month of September in order to write the serenata or rather theatrical cantata for the marriage of S.A.R. Archduke Ferdinand, a meeting which is so much more an honour since the older of the Maestros, Signor Adolf Hasse, called the Saxon, will write the opera and the younger Maestro the serenata. A certain Signor Abate Porini [Parini] is at the moment writing the poetry for

this cantata, which, as they write me from Vienna, will be finished the middle of next month and will be entitled *Ascanio in Alba*.[7]

This meant that father and son were once more off to Italy. They left Salzburg on 13 August 1771, in ten days were back in Milan, and on the 31st were visiting with Hasse.[8] Their lodgings were quite 'musical' but no doubt disturbing as Wolfgang wrote to his sister on 24 August, the day after they arrived: 'Above us is a violinist, under us is another, next door a singing teacher gives lessons, in the last room next to ours is an oboist. That's delightful for composing!'[9] But compose somehow he did.

Giuseppe Parini (1729–1799),[10] the librettist for *Ascanio in Alba*, was not, at least in name, unfamiliar to the Mozarts. His had been the translation of Racine's play used by Vittorio Cigna-Santi as the basis for *Mitridate, Re di Ponto*; more pertinently, he was the critic for the *Gazzetta di Milano* who had written so favourably about Wolfgang's music and the performance of the opera.[11] Parini, an abate and a member both of the Milanese Accademia dei Trasformati (as was Cigna-Santi) and the Roman Arcadia, was not simply a librettist. One of Italy's most celebrated poets, this keen observer of contemporary behaviour and customs of the Milanese aristocracy was an author mainly of essays and sonnets which recounted what he saw, such as *Il Giorno* which describes the behaviour of the spoiled young noble and includes many telling passages which bemoan the loose morality of the eighteenth century. A follower of current developments of the Enlightenment and a moralist, Parini allowed himself to be persuaded by Count Firmian, his protector, into writing a laudatory text for the young ruler's wedding celebrations.

The *festa teatrale*, which is what Parini called his work,[12] was a typical seventeenth- and eighteenth-century genre, frequently heard at the court of Vienna.[13] Written by court poets to celebrate births, marriages, name days, etc. of the reigning family, a *festa teatrale* would often be based on mythology and make use of allegory to honour the noble whose celebration it was. Similar to the contemporary *azione teatrale*,[14] both genres were a sort of opera in miniature: that is, they were usually not as long as an opera but longer than a simple cantata or serenata. The normal number of *personaggi* for a *festa* was six although one finds *azioni* with only two or three characters. While the *festa teatrale* could have had any number of scenes or parts, the *azione* properly had two parts as does *Ascanio in Alba*. Probably the first *festa teatrale* at Vienna was *L'inganno d'amore* by Antonio Bertali in 1653; some 30 examples were then provided by Antonio Draghi and others by Johann Joseph Fux. Metastasio wrote eleven *feste teatrali* some of which were set to music more than once, and Parini supposedly followed his models when working on *Ascanio in Alba*. Although the Metastasian conventions were obviously adhered to by Parini, he unfortunately lacked the master's poetic skill in making the simple plot come alive.

The libretto begins by requesting that Venere (Venus) be seen descending from the clouds accompanied by genies, graces, and her son Ascanio. She then says to him that she would like to see him married to Silvia, a lovely nymph and descendant of Hercules. First, however, they must test Silvia's virtue. Ascanio is delighted with the idea of marriage but is impatient at the delay. Now Fauno comes onto the scene accompanied by other shepherds and they all praise the invisible-to-them Venere and her goodness. Next we see Silvia with Aceste, the High Priest, who informs her that Venere intends for her to marry Ascanio and for them to found a New City with their children. Cupido (Cupid), though, has shown Ascanio to Silvia and since then she has been in love with the nameless youth. Aceste reassures her that all will end well; when they leave to prepare to make sacrifice to the Gods, Ascanio sings an aria declaring his love. During the following ballet, the nymphs and graces change the woods into a temple, the first edifice of the New City. At this point Silvia sings an aria in which she expresses her desire to be joined with her unknown love; when Ascanio next appears she recognizes him as the youth of her dreams, but when he pretends not to know her she faints. Ascanio takes this opportunity to lament his not being able to reveal himself to her. When Silvia awakens she expresses not only her anguish but also her determination to remain constant to her responsibilities. Ascanio now throws himself at her feet but Silvia rejects him and leaves as the young God sings her praises. The test of Silvia being thus over, Venere appears with the nymphs and shepherds and gives Ascanio to Silvia. After the couple and Aceste sing of their happiness in a trio, Venere encourages them to behave properly towards their subjects. The *festa teatrale* ends with a chorus of praise and thanksgiving to Venere.

The libretto was filled with allusions to the spouses Archduke Ferdinand of Austria, Maria Theresa's third son and brother to Leopold, Grand Duke of Tuscany and future Emperor; and Princess Maria Beatrice Ricciarda of Modena, daughter of Rinaldo d'Este, Hercules III, and their families, as Jahn has pointed out:

The description which Fauno gives of the guardian divinity of the country, and the address of Aceste to Venus as she departs, contain so many illusions to Maria Theresa that non-recognition was impossible. Silvia, too, of the race of Hercules (the name of Ercole was common in the family of D'Este), the pupil of Minerva and the muses, the pattern of virtue and modesty, is undoubtedly the Princess Beatrice, whose intellect, literary cultivation, and amiability were universally admired. There was less to be said of the Archduke Ferdinand; nothing could be made of him but a fair youth with rosy cheeks. It is worthy of note that although mutual liking founded on beauty and spiritual endowments is highly extolled, yet, as became a royal wedding, the subjection of inclination to duty is made the theme of highest praise.[15]

The responsibility towards one's subjects was certainly an aspect the enlightened Parini could not help emphasizing; it was also Maria Theresa's philosophy and therefore expected of Ferdinand as well. The Ideal State is suggested by the poet but was made visual by the 'Inventors and Painters of the Scenery', the Galliari brothers, in their realization of an idyllic atmosphere. The description of the opening scene which one reads in the libretto is as follows:[16]

A spacious area, intended for the solemn pastoral gatherings, outlined with a crown of very tall and leafy oak trees, which beautifully distributed within here and there provide a very fresh and sacred shadow. Alongside the series of green trees are mounds of earth, formed by nature and made into various shapes by art, which allow the shepherds to seat themselves with lovely irregularity. In the middle an outdoor altar rises, in which one sees the legendary animal sculptured, from which one says the name the City of Alba gets its name. In the spaces which open between one tree and another a delicious and smiling countryside dominates, scattered with a few huts and encircled in the near distance by lovely hills, from which descend copious and limpid streams. The horizon ends in very blue mountains, the peaks of which are lost in a very clear and serene sky.

In the early eighteenth century, stage settings, even of a garden or sea or somewhere in the Underworld, were designed with emphasis on structure, and were actually drawings of architecture. Francesco Algarotti complained that sets were often only 'labyrinths of architecture where truth disappears'.[17] They were generally made to direct the eye of the beholder through the rigid rules of perspective to an invisible central point far in the distance. If singers moved about towards the back of the stage they were at odds with the size of buildings, objects or figures painted on the set which had been made to conform to the diminishing distance. Often a set would have its only exit onto the stage at the back and as Algarotti remarked, 'Then the characters appear as towering giants, as they are seen against the back of the set. . . . And these giants later get smaller, becoming dwarfs as they gradually come forward.'[18]

The Galliari brothers, who had also designed the sets for Wolfgang's *Mitridate*, began their careers by accepting the rich heritage of their profession and concerned themselves with making decorative scenery rather than sets which conformed in any individual way to the sense and atmosphere of the drama on which they were working. This was, though, the period of *opera buffa* with its concern for reality rather than stylization; and the new approach was to be found not only in the plots and music but also in the scenery for such works. Other areas of theatre could not help but be influenced by its 'naturalism' and the Galliaris, called to work in Turin (1762), Innsbruck (1765), Vienna (1767, 1770), Parma (1769), Berlin (1772), Paris (1777) as well as Milan, were made keenly aware of the changes through their many experiences.[19] Beginning with *Enea nel Lazio* done for Turin in 1760, one finds them designing their *scena quadro* with a feeling for the play in which it is to be used. From now on their scenery attempted to imitate the real in nature, not nature stylized; or actual environments, not simply those idealized architecturally.

The careful description of the opening scene for *Ascanio in Alba* does not stress perspective or structure; rather it emphasized the green and peaceful country atmosphere in which one is to see Venere and her entourage descend, all explicitly detailed by the Galliaris but with an intent to achieve a casual result. As stated, the scene was to seem as though it were formed by nature although actually made by art.[20] Another point to be noted is the indication in the libretto that the dancers, during one of their ballets, are to change the set from the woods to a temple. It was not an uncommon practice to have the scenery changed in front of the audience – it provided an element of delightful surprise – and it was possible to do so easily due to the developed technique of raising and lowering flats through a system of weights. Another 'marvel' of the evening was surely the sight of Venere and Ascanio with their genies and graces all descending from the 'very clear and serene sky', this time the credit going to Carlo Giuseppe Fossati, 'Machinista'. Such machines were also the result of advanced engineering and had played an essential role in Baroque opera where Gods and Goddesses had to be transported to or from Heaven and Hell. One must admit that the typical 'fantastic' opera libretto was possible thanks to the Italian theatrical engineers, of whom the Venetian Fossati was one of the last.

As for Wolfgang's participation in *Ascanio*, he began composing only at the end of August, as Leopold wrote to his wife on 31 August 1771, since that was when he received the libretto:

> The poetry has finally arrived, for which however Wolfgang has not yet done more than the overture, namely a rather long Allegro; then an Andante, which must be danced at the same time but only by a few people; then for the last Allegro he has done a sort of contradance and chorus, to be sung and danced at the same time.[21]

Wolfgang's involvement with ballet was not to be confined to what was to be danced during the opera itself but, as Leopold wrote, he 'must also compose the ballet which is to join together the two acts or parts' of *Ascanio in Alba*.[22] For *Mitridate, Re di Ponto* Leopold and Wolfgang had only to suffer through the long ballets presented between the acts of Wolfgang's opera, but now the young man had to compose them as well.

By the time of *Ascanio*, ballet was no longer an entertainment in which nobles and professional dancers and acrobats all appeared together, as they had in the *ballet de cour*. The construction of opera theatres allowed for a different sort of dance than the slow, stately movements which always took into account the viewing point of the ruling prince or king seated somewhere along one of the shorter sides of the grand salon. At first the dancers' problems were those of the singers: stage space and how much of it could actually be used. For a long time choreography aimed at graceful gestures by groups outlining symmetrical patterns, even if the *corps de ballet* was supposed to be monsters from Hell. A comparative history of dance and set designing would show that both exhibited comparable progress from stylization to naturalism, with a new approach to dance being affirmed in the pantomime ballet of the Florentine Gasparo Angiolini, *Don Juan ou Le Festin de pierre*, set to music by Gluck in Vienna in 1761.[23]

Dance was no longer to be just a series of interesting movements, it had to tell a story, to communicate. Later to become an international world, ballet was initially dominated by Italian families of dancers and choreographers who brought their art to all the important courts and cities, certainly with great success to Vienna and Milan as has been seen. At the time of *Ascanio in Alba*, one of Vienna's leading choreographers was Jean-Georges Noverre (1727-1810)[24] who had begun his career dancing for Favart at the *opéra-comique* in Paris where, after performing throughout Europe, he was called in 1754 as *maître de ballet*. Garrick, for whom he danced and choreographed for many years in London (he was at both Drury Lane and the King's Theatre), called him the 'Shakespeare of the dance,' and in Vienna, where Noverre had been called as Court *maître de ballet* in 1767, *L'Almanach théatrâl de Vienne* wrote of him in 1772: 'He knows how to cause each and every passion in the spectator through movement and only pantomime.' As much as his dancing and choreography, it was Noverre's theories on ballet expressed in his *Lettres sur la Danse* which caused a sensation in artistic circles. He wrote:

A well-set ballet is a living painting of the passions, morae, habits, ceremonies and customs of all the races on earth; as a consequence it must be a pantomime in every sense and must talk to the soul through the eyes. When it is deprived of expression, of striking scenes and powerful situations, it then offers only a cold and dull performance. This type of composition cannot be of mediocre quality; as in painting it requires a kind of perfection which, the more it attempts a faithful imitation of nature, the more difficult it is to ˙achieve.[25]

Clearly Noverre's ideas were in keeping with those of eighteenth-century naturalism and its desire for a true expression of sentiment. His period in Vienna, home of the pantomime ballet, was very fecund: in fact, between 1767 and 1774 he put on more than 50 ballets, something like seven or eight a year. While he was transferred to Milan in 1774 (where he stayed till 1776 when the theatre burned and he became *maître de ballet* at the Paris Opéra), in 1771 at the time of *Ascanio* he was still officially in Vienna. However Charles Le Picq (1749-1806), dancer and choreographer, a disciple of Noverre who followed him to London and Paris and who faithfully executed Noverre's artistic wishes, was one of the two choreographers who worked on Wolfgang's opera. Therefore a certain adherence to style and faithfulness of execution 'à la Noverre' was assured. Moreover, Le Picq, who would also have been the *primo ballerino* (with his wife, Anna Binetti, as *prima ballerina*), was a vivacious performer and known for the lightness and fluidity of his movements and quite arresting style.[26] Unfortunately, nothing is known about Giovanni Favier, *Ascanio*'s other *Maestro di ballo*.

In this opera, then, Wolfgang could not ignore the dance since he had to compose for it. As Leopold wrote, the entertainment was to be a longer affair than expected as it would be 'lengthened due to the two large ballets performed between the first and second act, each of which lasts three-quarters of an hour'.[27] These were, of course, in addition to the dancing which was to take place during the course of the opera. Because of exposure to these new ideas and need to respond to them, *Ascanio* must have been a new and important experience for Wolfgang even though his letters and those of Leopold, as unfortunately was usual, do not reveal specific compositional problems. That both father and son were concerned about the ballets and that Wolfgang had to write with specific regard for the dancers, however, is quite clear from Leopold's repeated mentioning of dance.

On 13 September 1771 Leopold was able to write to his wife:

In twelve days Wolfgang, with the help of God, will have completely finished the serenata, which is in reality an azione teatrale in two parts. The recitatives with and without instruments [i.e. *secco* and accompanied] are all finished, as are also the choruses, which are eight, and of which five are also to be danced at the same time. Today we saw the dance rehearsal and greatly marvelled at the hard work of the two ballet masters Pick [Le Picq] and Fabier [Favier].

The first appearance is Venere, who comes out of the clouds accompanied by genies and graces.[28]

Leopold went on in his recounting of Wolfgang's work to describe more specifically what the dancers' role would be in his son's opera:

The Andante of the Symphony will be danced by eleven women, namely eight genies and three graces, or eight graces and three goddesses. The last Allegro of the Symphony is a chorus of thirty-two choristers, namely eight sopranos, eight contraltos, eight tenors and eight basses, and will be danced at the same time by sixteen people, eight women, eight men.[29]

More interrelationships between chorus and dancers followed, all Wolfgang's responsibility, as Leopold continued to report:

Another chorus [i.e. besides the *Allegro* of the Symphony] is of shepherds and shepherdesses, who are again other people. Then there are choruses for shepherds, that is of sopranos and contraltos. In the last scene all the choristers and dancers of both sexes are together, genies, graces, shepherds, shepherdesses, and these all dance the last chorus together. Here the solo dancers are not included, namely Mr Pick [Le Picq], Mrs Binetti, Mr Fabier [Favier] and Miss Blache. The short solos during the choruses, which are sometimes for two sopranos, sometimes alto and soprano, will also be intermingled with solos by the male and female dancers.[30]

From Leopold's description one would expect Wolfgang to have been very involved with the choreographers, but neither the collaboration with them nor with Parini (whom Wyzewa and Saint-Foix considered 'the only great and true poet [Wolfgang] had occasion to know during his life')[31] is referred to in any professional detail. In any event, the undescribed problem of writing for dancers was combined with that of composing for chorus, another new experience for Wolfgang since theatre choral music could not be of the type he was accustomed to write in his masses or the occasional cantata such as his *Grabmusik*. The chorus was much appreciated in Vienna and occupied a prominent part in any *festa teatrale*; this was in contrast to Naples, for example, where the audience always preferred solo voices in its productions. From this aspect, too, *Ascanio in Alba*, although seemingly an Italian work, reflected the taste of its patrons, the Austrian court. At least Wolfgang had 32 people in the *Ascanio* chorus which meant a full sound would have been possible even if, given their number and the possibly confusing movement of dancers around them, intricate part-writing would not have been sensible. Certainly the stage was quite crowded at times with 32 choristers and 16 dancers, 48 people not

including the principals, as Leopold wrote there were to be in the last
Allegro of the symphony and the closing scene of the opera. This would
have been one more reason for the Galliaris to make their sets realistic,
enabling all to walk or dance about the stage without causing ridiculous
conflict by being out of proportion with the scenery painted according
to an idealized and fast-diminishing distant focal point.

Busy as he must have been with ballet and choral music, Wolfgang
could not neglect the music for the real stars of the *azione* or *festa*
teatrale, the solo singers. The cast, as Leopold communicated to his wife
at the end of the above letter and as one finds in the libretto, was as
follows:

VENERE—Geltrude Falchini (*seconda donna*, soprano)

ASCANIO—Giovanni Manzuoli (*primo uomo*, mezzo-soprano)

SILVIA, nymph of the family of Hercules—Antonia Maria Girelli-
Aguilar (*prima donna*, soprano)

ACESTE, Priest—Giuseppe Tibaldi (tenor)

FAUNO, one of the principal shepherds—Adamo Solzi (*secondo uomo*,
soprano)

CHORUS OF GENIES, SHEPHERDS AND SHEPHERDESSES

Wolfgang was among friends with his singers. Manzuoli, presently in
the service of the Grand Duke of Tuscany (Leopold, the groom's
brother), was known to Wolfgang from London and from more recent
contact in Florence on the Mozarts' first trip to Italy, and he was a keen
supporter of the young man. Tibaldi, who, as Leopold wrote to Count
Pallavicini, 'honoured my son by coming every morning to see him
write',[32] was obviously also in Wolfgang's camp.

Finally actual rehearsals for the singers began even though Wolfgang
still had two more arias to write.[33] On 21 September was the first
rehearsal of Hasse's opera, the main work of the festivities, *Ruggiero*,
which was to be his last opera as it was Metastasio's last libretto: their
long careers were intertwined to the very end.[34] On the following
Monday there was to be the first recitative rehearsal and on 27 September there was an *a cappella* chorus rehearsal. By the full rehearsal on 28
September Wolfgang had finished the opera and the rehearsal went
well enough for Leopold to hope, once again, for his son to enjoy
success. He wrote, 'I know what he has written and what kind of effect
it will have, and it is agreed that he has written well and right good for
the singers as well as for the orchestra.'[35] Another rehearsal of *Ascanio*
took place on 4 October and *Ruggiero* was rehearsed on 5 October.
There were two days rest and on 8 October it was Wolfgang's turn
again. However from 8 to 11 a.m. nothing could be done in the theatre
as the dancers rehearsed then. On 11 October *Ascanio* had its fourth full
rehearsal, by which time *Ruggiero* was up to its seventh. On the 14th

Wolfgang had his last rehearsal because, as Leopold explained to his wife:

> On the evening of the 15th the Duke [Ferdinand, the groom] arrives: then there is the marriage act, after the marriage act handkissing [i.e. greeting] at Court, then two hours of music, then eating, etc. On the 16th there is the opera [*Ruggiero*], on the 17th the serenata [*Ascanio*]; on the 18th, 19th, 20th there is nothing because of the anniversary of the death of His Majesty the Emperor [Ferdinand's father and Maria Theresia's husband]. Monday the serenata, etc., etc.[36]

But finally it was opening night and Leopold was happy:

> Then on the 16th was the opera and on the 17th the serenata, which was so astoundingly well-liked that it must be repeated today [19 October]. The Duke has ordered two copies. All the courtiers and other people speak to us continually on the street to congratulate Wolfgang. I'm sorry, but Wolfgang's serenata has so beaten Hasse's opera that I can't describe it.[37]

When *Ascanio* was performed again on 24 October, once more with the Duke and Duchess in the audience, they clapped so much that two arias by Manzuoli and Girelli-Aguilar had to be repeated.[38] The same day had been exciting for another reason: free food and wine had been distributed to the people and the Mozarts narrowly escaped injury when one of the scaffoldings erected for spectators fell, injuring or killing over 50 people.[39] Undaunted, the *festra teatrale*, which Leopold insisted was 'actually a small opera [since] an opera in music itself is not longer',[40] went on to have probably two more performances, its fourth and fifth, on 27 and 28 October, quite a run for a work intended simply as a secondary event in the celebrations.[41]

As to the music itself, Leopold said Wolfgang had composed it in 15 days.[42] However Wolfgang had already done the overtures by the beginning of September; on 21 September two more arias still needed writing. Probably three to four weeks would be a more honest reckoning although it would still be little time for a 15-year-old boy. As suited the occasion and spirit of his collaborators, Wolfgang provided a rather mixed musical setting for the libretto. More clearly, while the style in general is related to that of *opera seria*, it results in being brilliant and festive rather than pompous. Moreover it untypically contains (although not exclusively) relatively short arias which, however, still have *fioriture*. As noted, the work is also full of chorus and ballet, again not usual *opera seria* fare.

The three opening sections of the *festa teatrale* must be considered the overture as they follow one another without interruption; but, as has already been indicated, two were also sung and danced. First there is the

Allegro assai which is purely instrumental; next is No. 1, *Andante grazioso*, 'that the graces dance'; directly after is No. 2, *Allegro*, 'Chorus of genies and graces, sung and danced'. As Leopold recognized in his letter of 13 September,[43] they are three fast-slow-fast movements of an Italian symphony but during which dramatic action takes place. One does not know whose idea it was – Wolfgang, Parini, or one of the choreographers – although one suspects the more theatrically expert Parini to have been the originator of such a fluid and visually attractive way of getting into the drama.[44] Unfortunately Wolfgang's ballets performed between the acts of *Ascanio* are lost; but one can say that probably every time the chorus was performing in the course of the opera, someone was dancing since Leopold, writing specifically about the symphony and closing chorus which was sung and danced, noted that 'the short [vocal] solos during the choruses ... will also be intermingled with solos by the male and female dancers'.[45] Again to our misfortune, we have no idea what choreography was designed for them.

Choral music, moreover, plays a great part in *Ascanio in Alba* (which therefore implies the equal importance of the dance). Sixteen of the 33 numbers of the opera, in fact, are for chorus. Again as Leopold wrote home, various voice combinations were used: sometimes all shepherds and shepherdesses sing SATB music, sometimes only the tenors and basses are called upon, or only two soprano soloists from the chorus, and so forth. The music is generally homophonic with an occasional phrase of simple polyphony, the sort of texture one would expect in music which was to provide more or less an aural accompaniment to a visual entertainment. Due to their frequent repetitions, some chorus numbers serve to unite the opera in *ritornello* fashion: No. 2, No. 4, and No. 18 are the same four-part 'chorus of genies and graces', 'Di te più amabile' (More lovely than you: example 1); No. 6, No. 7, No. 10, No. 11, No. 15, and No. 26 are the same 'chorus of shepherds' for tenors and basses, 'Venga, venga de' sommi eroi' (Come, come of great heroes), pleasant music based on their moving along together in thirds; and No. 28, No. 29, and No. 30 are the same SATB 'chorus of shepherds, nymphs and shepherdesses', 'Scendi celeste Venere' (Descend heavenly Venus), with a change of text in No. 29 to 'No, non possiamo vivere' (No, we cannot live). As a matter of fact, the only choruses which do not repeat are No. 9 'Hai di Diana il core' (You have the heart of Diana) for shepherds, shepherdesses, and nymphs; No. 20 'Già l'ore sen volano' (Already time flies) and No. 24 'Che strano evento' (What a strange event) both for shepherdesses; and No. 33, the 'Final chorus for genies, graces, shepherds and nymphs', 'Alma Dea tutto il mondo governa' (My Goddess governs all the world).

No. 6 and No. 7 exhibit, in addition, an ABA form since the section between them is in recitative; No. 10 and No. 11 are also joined by *secco*

Example 1

recitative. However a much more interesting da capo type of structure is evidenced in No. 9, 'Hai di Diana il core', which is one of the few non-repeated ensembles in *Ascanio*. The number opens with an instrumental introduction of 20 bars, *Allegro comodo*, which served to bring the 'Chorus of Shepherds, Shepherdesses or Nymphs' on stage; next there is another *Allegro comodo* but which now presents a ballet accompanied by a homophonic and syllabic four-part chorus; as the dance continues a three-part section for SSA women follows; now there is a return of four-part music for all but this time in polyphony; next is a second three-part section but this one SST for mixed voices; lastly there is a repeat of the opening four-part homophonic music. The number, accompanied by an active and musically independent orchestra of oboes, horns, and strings, is exceptional in *Ascanio in Alba* both for its length and variety.

As for the arias, all but two are in some variety of the traditional *opera seria* tripartite form: No. 22 'Al mio ben mi veggio avanti' (I stand

Example 1 (contd.)

(contd. overleaf)

before my beloved) for Ascanio follows an ABCB scheme; No. 13 'Sì, ma d'un altro amore' (Yes, but of another love) is a cavatina for Silvia in a single repeated section. Generally (in eight of the 13 arias), the short, or single section ABA' is to be found, such as Wolfgang employed for No. 3, Venere's 'L'ombra de' rami tuoi'; No. 5, Ascanio's 'Cara, lontano ancora'; No. 8, Fauno's 'Se il labbro più non dice'; No. 12, Aceste's 'Per la gioia in questo seno'; and so forth throughout the opera. These arias are therefore shorter than those associated with grand *opera seria* and also less florid quantitatively, although they are interesting and difficult enough to have been able to attract the attention of the audience (example 2 from No. 8). At the same time, Wolfgang inserted two sectional ABA arias, one for Ascanio and one for Silvia and in moments when a truly contrasting middle section is dramatically pertinent: No. 16 'Ah di sì nobil alma' and No. 23 'Infelici affetti miei.' In two instances he also set arias in the elaborate AA'BA' or *dal segno* form, again when

Example 1 (contd.)

dramatically they could logically be accepted: No. 19 'Spiega il desio le piume' (Desire opens its wings) for Silvia whose joys at the thought of her beloved overflow at this moment; and No. 21 'Dal tuo gentil sembiante' (From your lovely face) for Fauno who tries to reassure Silvia all will be well.

While he does not attempt characterization in *Ascanio*, Wolfgang does try, through the usual technique of word painting, to express single words or phrases, and some examples are worthy of note. For example, Ascanio begins one aria (No. 5) with a *messa di voce* on the word 'Cara' (Dear one), an appellation Wolfgang extends over more than two bars. While he stresses the affectionate word by sustaining its first syllable, the orchestra underlines his sentiments with a lovely ascending phrase (example 3).[46] Another example is in the above-mentioned No. 13 where strings and oboes furnish an undulating accompaniment to Silvia's words, 'Yes, but I feel the flame in my heart of another love' which helps one to imagine the interior flame. Again, in

Example 2

No. 14 'Come è felice stato' (How happy it was) when Silvia sings that
her heart is palpitating ('va palpitando il cor'), the strings play repeated
notes *staccato* and the vocal part separates the syllables with pauses, all
with the intent of simulating heart beats (example 4).

Great attention seems to have been given by Wolfgang to the
accompanied recitatives which, since they were typical of the *festa
teatrale*, are used amply by him for the first time in *Ascanio in Alba*.
They are longer than his earlier examples of the genre and show
frequent changes of tempo which attempt to reflect the various changes
of sentiment and mood expressed in the text. Wolfgang uses the

Example 3

Example 4

orchestra in these cases not only to underline the sense of the words but
also to try and communicate somewhat stronger emotions, which was
exactly why any eighteenth-century composer would have substituted
the continuo harpsichord and cello instruments with orchestra. John
Brown expressed contemporary thinking on it quite clearly:

> Here, too, [in accompanied recitative] the whole orchestra lends its
> aid; nor are the instruments limited to the simple duty of supporting
> and directing the voice. In this high species [i.e. impassioned type] of
> recitative it is the peculiar province of the instrumental parts, during
> those pauses which naturally take place between the bursts of passion
> which a mind strongly agitated breaks into, to produce such sounds
> as serve to awake in the audience sensations and emotions similar to
> those which are supposed to agitate the speaker. Here, again, another
> fine distinction is made by the Italians, between the descriptive and

the pathetic powers of music. These last are proper to the voice, the former to the orchestra alone.[47]

A good example of Wolfgang's handling of the accompanied recitative in *Ascanio in Alba* is the one before No. 5 where there are eight changes of tempo (*Andante; Allegro; Andante; Andante, un poco Adagio; Più andante; Un poco Adagio; Un poco Allegro; Andante*) which try to follow Ascanio's various feelings as he struggles with himself not to reveal who he is to Silvia (example 5).

Ascanio in Alba is not at all in the style of the 'grand' *opera seria* as was

Example 5

Mitridate, neither does Wolfgang attempt characterization as he did in *Mitridate* and *La finta semplice*. The work was simply a pastoral spectacle or, as Leopold once called it, a cantata,[48] indicating with this term the emphasis that Wolfgang (and the genre itself) placed on the lyrical, and not on the dramatic, quality of the composition. Nevertheless, it was a great success. *Il Ruggiero* by Hasse, on the other hand, was not. Certainly *Ascanio* was more attractive visually with all its dances, although *Ruggiero* had the usual ballets between its acts;[49] but the work by the older master had no chorus and no ensembles, either. This aspect, though, was due to Metastasio who had followed an old format in the *opera seria* and favoured only solo voices. Hasse, for his part, responded in the traditional manner. While his writing is always competent for the voice and orchestra, at the same time there is nothing especially noteworthy in the series of da capo arias he composed. To be sure, the voice is always given absolutely singable music; as a matter of fact, even the recitatives are more lyrical than discourse-like with the accompanied recitatives quite the most passionate sections of the opera. But perhaps it was just this quality of reliable soloists offering aria after aria which precluded any spontaneity and shifted attention from a standard Hasse opera to a varied work by young Wolfgang.

At any rate, the young spouses enjoyed *Ascanio* so much that Ferdinand was prompted to write his mother asking if he might hire Wolfgang and make him a permanent member of his court. Maria Theresa's answer revealed that, although she herself had been trained as an adequate performer, she had no deep understanding of music and its role in human life. Her cold and insensitive attitude towards Wolfgang expressed in a letter of 12 December 1771 was as follows:

> You ask me if you can take into your service the young Salzburger. I don't know how you can think you need a composer or other useless people. If that however pleases you I will employ him for you. What I am saying is to try and prevent you from taking in useless people and from giving positions to that sort of person. Once in service, it is a debasement of the service itself to see these people going around the world like beggars.[50]

Needless to add, Ferdinand did not hire Wolfgang and his two successes in Milan produced no permanent position. There was yet another opera to do at the Regio Ducal Theatre, however, and so father and son could still hope for something more from it than the gold watch set with diamonds which had her portrait that the Empress gave the young composer.

Chapter Seven : Notes

1. K. 111 in *WAM*, Serie V, 6, and *NMA*, Serie II, 5, bd. 5.
2. On 5 January 1771: see *Dokumente*, pp. 117-118.
3. Relative documentation for the period is in *Dokumente*, p. 118 ff. Also see Raffaello Brenzoni, 'Nel Veneto' in *Mozart in Italia*, pp. 136-145. It was probably on this trip to Turin that the Mozarts met Quirino Gasparini.
4. See their exchange of letters in *Dokumente*, I, pp. 119 and 120-121.
5. *Dokumente*, p. 121. While in Venice the Mozarts met Count Giacomo Durazzo, the Genoese nobleman who had been so useful to Gluck in Vienna and who was now Ambassador in Venice: see *Briefe*, I, p. 424.
6. It was also during this period that Wolfgang began his oratorio *Betulia liberata* intended for Padua but apparently never performed: see *Dokumente*, p. 119.
7. Letter dated 19 July 1771: *Briefe*, I, p. 428.
8. Hasse had arrived on the 30th: see *Dokumente*, pp. 121-122. On the Mozarts' second trip to Italy, also see Guglielmo Barblan, 'Compositore aulico' in *Mozart in Italia*, pp. 149-161.
9. *Briefe,* I, p. 432.
10. Much of the following information is based on Riccardo Allorto's biography of Parini in *Enciclopedia dello Spettacolo*, VIII, col. 1678-79.
11. See note 58 of Chapter VI here and the relevant passage in the text.
12. On his libretto, see the title page in *Dokumente*, pp. 122-123. Luigi F. Tagliavini in the introduction to his critical edition of *Ascanio in Alba* in *NMA*, pp. vii-viii, clears up the incorrect attribution of the libretto to Claudio Nicolò Stampa.
13. See Riccardo Allorto's description of the genre in *Enciclopedia dello Spettacolo*, V, col. 233, and Raymond Monelle, 'Gluck and the *festa teatrale*', *Music Letters* 54 (1973), p. 308 ff.
14. Discussed by Remo Giazotto in *Enciclopedia dello Spettacolo*, I, col. 1193, and Monelle, *idem*.
15. I, pp. 186-187. Jahn continued with another more personal note: 'The union had not been consummated without difficulty, and some anxiety was felt as to the relations of the young couple.'
16. A copy is in the Santa Cecilia Conservatory Library, Rome.
17. II, p. 305.
18. *Ibid.*, p. 311.
19. For a calendar of their activities from 1765 to 1773 see Mercedes Viale Ferrero, *Lo scenografia dalle origini al 1936* tomo 2, vol. III of *Storia del Teatro Regio di Torino* (Turin, 1980), pp. 257-258. The whole section is a valuable summary of their work but for more details see her book *La scenografia del '700 e i fratelli Galliari* (Turin, 1963).
20. On some of the Galliaris' work also see 'Fabrizio e Bernardino Galliari: la scena quadro' (pp. 124-127) and '*Enea nel Lazio*: Il melodramma e l'antichità classica' (pp. 161-167), this last by Mercedes Viale Ferrero, both in *Illusione e Pratica Teatrale*, *op. cit.* Several sketches are included at the end of the volume. Parini's *Descrizione delle Feste celebrate in Milano per le nozze delle LL. Altezze Reali l'Arciduca Ferdinando d'Austria e l'Arciduchessa Maria Beatrice d'Este* (Milan, 1825) complimented the scenery of *Ascanio* especially: see Tagliavini, p. ix.
21. *Briefe*, I, p. 433.
22. *Ibid.*, p. 435, letter of 7 September 1771. The autograph for this ballet is lost; in fact

only a copy of the bass part exists in the West Berlin Staatsbibliothek Preussischer Kulturbesitz. Tagliavini has included this bass part in the Appendix to his edition.

23. One of the few studies devoted to Angiolini is the little-documented *Il balletto pantomimo del Settecento: Gaspare Angiolini* by Lorenzo Tozzi (Aquila, 1972).

24. *Dokumente*, p. 122. The statement that Noverre came to Milan for Wolfgang's *Ascanio* is corrected in *Addenda*, p. 20.

25. On Noverre see Lillian Moore's article in *Enciclopedia dello Spettacolo* VII, col. 1243-1248, from which the above citation has been translated (col. 1245).

26. For an account of Le Picq's career see the article by Marie-Françoise Christout in *Enciclopedia dello Spettacolo*, VI, col. 1409-1410.

27. 21 September: *Briefe*, I, p. 438. The choreographers were each responsible for one of the ballets: the first was by Le Picq, the second by Favier.

28. *Briefe*, I, p. 436.

29. *Idem.*

30. *Ibid.*, pp. 436-437.

31. Teodor de Wyzewa and Georges de Saint-Foix, *Wolfgang Amédée Mozart. Sa vie musicale et son œuvre* (Paris, 1912), I, p. 396.

32. On 30 October 1771: *Briefe*, I, p. 447. Wolfgang felt the tenor had a forced production: see his letter of 7 January 1770 in *Briefe*, I, p. 301.

33. As Wolfgang wrote to his sister on 21 September: *Briefe*, I, p. 439.

34. On *Ruggiero* see Metastasio's letter of 26 December 1771 to Coltellini wherein he refers to it as 'this late effort of my tired and exhausted inventiveness': *Lettere del Signor Abate Pietro Metastasio*, Tomo IV, p. 111.

35. 28 September: *Briefe*, I, p. 440.

36. 12 October: *ibid.*, I, p. 444. The notices of the rehearsals are in Leopold's letters beginning on 21 September: *ibid.*, p. 437 ff and in *Dokumente*, p. 122. The most complete source of reference for the wedding festivities is Parini's *Descrizione ...* quoted from by Tagliavini, p. viii ff.

37. *Briefe*, I, p. 444. Parini also referred to his work as a 'serenata' in his *Descrizione ...*' p. 747. Klaus Hortschansky, who also places *Ascanio* in the tradition of the serenata, discusses the differences between the various genres according to contemporary theoretical and poetical sources: see his 'Mozarts Ascanio in Alba und der Typus der Serenata', *Analecta musicologica* 18 (1978), pp. 148-158.

38. Letter of Leopold to his wife of 26 October and Wolfgang's postscript: *Briefe*, I, pp. 445-446.

39. *Idem.*

40. On 21 September: *op. cit.*, p. 438.

41. *Dokumente*, p. 122. To celebrate the wedding, in addition to the operas and free food and wine distributed to the people, there was a gorgeous procession of servants dressed in the costume of the surrounding peasantry on the 19th; races for horses on the 27th; and for chariots on the 28th: see Jahn, I, p. 137.

42. In a letter of 30 October to Count Pallavicini: *Briefe*, I, p. 447. Wolfgang had actually received the libretto 29 August but on 5 September Parini wanted it back to make some revisions. Probably Wolfgang had begun to compose at least the recitatives by then: see Tagliavini p. viii and note 21 here.

43. *Op. cit.*, p. 436.

44. Wolfgang composed another finale for the overture (K. 111a/120) at the end of October-beginning of November 1771 which replaced the chorus 'Di te più

amabile' thus allowing the piece to be used as a proper symphony: see Köchel 6, pp. 135-136, and Georges de Saint-Foix, *The Symphonies of Mozart* (London, 1948), pp. 30-31. The autographs of the opera and the new finale are in the Staatsbibliothek Preussischer Kulturbesitz in West Berlin.

45. Letter of 13 September, *op. cit.*, p. 437.
46. A similar opening is to be found in *Mitridate, Re di Ponto*, Sifare's 'Soffre il mio cor con pace' (No. 2). It was in fact a not uncommon aria beginning and Tagliavini in his 'L'Opéra italien du jeune Mozart', *op. cit.*, pp. 149-150, quotes just such a setting of the word 'Cara' by J. C. Bach in *Adriano in Siria*.
47. Pp. 16-17. At the end of this passage, Brown gives examples of various scenes he has heard orchestral music describe (p. 18 ff).
48. Letter of 21 September 1771: *Briefe*, I, p. 437.
49. These were *La corona della Gloria* and *Pico e Canente* by Le Picq and Favier respectively: see Jahn, I, p. 136.
50. *Dokumente*, p. 124. Maria Theresa continued her remarks with, 'He already has a big family', a strange comment since she had met the actually small family. Clearly she was afraid of having too many mouths to feed.

CHAPTER EIGHT

Il sogno di Scipione[1]

EVEN BEFORE the Mozarts left for Milan and the performance there of *Ascanio in Alba*, Wolfgang had completed another work, this one intended to celebrate the fiftieth anniversary of the ordination of Prince Archbishop Sigismund Christoph von Schrattenbach, in whose employment were both Leopold and Wolfgang. The event was to be on 10 January 1772, and Wolfgang worked on the music between April and August of 1771.[2] He had chosen as his libretto *Il sogno di Scipione*, a text Metastasio had written earlier to honour his own patron, Charles VI, on his birthday in 1735[3] and which had already been set six times before. Wolfgang left the dramatic serenata intact merely substituting 'Carlo' with 'Sigismondo' in the final chorus. But then there was the *festa teatrale* to do for Archduke Ferdinand and father and son were away from Salzburg for four months from August to December 1771. After *Ascanio in Alba*, Wolfgang next composed three four-movement symphonies sometime between Milan and Salzburg (where he and Leopold arrived back on 15 December 1771) which are Italian symphonies but with a minuet added in the typical 'classical' form (K. 111b/96, 112, 114); he also did several sonatas (K. 124A. 124a/144, 124b/145, 124c). March 1772 saw as well the composition of his first *Litaniae de venerabili altaris sacramento* (K. 125) for four voices and oboes (and/or flutes as was the custom), horns, 'clarini', bass and organ in addition to the usual strings, a work very much in the Salzburg tradition; he also wrote several songs to German texts (K. 125d–h).

Soon after the Mozarts' arrival back in Salzburg on 15 December, their very lenient Archbishop von Schrattenbach had died and, in a few months, on 14 March, his successor Hieronymous Colloredo was appointed[4] and installed on 29 April as the new Prince Archbishop.[5] The event may have seemed harmless at first to the Mozart family, but it would soon prove disruptive to the way of life the understanding von Schrattenbach had allowed them to enjoy. An immediate consequence of Colloredo's arrival in Salzburg, however, was that Wolfgang's setting of *Il sogno di Scipione* was given in his honour instead, with the name of his former patron 'Sigismondo' necessarily changed to 'Giro lomo'. This was at the beginning of May[6] in the Prince Archbishop's Residenz Palace.

Whereas *Die Schuldigkeit des ersten Gebotes* had been performed in the Rittersaal, probably *La finta semplice* and *Il sógno di Scipione* were seen in the room next to it, the Konferenzsaal, where Wolfgang performed most of his music as the Hoftheater was not completed till 1775. One of many salons overlooking the Residenzplatz on one side and the inner court on the other, the red-damasked Conference Hall is rather square and, like the Rittersaal, of modest proportions. As is true of the entire palace, Italian decoration prevails and grand scenes of Alexander the Great painted by Altomonte on the ceiling dominate the room.[7] All in all, while not a proper theatre, it was still a very elegant setting for Wolfgang's celebrative piece about the Roman consul Scipio Aemilianus Africanus (185/4-129 B.C.). The younger son of Lucius Aemilius Pallus, under whom he served at the battle of Pydna in 168 B.C., Scipio was adopted by Publius Cornelius Scipio, the elder son of Scipio Africanus, whose name he then assumed. Throughout his military career Scipio was known for his integrity, personal bravery, and honesty, qualities Metastasio also attributes to him although, unfortunately for the drama, merely by implication rather than action. The poet based his account on Cicero's *Somnium Scipionis*, incorporating a myth of Silius Italicus who in the fifteenth book of his *Punica* has Virtus and Voluptas appear to Scipio.[8]

It was to be expected that Wolfgang would have eventually chosen an opera text by Metastasio (1698-1782), 'the favourite author of the century, whose name is heard gloriously from Cadix to the Ukraine, and from Copenhagen to Brasil' and who was recognized as 'the singular and preferred poet of composers'.[9] As a gift from Count Firmian Wolfgang had received the complete works of Metastasio;[10] he had set several of the texts as recitatives and arias as well as the oratorio *Betulia liberata*, and he had seen many of his serious operas on his travels. As far as *opera seria* was concerned, no one was Metastasio's equal. Arteaga dedicated several pages to him in his discussion of Italian opera, summing up the special qualities which made Metastasio's poetry so suitable for music in the following manner:

No one better than he has known how to bend the Italian language to the nature of music, now making the sentences of recitative vibrate; now leaving aside those words which because they are too long, or have an awkward and sustained sound are not suitable for song; now often using shortened words and those forms which end in an accented vowel, such as *ardì, piegò, farà* which greatly help to smooth out the diction; now artificially mixing seven-syllable lines with those of eleven syllables to give the sentence variety which suits

the harmonic interval and the pace of who has to sing it; now cutting
the verses in half in order to shorten the sentences and render the
pauses more sweet; now using rhymes discreetly but not in a fixed
way, according to the pleasure of the ear and to avoid excessive
monotony; now finally with singular ability suiting the diversity of
the metres to the various passions, making use of short lines for the
affections which express listlessness so that the soul, so to speak, does
not have the force to finish the sentiment. . . . No one better than he
has understood the needs of opera accommodating the lyrical style to
drama in such manner that neither the embellishments of the one
ruin the [theatrical] illusion of the other, nor the naturalness of the
latter thwart the ability to describe of the former.[11]

While Arteaga's judgement is not to be negated, it must be said that
even though such skill with language may have resulted in beautiful
poetry, it did not always achieve brilliant drama.

The libretto of Metastasio's *Il sogno di Scipione* presents the leader
asleep in the Palace of Massinissa (where the real Scipio was on a military
mission in 150 B.C.); in a dream Scipione is made to see Fortuna (Fortune)
and Costanza (Constancy) who urge him to choose one of them as his
protectress. When he asks for time to reflect, Fortuna becomes impatient
but the more understanding Costanza reveals to him that he has been
brought to Heaven to see his courageous ancestors. A Chorus of Heroes
then appears and Publio, his famous stepfather, comes forth and describes to Scipione the rewards of an honourable life. His real father
Emilio also appears and tells him of the futility of Earth. When Scipione
asks to remain with them in Heaven, he is told that he must first earn
his reward by living an exemplary life; he then asks their advice in
choosing the right guardian Goddess but they say that it must be his
own decision. Resisting the attractions of power offered by Fortuna,
Scipione finally decides in favour of Costanza and an honest life. Hearing this, Fortuna threatens him with terrible visions and a storm, but he
remains firm. Scipione then returns to Earth where he awakens and
reasserts his intention to follow Constanza. To end the piece there is a
Licenza for chorus in praise of the new Prince Archbishop Colloredo,
the supposed real-world Scipio.[12]

To perform the work, Wolfgang requested the following, unfortunately unvaried, voices:

SCIPIONE—tenor
COSTANZA—soprano
FORTUNA—soprano
PUBLIO, Scipione's stepfather—tenor
EMILIO, Scipione's real father—tenor
CHORUS OF HEROES

Not only does he employ just two soloist ranges, soprano and tenor, but Wolfgang makes no use of the castrato voice. Obviously these were not choices decided upon by him but by circumstance. Von Schratten-bach had let the castrato tradition at Salzburg die out,[13] which was why Wolfgang was obliged to learn to write for the voice in Italy and why none is employed in *Il sogno di Scipione*; at the same time, without doubt two good sopranos and three tenors were available in the city, which again is why he scored for these voices.[14] Idealized writing was not possible in the eighteenth century, nor would it have been sensible; as always, scoring, and often even style, were the results of Wolfgang's adjustment to his resources.

The celebrative *Il sogno di Scipione* is obviously even more undra-matic than *Ascanio in Alba*. The text suggests no stage movement apart from the entrance of the Chorus of Heroes, and the performers could easily have remained fixed in one position as they sang. There is no ballet and only two very simple homophonic choruses. The only answer as to why such a static work should have been requested is to be found in the type of court occasion to be celebrated and in the sober genre, both poetically and musically, generally composed for it. More than was the case with *Ascanio in Alba*, an opera as such was not what either Metastasio or Wolfgang intended to write in *Il sogno di Scipione*. Rather they were called upon (Metastasio in Vienna and Wolfgang in Salzburg) to provide something for a festive court occasion. The most special text and music that they could offer was that associated with opera since, from its creation, opera had been employed as the chief entertainment when a court wanted to celebrate an important event. However, occasions such as commemorating an annually recurring birthday did not necessarily call for a poet's most sublime dramatic effort, just something pleasant and relevant which had merely dramatic overtones so as to allow the composer to employ operatic forms and style in his setting of the text.

These *feste teatrali* or *azioni teatrali*, as Metastasio defined *Il sogno di Scipione*,[15] were often done only in the presence of the court and were therefore somewhat intimate entertainments. Although the first *Scipione* with music by Luca Antonio Predieri was given in the Vienna Favorita Theatre, others were not, such as another *azione teatrale* by Metastasio from the same year (1735), the non-historical fantasy *Le Cinesi*, set to music by Johann Georg Reutter, Jr, which was given simply in the private apartments of Maria Theresa (only an Arch-duchess at the time) and her sister Marianne; moreover, it was not even the main entertainment but served merely as an introduction to a ballet on a similarly oriental subject. While *Le Cinesi* had only three characters (augmented to four when it was repeated in 1753),[16] Metastasio's *Il sogno di Scipione* had five plus a Chorus of Heroes which meant conversation and conflicting opinions and behaviour, i.e. dramatic overtones, were possible. The setting is classical and was therefore interesting to an eighteenth-century audience recently made aware of antiquity through archaeological discoveries, most importantly, the main character was made to choose a less rewarding but more noble way of life, thus suggesting by association that the most important member of the audience, the Emperor and later both Prince Archbishops, were doing the same. Wolfgang would have found it difficult to break out of the static and undramatic scheme established by Metastasio in *Il sogno di Scipione*.

As Algarotti in his essay on opera suggested:

> One can almost say that the success or failure of the drama depends on the libretto. It is the plan of the building; it is the canvas on which the poet has outlined the painting, which must then be coloured by the composer. The poet directs the dancers, machinists, painters, those who are in charge of the wardrobe; he has the whole drama in mind, and even those parts which are not executed by him, he has nevertheless dictated.[17]

At the same time Wolfgang was not expected to break away from Metastasio's plan. It was sufficient for him to provide suitable operatic-type music for this concert in costume and this he did.

Not surprisingly, given that honour was expected to be paid through dignity, the style that Wolfgang chose for *Il sogno di Scipione* was that associated with *opera seria*. In great contrast with *Ascanio in Alba*, however, where the common form was the one-sectional da capo, here each aria of the opera proper (that is, excluding the *Licenza*) is of the elaborate AA'BA', or *dal segno*, structure first seen in *Mitridate*. Moreover, they are truly grandiose in style, too, and full of passages of great difficulty. They are also usually accompanied by the entire orchestra, that is not just with strings but with woodwinds and brass as well, all to make the music more important. Also, introductions to the arias are quite long, in the typical grand manner of *opera seria*. This in itself is not a fault; as John Brown pointed out, an orchestral introduction

> gives time to the singer to breathe, already, perhaps, fatigued by a long recitative; it often fills up, with propriety, a natural pause, and always finely prepares the audience for what is to come after, by enabling them, having thus once heard the strain, to listen with more intelligence, and, of consequence, with more interest and pleasure to the song.[18]

However, the first sections of arias are also long and, as the form demanded, textually very repetitive (four statements of the stanza was the rule) in order to achieve the desired musical length; second sections, on the other hand, set only a few words of text and presented them just once before the initial section, now abbreviated, returned. This results in heavy insistence both by the voice and the orchestra on the first section and gives the listener the impression that he is hearing the same text and music over and over. This latter feature was characteristic not just of Wolfgang and this particular form, but of *opera seria* music in general; it was certainly true of the works of great exponents of the genre, such as Hasse. At the same time, it was here that the singer's art of improvisation would have relieved any monotony.

In *Il sogno di Scipione* rather than attempting characterization Wolfgang limited himself to interpreting isolated words and ideas. For example in No. 1 'Risolver non osa' (It does not dare to decide) for Scipione, the musical phrase for the words 'che oppressa si sente da tanto stupor' (that feels overwhelmed by such wonder) is hesitating with the rhythm, broken up by rests, and chromaticism underlining a feeling of confusion and uncertainty (example 1). In the second section rapid

Example 1

forte-piano contrasts, a broken vocal line and *pizzicato* cellos and contrabasses reinforce Scipione's 'Delira dubbiosa' (Dubious, it wanders). When Emilio sings of 'a child who cries' in aria No. 6 'Voi colaggiù ridete' (You over there who laugh), he prolongs 'piange' while the orchestra also 'cries' with a descending chromatic line (example 2). *Forte-piano* effects and tremolo in the strings in No. 7 'Quercia annosa' (The old oak) bring Publio's fight 'against the opposition of twenty enemies' vividly before the listener. When in aria No. 9 Costanza sings 'Biancheggia in mar lo scoglio' (The rock whitens in the sea), her leaps outline the peaks of the rocks, while the second violins' weaving line suggests the sea. The word 'mare', sea, itself receives special word-painting treatment (example 3). Later, when Costanza sings of 'the tranquil and deep sea', the accompaniment is quieter with the violas sustaining as the violins and basses play an easy ♪♪ rhythm.

There are moments where Wolfgang manages to characterize a role,

Example 2

Example 3

but they seem actually the result of a coincidence between his expressing a single word and the personality of the protagonist. For example, in aria No. 2 'Lieve sono al par del vento' (I am as light as the wind) an arpeggiated vocal line and a series of semiquaver scales in the second violins presents us with a true Fortuna – powerful, authoritarian, capable of anger and resulting irascible acts; at the same time aria No. 3 for Costanza, 'Ciglio che al sol si gira' (Eyes which close at the sun), is written for strings alone which together with their lyrical music thus suits her mild temperament. Wolfgang orchestrated for strings alone not only for Costanza but also for the proud Fortuna, but in aria No. 8 where her opening words are 'A chi serena io giro' (To whom I turn serene). The text must be pronounced with calm control if it is to be effective, and it is certainly better underlined by the instrumentation chosen by Wolfgang. Naturally, though, the aria is dramatic rather than lyrical, with its abundance of *forte-piano* contrasts serving to illustrate 'dramatic' Fortuna's explanations about the contradictory alternatives of kindness and cruelty.

The accompanied recitative is used but once in *Il sogno di Scipione,* which is considerably less than in *Ascanio in Alba*; however, his expert handling of the genre reveals that Wolfgang is comfortable with it. The single example appears just before aria No. 11 where the recitative begins not with just strings, the usual accompanied recitative instrumentation, but with the entire orchestra in order to support Fortuna better as she threatens Scipione with adversity since he has not chosen her as his life's companion. The instruments are not employed at first to describe what she is saying; rather their task at the opening of the recitative is to enforce the sense of Fortuna's authority with strong chords. As she continues trying to frighten Scipione, however, and he sings: 'Heavens! What is it! What a bloody light! What clouds! What storms! What shadows are these! Ah, what thunder resonates in the turbulent spheres! A hundred arrows pierce my hair!', the orchestra attempts to interpret his various images and describe them with tremolos and excited and rapid scales which ascend and then break off frenetically one after another. Only at the end of the scene when Scipione decides to remain with Costanza no matter what violence Fortuna will throw in his path does orchestral quiet reign, Wolfgang thereby illustrating instrumentally what Scipione feels internally.

In addition to the examples already cited which demonstrate Wolfgang's awareness of the task at hand, that is the need to interpret Metastasio's drama even though a full-fledged operatic setting was not possible, there are two moments which reveal his acquired experience and show him striving for a dramatic continuity which is unexpected in this cantata-like piece. One is at the end of the conventional symphonic opening, written in two sections, where the final pianissimo chord becomes the initial chord of the following opening recitative.[19] This quiet transition from symphony to *azione* depicts the atmosphere of scene 1 and the sleeping Scipione perfectly (example 4); it also reminds one of Wolfgang's similar procedure in *La finta semplice* and *Ascanio in Alba* where the overture also continued directly without interruption into the action of the drama. That the effect pleased him is clear from his later use of it in *Die Entführung aus dem Serail* and *Don Giovanni*.

The other example of Wolfgang's particular sensitivity to the drama is in aria No. 10 'Di che sei l'arbitra' (Of which you are the arbiter): after Scipione ends his recitative with 'Ho già deciso' (I have already decided), Wolfgang does not waste time by having the usual long instrumental introduction to his aria but, instead, allows Scipione to proclaim immediately whom he has chosen. Wolfgang's departure from tradition is certainly dramatically valid as Scipione's strength and courage are not allowed to seem subsided by delaying his vocal entrance. His forsaking of an orchestral introduction to the aria was, moreover, in complete accord with eighteenth-century practice as reported by John Brown. After setting forth the reasons cited above for

Example 4

having an instrumental introduction, which the period called a *Symphony*, he then went on to explain when composers might instead eliminate one:

> The general *use* of the Symphony, renders the *omission* of it, on particular occasions, beautiful and striking. Thus, for example, at the end of a Recitative, or at the beginning of a scene, when the audience are expecting, as usual, the preparatory Symphony to the Air, they are suddenly surprised by the violent burst of some impetuous passion, which admitted of no possible pause.[20]

Il sogno di Scipione is a work which is often beautiful and at times quite expressive; nevertheless, it is not a true drama and Wolfgang used but a few of the musical story-telling means he had learned. In fact, one might say that he regressed and thought here in terms of an immediate and narrow interpretation of the text rather than in terms of dramatic unity. One must conclude that the occasion required him to compose a more conventional work than he was capable of producing. *Il sogno di Scipione* shows us Wolfgang called to do a routine job at home in provincial Salzburg and responding well to the task.[21] More to the point is the fact that his patron, the new Prince Archbishop Hieronymus Colloredo, must have been pleased by this piece presented in his honour as he agreed to remunerate Wolfgang's position of Konzertmeister which the boy had held formerly without pay;[22] he also agreed that father and son could make yet another trip to Italy, actually one projected as early as March of 1771, where another Mozart opera was to be performed in December 1772.

1 Wolfgang Mozart in court dress

CONVENIT IGITUR---IN GESTU NEC
VENUSTATEM CONSPICUAM, NEC TURPI
=DINEM ESSE, NE AUT HISTRIONES,
AUT OPERARII VIDEAMUR ESSE. *Off. Rhet: ad: Her:*
Lib. 3. XV.

G. Eichler delin.   *Jac. Andr. Fridrich Sc. A.V.*

2 Leopold Mozart

Ansicht Haus von Denkirdaten Gasthof zum Gold unen Schiff gegen die Domkirche, die Hochfürstl. Residenz u. g Haupswache in Salzburg.

3 Residenz Square, Salzburg

4 Giuseppe Parini

5 Wolfgang's autograph of *Die Schuldigkeit des ersten Gebotes*
6 Wolfgang's autograph of *Ascanio in Alba*

7 Scenes from *Lucio Silla*

PETRVS METASTASIVS
ROMANVS

8 Pietro Metastasio

Der Thumb oder Haupt-Kirche zu Salzburg.
wie selbe gerad gegen über in dem Baüer oder denen Bogen im gesicht fällt.

Le Dome ou L'Eglise cathedrale de Salsbourg.
comme elle se presente vis a vis dans l'apartement au dessus des arcs ou portiques

9 Salzburg Cathedral

While Prince Archbishop von Schrattenbach was very strict in moral matters, Colloredo would be seen by the Salzburgers to allow greater freedom in church affairs. However, although he cared for the splendours of his court more than his predecessor, and in spite of his being a musician himself, music declined at Salzburg rather than improved during his reign. At the same time he was a man of his period and carried out important, enlightened reforms. Unfortunately for all, and certainly for the Mozarts, in the words of Jahn:

> [Colloredo] was self-willed, parsimonious, and unscrupulous. He seldom expressed satisfaction with his officials. His disdainful mode of address to all but those of the highest nobility, and the irritable tone of his conversation, kept all about him in timid subordination.[23]

Jahn continued that Colloredo would prove to be anti-Salzburgers, anti-small people, anti-independence: in short, automatically anti-Wolfgang, as he fitted into all of these categories.

At the date of *Il sogno di Scipione* the Prince Archbishop was probably too delighted with his new position to take much notice of the mere musicians in his employ, but he would have occasion in the future to get to know them and, unfortunately, to register his disapproval of Leopold and Wolfgang.

Chapter Eight : Notes

1. K. 126 in *WAM*, Serie V, 7, and *NMA*, Serie II, 5, bd. 6.
2. For a clear explanation of the problems involved in dating *Scipione*, see Josef-Horst Lederer's introduction to his critical edition of the opera in *NMA*, p. vii ff on which the information presented here is based.
3. It was performed again for Franz I's name day in 1743: *Dokumente*, p. 127.
4. Schneider and Algatzy, p. 33.
5. *Idem* and *Dokumente, idem.*
6. The exact date is unknown.
7. Today portraits of Wolfgang's two prince archbishops, von Schrattenbach and Colloredo, hang on the walls.
8. See Jahn, I, p. 190. At the time of Metastasio's libretto Charles VI had just suffered severe defeat in Italy, and the poet alludes to his difficulties.
9. Arteaga, II, pp. 78 and 80.
10. See note 19 in Chapter VI.
11. *Ibid.*, pp. 83–84 and 89.
12. Wolfgang had composed two versions of the *Licenza*, the first (No. 11a) for von Schrattenbach in 1771; and the second (No. 11b) not in 1776 as stated in Köchel 6, p. 151, but for Colloredo in March–April 1772: see Lederer, p. ix.
13. Jahn, I, p. 236.
14. The scoring is similar to that of *Die Schuldigkeit* which was for three sopranos and two tenors.

15. See Chapter Seven for a brief description of the genres.
16. See Metastasio's letter to Calzabigi on this addition in *Lettere del Signor Abate Pietro Metastasio*, Tomo II, p. 106.
17. II, p. 262. On the libretto in general read there pp. 262-269.
18. P. 31.
19. Wolfgang later composed another closing section so that the overture could be performed as a proper symphony (K. 141a/161 and 163).
20. Pp. 31-33.
21. C. B. Oldman, 'Mozart', *Grove's Dictionary of Music and Musicians*, V, p. 928, on Wolfgang's *Scipione* says 'his setting is one of the dullest things he ever wrote'. The autograph score is now in the West Berlin Staatsbibliothek Preussischer Kulturbesitz.
22. *Dokumente, idem*.
23. I, p. 343.

CHAPTER NINE

Lucio Silla[1]

AFTER THE SUCCESS of *Mitridate, Re di Ponto* and apparently even before he was officially invited to compose *Ascanio in Alba*, Wolfgang received a second opera contract from Milan. Dated 4 March 1771 it read:

> It is agreed for Signor Amadeo Mozart to set to music the first drama which is to be presented in this Regio Ducal Theatre of Milan in Carnival of the year 1773. ... It is agreed that the above named Signor Maestro must send all the music for the recitatives within the month of October of the year 1772 and must be in Milan at the beginning of the following month of November to compose the arias and assist at all the rehearsals necessary for the above mentioned opera.[2]

The commission was obviously important to Wolfgang as it was another opportunity for him to become known both to the Italian and Viennese musical worlds as Milan was under Austrian domination. It was to be only the first opera of the season, whereas the more important was the second, but still he was only a young man, it was for one of the world's great theatres, and they were paying him 130 *gigliati*, 30 more than he had received for *Mitridate*, which meant that his career was progressing financially,[3] too. However, before composing *Lucio Silla*, the libretto eventually decided upon, and setting out with his father on their trip to Italy, Wolfgang was occupied with much other music between the time he received the contract and the actual performance of the opera.

As has been recounted, *Ascanio in Alba* and *Il sogno di Scipione* were attended to. After this latter work of May 1772 Wolfgang composed several symphonies (K. 128, 129, 130, 132, 133, 134), a *Regina Coeli*, for four voices and orchestra as was much of his Salzburg sacred music, as well as some lighter music, six minuets and trio (K. 130a/164). Then, as his contract stipulated, Wolfgang finished the first set of recitatives for *Lucio Silla* in October 1772,[4] and set off with his father on the 24th for Italy[5] so as to be at the theatre in time to start composing the arias in November, again as the contract bound him to do. In October-

December he was dedicating himself to writing quartets as well, actually a set of six (K. 134a–155 ff) which he began so as to while away the days spent waiting for the singers to arrive.[6] One understands how easily a composer could have become nervous or bored or both in that interval between reading the libretto, when quite naturally his creativity was stimulated, and actually composing the music, which was possible only once the singers and their particular 'instruments' were familiar to him. In the case of *Lucio Silla* events were unusually delayed and the singers arrived late, as one learns from Leopold's letters home.

Little more than a month before the opening, he complained quite understandably: 'Of the male and female singers no one is here but Signora Suarti [Suardi], the secondo uomo and the last tenor. The primo uomo Signor Rauzzini arrives today. De Amicis will arrive either the end of this month or the beginning of the next.'[7] Finally on 21 November and the silver anniversary of his marriage Leopold could report to his wife not only that he was thankful for the 25 years they had had together ('good things need their time') but also that 'the primo uomo Signor Rauzzini has arrived';[8] unfortunately on 28 November the *prima donna* Anna de Amicis-Buonsolazzi had still not turned up.[9] This was perhaps not so worrying for Wolfgang as he was already familiar with her voice, having heard her in Jommelli's *Armida abbandonata* when he was in Naples; he had commented afterwards that she 'sings incomparably well'.[10]

Something could still be composed, though, as Leopold assured his wife: 'In the meantime Wolfgang has enough to do to write the choruses, of which there are three';[11] he also set Rauzzini's first aria, 'Il tenero momento', 'which is, however, incomparable, and he sings it like an angel';[12] and finished the overture.[13] A new problem arose when the tenor Cordoni, who was to sing the title role, became ill and the theatre had to find someone else. It was already December and Leopold worried that it would not be an easy task to substitute him as the role required someone 'who must not only be a good singer but a good actor and a good-looking person in order to present Lucio Silla with distinction'.[14]

Wolfgang went ahead without him, although slowly, and had to write home on 5 December, 'Now I still have fourteen pieces to do, then I will be finished.' In good humour he continued: 'Happily one can count the trio and duet as 4 pieces.'[15] De Amicis had arrived only the day before and, exerting her dictatorial power as *prima donna*, demanded more spectacular music from young Wolfgang, a desire he quickly gratified. Leopold proudly wrote that his son had composed quite special passages in her main aria, 'all new and completely unusual and amazingly difficult'; happily for all, Leopold confirmed that 'she sings them in such a way that one must be astounded'.[16]

After much seeking, the only tenor who could be found was Bassano Morgnoni, a church singer from Lodi, and he was expected to arrive as late as 14-15 December; till then Wolfgang could not begin his arias. In the meantime rehearsals for the rest of the cast had to proceed without him with the first recitative and instrumental rehearsals taking place on 12 December. Finally, on 17 December, which was several days later than he was expected, the tenor arrived, and Leopold communicated home that already on the very next day 'Wolfgang wrote two arias for him'.[17] Creativity could not afford to wait for inspiration under such demanding and last-minute conditions. One wonders what sort of method Wolfgang employed for getting an idea, and quickly at that, of the vocal capacity of a singer who was new to him and whom he had not heard in performance: did he ask him to sing an aria or two, or were a few scales and trills sufficient? Once again the letters are silent on these technicalities. One supposes Wolfgang to have completed Silla's necessarily reduced part immediately after Leopold sent off his letter since on the following days, 19-20-22 December, the first orchestral rehearsals took place and on 23 December there was the dress rehearsal. As one might expect, the theatre was closed for Christmas Eve and Christmas Day but then on Saturday 26 December Wolfgang's opera had its first performance.[18]

Writing home a few hours before the opening, Leopold was quite optimistic as he felt the dress rehearsal had gone well.[19] But it was a long opera, four full hours not counting the ballets[20] of which there were three as usual, and it was put on two hours later than scheduled due to the delayed arrival of the Archduke, who had not only got up late from table but then took a long time over five letters to the court of Vienna with his New Year's greetings: as Leopold wrote, Ferdinand 'writes very slowly'.[21] The irritated and tired audience, having arrived an hour before the announced time and therefore in the theatre three hours before hearing a note of music,[22] was not in a receptive mood for the opera-plus-ballets which went on till two in the morning. The orchestra was also annoyed by the delay and late hour. Things did not go well with the performance itself either.

First there was the tenor who had barely learned his part; moreover, being mainly a church singer, he had had very little stage experience and moved in a way so as to make the audience laugh at him. Equally disruptive was the fact that he and the *prima donna* did not get on, and after their first scene together, she did not sing well due to her aggravation with him.[23] The *primo uomo*, Rauzzini, too, played his part in annoying her: he had had the Archduke told that he was nervous and might not have been able to sing unless the court encouraged him whereupon, at his entrance, the Archduchess warmly applauded. The jealous and offended de Amicis was not placated till the next day when their Highnesses invited her to an hour-long audience during which they reassured her of their appreciation of her talents. All in all, opening night was not of the sort Wolfgang and Leopold had hoped for.

These sad events Leopold reported home on 2 January 1773.[24] However, he went on to say that, fortunately, on succeeding evenings things improved and the theatre was 'so full that one can scarcely squeeze in'; de Amicis now 'had the upper hand since most of her arias were repeated'.[25] His favourable account continued on 9 January: 'The opera, God be praised, goes so incomparably well that the theatre is amazingly full each day, but so many people would not come to the first opera if it were not such an enormous success. Daily arias are repeated, and after the first evening the opera has received and enjoyed more applause each day.'[26] In fact, one spectator, Count Castelbarco, was so delighted with the opera that he gave Wolfgang a gold watch and chain.[27] By 16 January, Leopold was able to boast that *Lucio Silla* had had 17 performances and would probably be given 20 in all; since they were actually more than were expected, the opening of the second opera, Paisiello's *Il Sismano nel Mogol*, had to be postponed.[28] Wolfgang's opera in the end enjoyed 26 performances, all to full houses, certain proof of its success.[29]

For this opera Wolfgang was collaborating with a new librettist, the Italian poet Giovanni de Gamerra,[30] a rather strange character. Born in Leghorn[31] in 1743, de Gamerra studied law at the University of Pisa. Deciding against a career in the Church,[32] he joined an army regiment stationed at Milan. In 1768, by which time he was a Lieutenant and a writer of some renown, he published a minor poem, *Campo Boemo*, which had the good fortune to be praised by Metastasio with whom he must have come into contact when his regiment in the meantime was transferred to Vienna. An illness forced de Gamerra to leave the army, and he returned to Milan where he wrote his first play, *I solitari*, in 1770. It initiated a new 'tearful' genre, the *lacrimoso* type of drama for which de Gamerra became renowned. The poet had obtained a position at the Austrian court by the time Wolfgang was invited to compose his opera for Carnival of 1773, and it was therefore only logical that he be asked to supply the libretto. The same year saw the publication of his *Corneide*, and in 1775 he was named *Poeta cesareo* and presented at the Viennese court by Metastasio. But for some mysterious reason, in 1777 de Gamerra suddenly left Austria and returned to Leghorn where, poor and sick, he fell in love with a young aristocratic girl, Teresa Calamai. When her family opposed their marriage, the poet left for Naples only to be called back by her sudden sickness and death. Although he later married Anna Verace, and lived hand to mouth either in Pisa or Florence, he never forgot his first love and managed to dig up her skeleton and keep it at home! In 1786 he sent his plan for a reform of the theatre to

Ferdinand IV at Naples who invited him to direct the court theatre but then, disliking the sad dramas in which de Gamerra excelled, dismissed him. In 1793 the writer published his reactionary poem *Batania e la Belgica liberate* and for this protest against the revolution, the Austrian court made him their theatre poet. In 1802 he retired to Vicenza and lived comfortably on his pension till his death in August 1803.

As Leopold wrote home, de Gamerra, after finishing *Lucio Silla*, 'sent the poetry to Abate Metastasio in Vienna' to look over,[33] a kind gesture of respect to his mentor; however, Metastasio apparently found that there was a great deal which could be improved as 'he corrected and changed much, and replaced an entire scene in the second act'.[34] For Wolfgang it meant rewriting music,[35] certainly many recitatives, another source of irritation to Leopold which the boy, however, seemingly took in his stride. In spite of Metastasio's attempts to improve de Gamerra's libretto, it remains an illogical plot albeit typical of eighteenth-century *opera seria* in its outline: a complicated love story of strong passions and tense, often mortal, situations set in the classical past.

Cecilio, a senator banished by Silla, has secretly returned to Rome to see his fiancée Giunia, the daughter of Cajo Mario. His friend Lucio Cinna tells him that Silla has had it rumoured that Cecilio is dead in order to obtain Giunia's hand for himself, and advises Cecilio to meet Giunia in the cemetery where she goes to pray for her dead father. In the meantime Silla, having been rejected by Giunia, decides to kill her. We next see Cecilio at the dark cemetery, surrounded by statues of Roman heroes, awaiting Giunia who arrives accompanied by youths and virgins asking revenge against Silla. When she is left alone, Cecilio presents himself to her: at first she mistakes him for a phantom but then, recognizing him, the two rejoice in a duet.

In Act II the Counsellor Anfidio advises Silla to declare Giunia his betrothed publicly as she cannot oppose him before the people. When he agrees, Silla's sister Celia admits she has been unsuccessful in her attempts to win over Giunia for him, thus suggesting marriage as perhaps not sensible at the moment; she then asks for permission herself to marry Cinna to which Silla agrees. Just as Silla leaves, Cecilio rushes in set to kill him in obedience to a dream; Cinna advises him to wait. He also next tries to convince Giunia to pretend to acquiesce to Silla's wishes and then to kill him in bed, but the girl cannot bring herself to commit murder and Cinna resolves to kill Silla himself. Now Giunia tries to calm Cecilio and convince him to stay hidden; and Celia tries, in turn, to get Giunia to agree to marry Silla. At the Campidoglio Silla publicly declares his marriage to Giunia but she, at his words, tries to kill herself. At the same time Cecilio rushes in to kill Silla but is disarmed. Cinna has also come in with his sword unsheathed, but realizing the plan has failed, says he had come to protect Silla. A trio for Giunia, Cecilio, and Silla ends the scene.

In Act III the enchained Cecilio asks Cinna to revenge him. When Anfidio takes Cecilio before Silla, Giunia, who has sworn to kill herself before Cecilio is killed, is also present. Silla then tells the public that he shall have revenge and his beloved both that same day. Giunia cries out that he is about to kill her betrothed and appeals to the people for justice. Seeing no way out, Silla pardons everyone and unites Cecilio and Giunia. Moved by guilt, Cinna confesses his participation in the plot to kill Silla, but he is also pardoned; Silla then gives him Celia. Next Anfidio is excused for his bad counsel and Silla steps down as dictator thus restoring freedom to Rome.

The long and varied military career of the actual Roman general Lucius Cornelius Sulla (130-78 B.C.), called Lucio Silla in Italian, did reveal him to be a great commander; as a statesman, although he carried through a vast programme of constitutional reform, actually a series of laws designed to re-establish the supremacy of the senate in the Roman constitution, his methods were devastating and caused great social unrest. In fact, after his reign as dictator, the people lived in fear of a *Sullanum regnum*, of being ruled by a second Sulla. He also resigned his dictatorship (in 79 B.C.) for reasons which are still not clear and which Julius Caesar later called 'elementary ignorance'. However, some scholars believe that Sulla was trying to establish not a republican form of government, but a principate of the type Augustus was later to set up; and that when his scheme was discovered, his supporters, led by Caecilii Metelli (Cecilio in the opera), turned on him and forced him to resign. It seems that this account of the affair with details taken from Plutarch, was de Gamerra's point of departure for his libretto.

His plot is without doubt complicated and is made even more so to the reader of the libretto by the similarity of the names, although this particular confusion would have been removed in the theatre where the presence of the actual characters would have made their identities clear. In spite of this annoyance, there is some logic to events, that is until the last act. Here, contrary to the character of Silla as revealed in Acts I and II, and without obvious reason, de Gamerra has him pardon all and, as though unexpectedly discovering himself guilty and without being asked, relinquish his position as dictator. The only word in defence of such an ending (even if the real Sulla's behaviour was equally inexplicable) is that it allowed the audience to go home smiling and convinced that 'all's well that ends well'; it was certainly not good theatre. Charles Terry, in discussing Johann Christian Bach's setting of the same subject for Mannheim in 1776, said of the libretto that 'public taste had outlived its venerable *clichés*, its classic heroes, magic gardens, imprisoned princesses, knightly paladins and wearisome *réchauffage* of the clas-

sics'.[36] Noting changes already apparent in eighteenth-century preferences, he thought 'Metastasio's [and de Gamerra's] pompous plati-
tudes fell heavily on the ears of a generation ready to find diversion,
romance, and distraction in the characters, or the happenings of an age,
less remote ... than the crude politics of a Persian or Roman General.'[37]
Be that as it may, theatres went on to produce such *opere serie* and
audiences to frequent their performances, perhaps less concerned over
the plot than they should have been as long as the music and singers
were good. Certainly Wolfgang and the librettists were all aided in
Lucio Silla by, in the main, a splendid cast:

LUCIO SILLA, dictator—Bassano Morgnoni (tenor)
GIUNIA, daughter of Cajo Mario and intended wife of Cecilio—
  Anna de Amicis-Buonsolazzi (*prima donna*, soprano)
CECILIO, proscribed senator—Venanzio Rauzzini (*primo uomo*, so-
  prano)
LUCIO CINNA, Roman patrician, friend of Cecilio and secret enemy
  of Lucio Silla—Felicità Suardi (contralto)
CELIA, sister of Lucio Silla—Daniella Mienci (soprano)
AUFIDIO, tribune of Lucio Silla—Giuseppe Onofrio (tenor)
GUARDS, SENATORS, NOBLES, SOLDIERS, PEOPLE, YOUNG MAIDENS

Charles Burney, for example, knew the voices of 'Giunia' and 'Cecilio' and described them in some detail. The first time he heard Anna
de Amicis-Buonsolazzi (born *c.* 1740) was in 1762 at the London Opera
House where she appeared in the comic pasticcio *Il Tutore e la Prysilla*,
captivating the audience in various ways:

> Her figure and gestures were in the highest degree elegant and
> graceful; her countenance, though not perfectly beautiful, was ex-
> tremely high-bred and interesting; and her voice and manner of
> singing, exquisitely polished and sweet. She had not a motion that
> did not charm the eye, or a tone but what delighted the ear.[38]

After her success in London, de Amicis 'held the first rank among
female singers in the serious operas of Naples and other great cities of
Italy'.[39] Going on to discuss her vocal technique, Burney wrote of her
'compass of voice' and the 'delicate and difficult expression and execution' of which she was capable.[40] Moreover: 'De Amicis was not only
the first who introduced *staccato divisions* in singing on the stage, but the
first singer that I had ever heard go up to E flat in altissimo, with true,
clear, and powerful *real* voice.'[41] He compared her with Lucrezia
Aguiari (1743-1783), the soprano Wolfgang had so marvelled at in
Parma that he sent a passage of her embellishments home,[42] affirming
that she, on the other hand, sang her high notes in falsetto.

Mozart's *primo uomo*, the Cecilio of *Lucio Silla*, was equally excellent. A Roman, Venanzio Rauzzini (1747–1810) was first heard by Burney in Munich the year before *Lucio Silla*, where he said the castrato was

> the first singer in the serious opera ... [was] of singular merit, [and] has been six years in the service of this court.[43] ... He is not only a charming singer, a pleasing figure, and a good actor; but a more excellent contrapuntist, and performer on the harpsichord, than a singer is usually allowed to be.[44]

Shortly after his Milanese performance, Rauzzini went to London where Burney heard him again in 1773. After remarking on the singer's skill as an opera composer,[45] he noted that the 'beautiful and animated young man' had a voice which 'was sweet, clear, flexible and extensive; being in compass more than two octaves'.[46]

Unfortunately Rauzzini did not have a large voice and so 'It was some time before his abilities were felt by the [London] public here, to the favour of which nothing can so speedily convey the merits of a singer as a *great* and powerful voice.'[47] Success was soon to be his, though, as 'his taste, fancy and delicacy, together with his beautiful person and spirited and intelligent manner of acting, before the season was over, gained him general approbation'.[48] By 1775 Burney was able to write: 'At this time, there was no male singer, *di gran grido*, in England, except Rauzzini, who more frequently pleased than surprised his audience.'[49]

As one would expect, Wolfgang's writing reflects the abilities of his singers. Anna de Amicis' music is extremely difficult (she insisted her young composer make the most of her technique, as Leopold wrote home),[50] especially her arias No. 11 'Ah, se il crudel periglio' and No. 16 'Parto, m'affretto' which abound in long, intricate *fioriture* demanding great skill for their execution.[51] Equally difficult are those entrusted to Rauzzini. For example his aria No. 14 'Ah, se a morir mi chiama' not only makes use of his two-octave range noted by Burney, but calls for an upward skip from a natural to a″ flat. All his numbers are exceedingly long and embellished but, referring to No. 2, 'Il tenero momento', Leopold remarked he sang like an angel.[52] Although Burney attributed the first use in the opera theatre of *staccato fioriture* to de Amicis, she must have soon been imitated by other gifted sopranos since Wolfgang composed such a line not for her but for Daniella Mienci, Silla's sister 'Celia'. As it is Wolfgang's first example of such writing in his operas, it obviously attests to this soprano's more-than-usual skill.

While it is not possible to discern anything in particular about Onofrio, Anfidio in the opera, or Suardi, the castrato who took the male role of Lucio Cinna, except that one sees from their music that they must have been well able to sing the brilliant arias typical of *opera seria*, Morgnoni must have been quite a disappointment to Wolfgang. As Leopold had insisted, the role of Lucio Silla called for a good actor, which Morgnoni was not; worse still was that Wolfgang must have automatically thought of his as a somewhat special role musically since Leopold, even before he knew who it would be, said the part called for a good singer.[53] In the end, and undoubtedly to suit the singer's limited abilities, Wolfgang confined Silla's arias to a restricted range and excluded any request of more than normal, straightforward singing from them. Cleverly, he tried to compensate for these shortcomings on the part of the singer by always accompanying him with a full and active orchestra.

Understandably, whatever his music, even a *cantabile* aria, would have revealed much about a singer: 'if he has voice, if he has feeling, if he has taste, if he has fancy, if he has science'.[54] And if he intended to ornament his music – and everyone, public and composer included, expected that he would, at least at the da capo repeats of an aria – he had to know music theory. As John Brown categorically stated, he 'ought to be a perfect master of the science of counter-point, that he may know precisely what liberties he may take with respect to the harmony of the other parts.'[55] There was always the danger, too, that the singer would demand bravura arias from the composer, not when they could be used with effect at some moment in the drama, but '*chiefly*, indeed, too often, *merely* to indulge the singer in the display of certain powers in the execution, particularly extraordinary agility or compass of voice'.[56] As Benedetto Marcello insinuated in his satire of 1720, *Il teatro alla moda*, an opera was the testing ground of the capacity to dominate of the librettist, composer, and singers, and Wolfgang was gaining valuable experience in learning how to assert his creativity in the fray.

Not even critics of eighteenth-century opera abuses, such as Stefano Arteaga, however, felt that embellishments were to be entirely eliminated; the composer was merely to control their insertion:

He must allow them whenever they truly correct defects in the composition or in sentiment, whenever they help in creating the dominating sentiment of the song, whenever they agree with the object imitated and with the situation, whenever they serve to aid the attention of the spectator by helping him to enter into the sense of the word or to feel the force and variety of the music better.[57]

Obviously the period felt that ornaments could aid in achieving music's desired expressive results; at the same time all, Arteaga included, justly complained that their overabundance or employment in unsuitable moments could have the opposite effect and weaken any expressiveness,[58] and it was this abuse which came under attack.

In spite of having traditional restrictions on his composing, *Lucio Silla* reveals that Wolfgang was actually able to express his individuality in a clearer way than ever before. This is apparent in the purely instrumental pieces as well, such as the overture and, even more evidently, in the instrumental interlude of Act I which accompanies the change of scene from Giunia's apartment 'surrounded with statues of the most famous Roman heroines', to the cemetery, an 'atrio, as dark as it is magnificent, which leads into underground rooms where,there are sumptuous monuments of the Heroes of Rome' (two of the seven suggestive sets designed for *Lucio Silla* by Fabrizio and Giovanni Antonio Galliari).[59] The overture has no defined dramatic association whereas this interlude is more programmatic and, by means of nine bars of fluctuating major-minor relationships, creates the supernatural atmosphere of the cemetery (example 1). The brief instrumental section is actually the beginning of a long, continuous scene for it goes directly into Cecilio's accompanied recitative 'Morte, morte fatal' (Death, fatal death), wherin his wonder and fear and finally relief at seeing Giunia lead without interruption to the chorus No. 6 'Fuor di queste urne dolenti' (Beyond these sad urns), lugubrious, homophonic four-part music for Giunia's companions in which, with a background provided by a full and active orchestra, the unexpected alterations in the voice parts communicate the horror of the death inflicted by the Romans. The choral number leads, once again directly, into a section for Giunia in which she grievingly invokes her dead father (see example 2 for Wolf-

Example 1

2 Oboes

Violin I, II
(plus Violas
and Basses)

Scena VII. RECITATIVO: Cecilio

Example 2

gang's use here of implied chromatic harmony). Another accompanied recitative follows, this time for Giunia and Cecilio which leads straight into their duet 'D'Eliso in sen m'attendi' (No. 7, Elysian fields await me), a brilliant piece which closes the act. In this last episode of continuity, that is in going directly from the accompanied recitative to the duet, Wolfgang once more reveals himself a participant in the most novel of eighteenth-century musical-dramatic trends. Noting moments in an opera when the orchestral introduction might have been done away with, John Brown mentioned just such a situation as that taken advantage of by Wolfgang: 'when, for instance, in an accompanied recitative, after a succession of very different emotions, some sentiment is supposed to take possession of the mind, related to that which is to be the subject of the Air, and to which it is afterwards led by a gradation of kindred emotions.'[60] Brown assured his reader that an audience would melt away at the imperceptible transition. Describing strong emotions, scenes of fear or unhappiness, with dissonance is a practice which did not originate with Wolfgang (the madrigalists of the *Cinquecento* made great use of their association); but it must be noted how well he, too, understood the possibilities inherent in chromaticism and in an age which preferred consonance and serenity in music. In addition, Wolfgang handled his enlarged musical vocabulary with perfect mastery.

A second indication of Wolfgang's increased ability in *Lucio Silla* is that he now uses musical ideas, first heard in association with a text, as recurring motives in a section which does not have that particular text; the result is that dramatic expression is not relegated to a single bar or phrase but permeates and unifies an aria. In No. 5 'Il desio di vendetta' (The desire for revenge) for Silla, the violin motive which suggests the idea of a 'fiamma', a flame, in the orchestral introduction (example 3)

Example 3

and that which the voice has to the words 'si m'infiamma' (yes, it in-
flames me; example 4) – precursors of numerous later instrumental
descriptions of fire, especially dear to Wagner – are used often throughout the aria in this way. Motives which evoke heart beats ('e sì m'agita
il petto', and yes it agitates my breast: example 5) are employed
in the aria in the same manner. One can find another 'dramatic' instrumental motive suggested by the text, 'Parto, m'affretto. Ma nel partire
il cor si spezza' (I leave, I hurry. But in parting my heart breaks) in No.
16 where the violins, in a hesitating line of *piano-forte* contrasts, convince us of the fear and trembling of death felt by Giunia (example 6).
Wolfgang has found a means by which the orchestra can either
communicate inexpressed thoughts or emotions, or is able to assure us
that a certain attitude or situation has not changed by returning to the
musical motive originally stated with certain words.

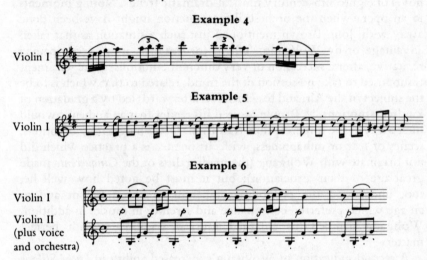

Example 4

Example 5

Example 6

Most noticeable in *Lucio Silla* is also a subtle 'Mozartian' treatment of
rhythm. An ample use of suspensions, of unexpected triplets, of phrases
which begin irregularly before or after a strong accent, and a more
mature understanding of harmonic rhythm permits Wolfgang to create
sophisticated dramatic effects and suggest deeper emotions. A specific
result of his new application of rhythm and implied awareness of its
multiple uses is that even the *Adagio* or *Grazioso* sections of the opera
have acquired a new calm allowing for a more lyrical flow to the
phrases, as in No. 14 'Ah, se a morir mi chiama' (Ah, if I am called to
die), for example.

Following the latest trends in eighteenth-century *opera seria*, Wolfgang scored not just for strings in *Lucio Silla* but for a more varied
ensemble. Of course his choice of instrumentation was in part decided

by the group at his disposal, the large orchestra of the Milan Teatro
Regio Ducale he had been able to work with also in *Mitridate* and
Ascanio. At the same time, his way of intensifying their sound by
employing the strings often in passages of continous semiquavers and
then, above this sonority, of offering the distinct and several colours of
brass and woodwinds to heighten the dramatic atmosphere revealed a
new competence in his orchestral writing. Wolfgang's next trip to
Vienna and exposure to that capital's excellent instrumental music (by
Franz Joseph Haydn, Dittersdorf, Vanahll, etc.) was to have a long-
lasting influence on him, but it was no doubt his experiences in Milan
which provided him with his solid foundation in orchestral techniques.

As far as form was concerned and as was traditional, most of the arias
of *Lucio Silla* are tripartite, in fact one finds here the same variants of
the structure noticed in *Mitridate, Re di Ponto*, Wolfgang's previous
opera seria for Milan. And as was occasionally the case in *Il sogno di
Scipione*, they are often less-evidently structured since middle sections,
which are quite short, are apt to be similar in musical content to opening
sections. The two most common of these aria forms in *Lucio Silla* are
quite complex AA'BA' (to be found in No. 5, Silla's impressive entrance
aria, 'Il desio di vendetta'; No. 8, Aufidio's 'Guerrier, che d'un acciaro';
No. 12, Cinna's 'Nel fortunato istante'; No. 15, Celia's 'Quando
sugl'arsi campi'; and No. 20, Cinna's 'De più superbi il core'. No. 19,
Celia's 'Pupille amante', is a truncated version, presenting only the
beginning AA') and the simpler ABA' (No. 1, Cinna's 'Vieni
ov'amor t'invita'; No. 2, Cecilio's 'I tenero momento'; No. 3, Celia's
'Se lusinghiera speme'; No. 11, Giunia's 'A se il crudel periglio'; and
No. 14, Cecilio's 'Ah se a morir mi chiama'). Other arias, however,
which do not return to previously heard material (such as that in an AB
structure - No. 10, Celia's 'Se il labbro timido' and No. 13, Silla's
'D'ogni pietà mi spoglio' - or in a single section as is No. 16, Giunia's
'Parto, m'affretto') are also to be found, although they are clearly in the
minority.

The noteworthy employment of the orchestra before the recitative
for Cecilio in Act I, scene 7, 'Morte, morte fatal' has already been
mentioned; another recitative worth citing is Cecilio's 'Dungue sperar
poss'io' (Then may I hope) in the second scene of the same act: its
quality is a foretaste of the Countess's recitative, 'E Susanna non vien' in
Le Nozze di Figaro due to its corresponding various changes of sentiment, its surprising individuality, and the intimate excitement expressed by the orchestra, in this case of the young man awaiting his
beloved and hoping not to be disappointed.

The choruses of *Lucio Silla* are simple and homophonic: No. 6,
noticed earlier for its remarkable harmony, is proof of Wolfgang's
sense of form, seen also in its ABA construction (chorus-solo-chorus),.

and of his feeling for dramatic continuity. Of the remaining ensembles,
the above-mentioned duet for Giunia and Cecilio (No. 7 'D' Eliso in
sen m'attendi') demonstrates exceptional eighteenth-century virtuosity: de Amicis and Rauzzini were asked on the word 'piacer' to sing a
long and difficult *fioritura* in thirds, an interval which for reasons of
intonation is always demanding although extremely beautiful and effective when well done (example 7). Another ensemble, the trio No. 18

Example 7

'Quell orgoglioso sdegno' (That proud disdain) for Giunia, Cecilio,
and Silla is again an application of Wolfgang's newly-acquired treatment of the motive, as well as his employment of counterpoint to
express both diverse thoughts (a technique which appeared in his operas
for the first time in the Act III finale of *La finta semplice*) as well as,
through imitation, of shared sentiments. True, the structure is very
simple; but it must be seen as a beginning which will lead to the trio of
the first act of *Figaro*. By concluding Act I of *Lucio Silla* with a duet,
Act II with a trio, and Act III with a quartet and a chorus, Wolfgang,
and de Gamerra one must add, have seemingly managed to involve
more characters as the drama progresses as well as to allow for increasingly more interesting act endings as the opera goes on.[61]

Lucio Silla attests to a growing musical maturity in Wolfgang since
his two preceding works *Ascanio in Alba* and *Il sogno di Scipione* (or
rather, as was suggested earlier, that he was not at liberty to use his
newly-acquired ability in these occasional and conventional operas). It
is a maturation which Dent observed in his other music of the same
period: 'A new note of passion appears in the slow movements of his
quartets and sonatas, which are often quite romantic in character.'[62]
Wolfgang's awareness of rhythm and harmony has widened, and he
implements his new capabilities with great success for a more complete
and dramatic realization of the libretto. His use of orchestral motives,
too, coupled with counterpoint and more discriminating instrumentation, creates a new operatic texture. *Lucio Silla* is Wolfgang's first opera
which suggests his future style in any clear sense and reveals his first
concrete intuition of the possibilities inherent in music to express
drama.

It may be said that in *Lucio Silla* Wolfgang abandoned conventional
writing to discover, through his own efforts, suitable musical means for

expressing a text. It is without doubt an *opera seria*; but it was composed with more than common flexibility. Perhaps it was the opera's new and unconventional aspects which, despite its evident popularity, kept the Milanese nobles from commissioning yet another work from the young Mozart. Or perhaps at 17 (he had celebrated his birthday on 27 January at the height of the opera's success) he was considered too 'old' to be interesting. Fate also played her part in impeding his return to Milan since the Teatro Regio Ducale was burned to the ground in 1776, never to reopen as such. Of course, in 1778 a new, and now public, theatre was opened, the famous Teatro La Scala, but Wolfgang was not invited to compose for it either. In spite of his enthusiasm for Italian opera – expressed many times but also in a letter of 7 February 1778 where he wrote: 'My one ardent wish is now to write operas; but they must be French, not German, and Italian rather than one or the other'[63] – Wolfgang was never to write another work for Italy and *Lucio Silla* was his last opera for the country whose music he so loved.

The Mozarts did not leave Milan immediately after Wolfgang's opera had ended its run, however, but stayed on instead to hear Paisiello's *Il Sismano nel Mogol*, the second opera of the season. In the interim Wolfgang composed the now famous brilliant motet 'Exultate, jubilate' (K. 165) for Rauzzini which the castrato sang on 17 January at Milan's Theatine Church.[64] Unfortunately, on the following days Leopold was in such pain with an attack of rheumatism that he had to take to his bed.[65] In fact, Wolfgang went alone to the first orchestral rehearsal of *Il Sismano*, writing home afterwards that, 'In this opera there will be 24 horses and lots of people on stage, and it will be a miracle if some accident does not happen. I like the music but I don't know if the public will like it since only those connected with the theatre have been allowed to attend the first rehearsals.'[66] On the opening night, 30 January, Leopold was still in bed, which meant that Wolfgang went again without him to the theatre.[67] The opera, Leopold wrote home after hearing Wolfgang's comments, was beautiful but, as one can believe thinking of all the horses as well as people involved, 'presented at great expense'. Leopold stayed indoors most of February trying to get warm in the cold room by wearing lots of clothes to bed.[68]

Finally, though, he was able to get up, and on 27 February he wrote that in the evening he and Wolfgang would attend Paisiello's opera together; afterwards they were going to a ball which was to begin at 1 a.m. and last till morning mass. Now that he was better, they would soon make arrangements for the trip home to Salzburg. Leopold concluded by saying what was in Wolfgang's heart, too: 'It is difficult for me to leave Italy.'[69]

Chapter Nine: Notes

1. K. 135 in *WAM*, Serie V, 8.
2. *Dokumente*, p. 119. On Wolfgang's last trip to Italy, see Guglielmo Barblan, 'Il *Lucio Silla* e un ignorato incontro con Paisiello' in *Mozart in Italia*, pp. 165-177.
3. *Idem*. On the value of the *gigliato*, see note 29 of Chapter VI here.
4. Some would have to be rewritten later due to changes in the libretto: see note 45 here. The autograph score of *Lucio Silla* disappeared after the Second World War (see Köchel 6, p. 163). Various eighteenth-century copies exist, such as the one by Dragonetti now in the British Library (which, however, lacks recitatives).
5. *Dokumente*, p. 127.
6. Letter from Leopold to his wife of 28 October 1772: *Briefe*, I, p. 457.
7. Letter of 14 November: *ibid.*, I, p. 460.
8. *Ibid.*, p. 462.
9. *Ibid.*, p. 464.
10. Wolfgang's letter to his sister of 5 June 1770: *ibid.*, p. 358.
11. Letter of 14 November, *op. cit.*
12. Letter of 28 November, *op. cit.*
13. Letter of 14 November, *op. cit.*
14. Letter of 5 December: *ibid.*, p. 465.
15. *Idem*.
16. Letter of 12 December to his wife: *ibid.*, p. 466.
17. Letter of 18 December: *ibid.*, p. 467.
18. *Idem*.
19. Letter of 26 December: *ibid.*, p. 469.
20. *Idem*.
21. Letter of 2 January 1773: *ibid.*, p. 471.
22. *Ibid.*, p. 472.
23. *Idem*.
24. *Ibid.*, pp. 471-472.
25. *Ibid.*, p. 472.
26. *Ibid.*, p. 473.
27. *Idem*. As Wolfgang was later to complain, people gave him watches when money or a position would have served him better.
28. Letter from Leopold to his wife: *ibid.*, p. 475.
29. Leopold's letter to his wife of 23 January: *ibid.*, p. 477.
30. He is named in the libretto, f. 3v. The following information is taken from *Dizionario Letterario Bompiani* (Milan, 1957), II, pp. 19-20.
31. As had another of Wolfgang's librettists, Marco Coltellini, the 'arranger' of the unfortunate *La finta semplice*.
32. Both Coltellini and Giuseppe Parini, author of Wolfgang's *Ascanio in Alba*, as well as Metastasio, who wrote his *Il Re pastore*, were clergymen, a somewhat mysterious fact in the case of Coltellini who had a family.
33. Letter of 14 November, *op. cit.*, p. 460.
34. *Idem*. In the libretto (f. 2) de Gamerra merely says that Metastasio has given the work his 'absolute approval'.
35. *Briefe*, idem.
36. *John Christian Bach*, p. 130
37. Pp. 130-131.

38. *General History*, II, p. 864.

39. *Ibid.*, p. 865.

40. *Idem.*

41. *Idem.*

42. In his letter to Nannerl of 24 March 1770: *Briefe*, I, p. 324.

43. *Germany*, I, p. 126.

44. *Idem.*

45. He wrote a *Piramo e Tisbe* and a *La vestale*: see Burney, *General History*, II, p. 880.

46. *Idem.*

47. *Idem.*

48. *Idem.*

49. *Ibid.*, p. 882. Rauzzini retired later to Bath, England, and in 1794 Haydn wrote a canon on the words 'Turk was a faithful dog, and not a man' which referred to the singer's dog. Rauzzini had quite a controversy, described by Burney, *ibid.*, p. 894 ff, over his affirmation that he had composed music for Sacchini's operas.

50. See note 16 here and the relevant passage in the text.

51. At a concert of 29 March 1783 given in Vienna, and to which the Emperor surprisingly came, Wolfgang wrote that 'the scene from my last Milan opera, *Parto m'affretto*' was sung by 'Mad.elle Täuber', obviously another soprano with special vocal abilities. This is another proof of the aria's success in the theatre if Wolfgang felt he could use it alone in concert. (*Briefe*, III, pp. 261-262.)

52. See note 12 here and the relevant passage in the text.

53. For Leopold's comments, see note 14 here and the relevant passage in the text.

54. John Brown, p. 43.

55. *Ibid.*, p. 47.

56. *Ibid.*, p. 39.

57. III, p. 41.

58. *Idem.*

59. These famous 'Inventors, and Painters of the Scenes' had also worked on Wolfgang's *Mitridate* and *Ascanio*. All seven of their sets are listed on f. 4v of the libretto (copies are in the Bologna Conservatory Library and the East Berlin Deutsche Staatsbibliothek). Several sketches are in the Bologna Pinacoteca Nazionale.

60. Pp. 32-33.

61. Although the *entr'acte* ballets to *Lucio Silla* (*Le gelosie del Seraglio, La Scuola di Negromazia, La Giaconna*) were once attributed to Mozart (K. 135a/Anh. 109, sketches in the Salzburg Mozarteum), Walter Senn doubted his authorship in the first ballet in 'Mozarts Skizze der Ballettmusik zu *Le gelosie del Serraglio* (KV Anh. 109/135a)', *Acta Musicologica* 33 (1961), pp. 169-192; recently Gerhard Croll in 'Bemerkungen zum *Ballo Primo* (KV Anh. 109/135a) in Mozarts Mailänder *Lucio Silla*', *Analecta Musicologica* 18 (1978), pp. 160-165, agreed the author to have been Joseph Starzer. Whose music was used for the other two ballets is not known but more than likely they were not by Wolfgang as traditionally one composer did the opera and another did the ballets. *Ascanio in Alba* had been an exception, but then it was not the usual sort of opera either, and already filled with ballet.

62. Edward J. Dent, *Mozart's Operas*, 2nd ed. in paperback (London, 1947), p. 24.

63. In a letter from Mannheim to his father: *Briefe*, II, p. 265.

64. Wolfgang's letter to his sister of 16 January: *ibid.*, I, p. 475; and *Dokumente*, p. 129.

65. On 23 January Leopold wrote to his wife that he had been in bed already eight days: *Briefe*, I, p. 476.
66. Letter to his sister of 23 January: *ibid.*, p. 477.
67. Leopold to his wife on 30 January: *ibid.*, p. 478.
68. His letter to his wife of 6 February: *ibid.*, p. 479.
69. His letter to his wife of 27 February: *ibid.*, p. 483.

CHAPTER TEN

La finta giardiniera[1]

ARRIVING IN SALZBURG on 13 March 1773, the Mozarts were in time to celebrate the anniversary of Prince Archbishop Colloredo's installation the next day.[2] After a few months, though, and taking advantage of the fact that the Archbishop was also to be away, father and son were off again, this time to Vienna. Leopold had not given up hope that Wolfgang could obtain a commision, or better still a position, in the capital; as a matter of fact, after Wolfgang's successes in Austria-dominated Milan, his expectations must have increased, and on 14 July 1773 they set out from Salzburg, hopeful as usual, and were to be away the entire summer.[3]

The Mozarts' first social call in Vienna was paid to the music lover who had been so kind to them on their last, not very satisfying, visit to Vienna at the time of *La finta semplice*, Anton Mesmer. They had their mid-day meal with the patron of Wolfgang's *Bastien und Bastienne* on the 17th and on the 18th with his cousin, School Director Joseph Mesmer; again on the 19th and the 26th they spent the whole day with the doctor[4] and were to keep up these frequent visits throughout the summer. Everyone, including Wolfgang, enjoyed playing Mesmer's recently acquired unusual instrument, a glass harmonica;[5] Leopold praised his house, too, writing home that 'the garden is marvellous with views and statues, theatre, bird house' and so forth.[6] In between these pleasant visits, however, Wolfgang found time to compose and, of course, to visit Maria Theresa. After their audience on 5 August, though, Leopold could only report to his wife that 'Her Majesty was very polite with us'.[7] Two days later Wolfgang gave a violin concert in the Kajetana Monastery Church and on the 9th his 'Dominicus' Mass (K. 66) was heard in the Jesuit church on the Hofplatz[8] with Leopold conducting.[9] At the end of July their *chéf* had come to Vienna but Colloredo left almost immediately for Laxenburg,[10] a summer court residence to the south of Vienna, and was not to return until 11 August, allowing Leopold and Wolfgang to relax a bit in his absence.[11]

It must have been in these months that Wolfgang met Tobias Philipp von Gebler who had written a play, *Thamos, König von Aegypten* which

was published in Prague and Dresden that same year (1773). Von
Gebler, a poet, Baron, and Chancellor at the Bohemian-Austrian office
in Vienna was clearly an important man. He was looking for someone
to write music for his play and it was probably in this period that his
first contact with the young composer took place, perhaps through the
good offices of Mesmer.[12] Certainly Wolfgang saw Noverre, the
famous choreographer with whose pupil he had collaborated in
Milan.[13] It was a period, too, of concern over the health of Florian
Leopold Gassmann (1729-1774), Imperial Court Composer since 1763,
but he vacated no position and Leopold had to write home on 4
September rather curtly that, 'Herr Gassmann was sick; he is now
better.'[14] Whether Leopold and Wolfgang attended the opera is not
certain although, knowing their keen interest in opera in general and in
particular those part of the Viennese scene, one might assume that they
did. Works by leading composers such as Galuppi, Salieri and Anfossi
were offered at the Kärntnertor Theatre and Burgtheater,[15] and ballet,
also extremely popular, could be seen almost every day in the capital.

While between friends, musical entertainments, and composing
Wolfgang was never at a loss for something to do, Vienna did not offer
him what he most desired and, once again, he left the city empty-
handed. Besides taking up their usual duties in Salzburg, Leopold and
Wolfgang were busy in late autumn moving house. The family had
been living on the third floor of a building owned by Hagenauer, in
Getreide Gasse in the oldest part of Salzburg. The apartment, which
had only a single bedroom, had been too small for the family for quite
some time. Already on 20 February 1771 Leopold had written to his
wife from Venice that he felt the place unsuitable, insisting that 'we
cannot continue to sleep all together like soldiers; Wolfgang is no
longer a seven-year-old child'.[16] Their move to a house in Hannibal
Platz,[17] previously owned by a dancing master who held dances and
masked balls there every year and which was still referred to as the
Tanzmeisterhaus, meant now having eight rooms at their disposal, a
sufficient number for the family to enjoy comfort and privacy and for
Wolfgang to be able to work undisturbed.[18]

On 6 December, however, after barely settling in, father and son
packed their bags again and departed, this time for Munich where
Wolfgang had been commissioned by Count Joseph Anton von Seeau,
Superintendent of Theatrical Entertainments in Munich, to do an *opera
buffa*, *La finta giardiniera*.[19] It is possible that his fellow Salzburger Count
Ferdinand Christoph von Zeil, Prince Bishop of Chiemsee, who was
enthusiastic about Wolfgang's talents, had exerted some influence in
obtaining the commision for him; and as Elector Maximillian III was
also interested in the young composer, it was difficult for Archbishop
Colloredo to refuse the Mozarts a leave of absence.[20] Presentation of

the opera was originally planned for 29 December, therefore their arrival in Munich was already rather late if Wolfgang had to compose the arias and the singers to learn them.

The situation there, as far as opera was concerned, was not as favourable to the composer as it was in Milan, where Wolfgang's music had always had several consecutive performances. In Italy an opera was given as long as an audience came to hear it; but in Munich things went differently, as Leopold related to his wife a few days after arriving:

Here it is like in Salzburg. One can perform an opera where one [the audience] pays not oftener than twice in succession, otherwise one would see too few people in the theatre; then for two or three weeks one must perform other operas, and then come back with the previous one, namely as one does with comedies and with ballets.[21]

Of course, there were advantages in this routine for the singers, as he went on to explain: Therefore they know at least twenty operas by heart due to this rotating, and in the meantime will study a new one.[22] For these reasons 'Wolfgang's opera will be offered therefore for Christmas [i.e. the season] and I believe on 29 [December] for the first time.'[23]

Some time during their stay in Munich, Nannerl was to come to spend Carnival with them, but the uncertain scheduling of the theatre made any assurance that she would see her brother's opera impossible.[24] Leopold was hoping that the work would be able to be performed in any event before the pre-Lenten festivities began, for reasons he made clear in the same letter:

Then once Carnival really begins, only unimportant light operas will be given in a small theatre set up in the Redoutensaal, where a group of masqueraders will be gathered and where there are several game tables, and where there will be only noise, masque-conversation and gambling at the many tables. Nothing worthwhile is ever presented then because no one would pay attention.[25]

Certainly it would be best for Wolfgang's opera not to be attempted in this confusion but rather in the normal Residenz theatre, quite an attractive setting as described by Burney: 'It is not large, having but four rows of boxes, fifteen in each; but it is more richly fitted up, than any that I had ever seen.[26]

In general Munich was an important music centre and, as Burney also noted, had 'a great number of modern musicians of the first class'.[27] Leopold and Wolfgang intended to have them properly informed as to Wolfgang's skills and sent home for two *Lytanien de Venerabili*, one by Leopold and a 'big Litany' by Wolfgang, which they intended to do on New Year's Day.[28] Unfortunately on 16 December

and for several succeeding days Wolfgang was in pain due to a bad
tooth and, as his face was quite swollen, could not leave the house.[29] In
spite of not feeling well, he had to attend the first rehearsal of *La finta
giardiniera* which happily, as Leopold recounted to his wife on 28
December, had favourable results. The opera

> was so very well liked, that they would like it postponed till 5
> January 1775 in order that the singers learn it much better; and when
> they have the music properly in their heads, which would have been
> too soon to do by 29 December, they can act more assuredly, and the
> opera will not be ruined. In brief, the composition of the music is
> liked amazingly well, and will be performed then on 5 January.
> Now there is only the production in the theatre, which ought to go
> as well as I hope, since the actors are not opposed to us.[30]

Although Burney had heard Venanzio Rauzzini in Munich, the
castrato who so distinguished himself as 'Cecilio' in Wolfgang's *Lucio
Silla*, he did not perform in *La finta giardiniera* as he was already settled
in London by that time;[31] also, castrati were generally not included in
an *opera buffa* except for special effects as was done in Wolfgang's
present comedy. After all, these artificial creatures did not really fit in
with this, the most down-to-earth musical genre of the Italian stage.
Even though they would have preferred to have been able to affirm
that *opera seria* was the more 'natural' genre, both Algarotti and Arteaga had to admit that in the eighteenth century greater expressiveness
was to be found in comic opera. As Algarotti wrote: 'There are, for
example, the *Intermezzi* and the comic operette where expression dominates as the main characteristic more than in another kind of entertainment.'[32] The reason for this he found in the simpler type of music
necessarily employed in *opera buffa* due to its less qualified singers:

> This perhaps because the composers, since there are only very
> mediocre singers, cannot write, given their [the singers'] talent, all
> the secrets of the art, all the treasures of the science; whereby they
> [composers] are forced to stick to the simple and to support nature.[33]

But for whatever external reasons, 'due to the truth contained therein,
that sort of music is in vogue and triumphs',[34] in spite of Algarotti's
intellectual and aristocratic surprise as *opera buffa* was 'reputedly
plebeian'.[35]

However true it might have been elsewhere, Munich did not have
particularly second-rate singers in its *buffa* company: while it is not
certain who performed in all the roles of *La finta giardiniera*, it is known
that Rosa Manservisi sang, and probably her sister Teresa as well, with
Rosa in the title role and Teresa in a second female part. With regard
probably to Teresa, since he says she was the second singer of the comic

company, Burney wrote that a 'Signora Manservisi deserves to be mentioned; her figure is agreeable, her voice, though not strong, is well-toned, she has nothing vulgar in her manner, sings in tune, and never gives offence'.[36] Rudhart, in his history of opera in Munich, wrote that Rosa, above average in voice, execution and personal appearance, was especially suited for *opera buffa* as was the bass in the cast, Rossi.[37] Of a tenor in the company, Signor Fiorini, Burney wrote: 'He has perhaps been a better singer than he is at present; but now, neither his voice, nor manner, had any thing interesting in it, though both were free from any common defects; for he sang in tune, had a shake, and was far from vulgar.'[38]

As to Algarotti's assertion that *opera buffa* was more natural than *opera seria*, the plot of La finta giardiniera would prove him correct, although 'simple' may not be the right adjective for the series of confused and amusing scenes straight out of the *commedia dell'arte* repertory and full of jealousy, love, and disguise. Some of these elements are seen even from the list of characters, offered here with the names of their possible first interpreters:

DON ANCHISE, Podestà of Lagonero, who is in love with Sandrina (tenor)—Signor Fiorini

MARCHESE VIOLANTE ONESTI, who is in love with Contino Belfiore; believed to be dead, she has taken the name of SANDRINA and is disguised as a gardener (soprano)—Rosa Manservisi

CONTINO BELFIORE, formerly in love with Sandrina and now with Arminda (tenor)—Johann Walleshauser

ARMINDA, Milanese noble woman, formerly in love with Cavalier Ramiro and now engaged to be married to Contino Belfiore (soprano)

CAVALIER RAMIRO, in love with Arminda but refused by her (soprano) —Tommaso Consoli

SERPETTA, servant to the Podestà and in love with the same (soprano)—Teresa Manservisi

ROBERTO, servant to Violante, who pretends to be her cousin, has taken the name of NARDO and is also disguised as a gardener; he is in love with Serpetta (bass)—Giovanni Rossi[39]

Possibilities for comedy are seen immediately in the relationships between characters and the ensuing events take full advantage of developing them. A year before the opera begins, the Marchese (Marquise) Violante Onesti was wounded in a fit of jealous rage by her fiancé, Contino (or 'little Count') Belfiore. Believing Violante dead, he fled Milan and went to Lagonero, where he promptly fell in love with Arminda, niece of Podestà Don Anchise, Mayor of Lagonero. At the same time, Violante, still in love with Belfiore in spite of his terrible jealousy, has come to Lagonero disguised as a gardener where, under the assumed name of Sandrina and together with her servant Roberto who now calls himself Nardo and also pretends to be a gardener, she is in the employ of Don Anchise. The opera begins with the preparations for the wedding of Belfiore and Arminda during which other amorous aspirations are revealed: Cavalier Ramiro would like Arminda for himself, the servant Serpetta would like Don Anchise, he in turn has taken a fancy to Sandrina (and amusingly likens his feelings to musical instruments), while Nardo likes Serpetta – all unrequited loves. In the following scene, after Arminda explains he must be faithful to Belfiore, he, quite pompously, boasts of his noble origins, naming as his ancestors Scipio, Marcus Aurelius, Muzio Scevola, etc. Then, after a scene in which poor Nardo is refused by Serpetta, Belfiore believes he recognizes his once-beloved in the gardener Sandrina and, in consequence, Ramiro hopes yet to win Arminda and Don Anchise fears he may lose Sandrina.

In Act II events complicate the situation. Ramiro has received word from Milan which accuses Belfiore of the murder of Violante and, worse, of dishonourably running away. To try and save him, Sandrina at first says that she is Violante but then, aside to Belfiore, she insists she is simply a friend of Violante. Belfiore is confused and desperate and believes himself mad. A short while later Serpetta announces that Sandrina has fled; actually she has been abducted by the jealous Arminda. Now all hunt for the gardener, but in the darkness they fail to recognize one another. Confusion reigns supreme as the most unexpected couples embrace. Finally Sandrina is found in the grotto where she has been abandoned, misunderstandings are cleared up, and Don Anchise and Ramiro are able to challenge Belfiore; however, he and Violante manage to elude everyone when they momentarily go mad.

In Act III Don Anchise decides to annul the marriage between Belfiore and his niece Arminda since the Contino is crazy; he then gives her hand to Ramiro. In the next scene, Violante and Belfiore, at first very tired and almost convinced that it has all been a bad dream, are taken by another fit of jealousy. But love arrests their tempers and they manage to calm themselves and return to the home of the Podestà where three couples then celebrate their marriages: Violante and Belfiore, Arminda and Ramiro, Serpetta and Nardo. Only Don Anchise is left alone to await another 'Sandrina'. The opera ends with everyone singing the praises of Violante, the Pretended Gardener.

The libretto for Wolfgang's *La finta giardiniera* had been set earlier in 1773–1774 for performance in Rome's famous Teatrō delle Dame by Pasquale Anfossi.[40] Unfortunately, its poet is not known although both Calzabigi (to the surprise of students of Gluck) and Coltellini have been proposed, without proof it must be added, for authorship. Most

likely it was Abate Giuseppe Petrosellini (1727-1799), a Groom of the
Chamber at the Papal Court and member of several literary academies.
He had written the *dramma giocoso L'incognita perseguitata*, which Anfossi
had set for the 1772-1773 Rome Carnival (and which Cimarosa, Paisiello, Piccinni, and Salieri would also make use of), and his comic style
there is akin to that found in *La finta giardiniera*.[41]

For Pasquale Anfossi (1727-1797), the libretto's first composer, Arteaga had much praise, saying that he was 'facile and fecund' in his
comic operas and enjoyed the same place among composers as Goldoni
did among comic writers.[42] Comparison between his setting of *La finta
giardiniera* and that by Wolfgang reveals him there to to be an able
composer but not quite the interpreter of comedy Wolfgang proved to
be. Perhaps it is his standard use of the orchestra and of rhythm that
distinguishes him from Wolfgang who showed in this opera that
variety of instrumental colour and flexible rhythmic patterns could be
employed for dramatic purposes. Proof of Wolfgang's ability with
comedy comes from another source at a later date, in June 1783, when
Anfossi's *opera buffa Il curioso indiscreto* was given in Vienna. As stated
openly in the libretto:

> The two arias on page 36 and on page 102 have been set to music by
> Signor Maestro Mozzart, to please Signora Lange, not because those
> written by Signor Maestro Anfossi were beyond her ability, but for
> other reasons.[43]

Wolfgang had actually composed three arias to replace those set by
Anfossi, two for Signora Lange and one for Herr Adamberger (K. 418,
419, 420); but while the second soprano aria was so well liked it had to
be repeated, the tenor aria was not done 'due to a trick by Salieri', as
Wolfgang wrote home.[44] In any event, in this case Wolfgang's comic
music was so preferred to Anfossi's that the singers obviously made a
fuss to do his instead.

At the same time there was known to the Mozarts a composer of
comic opera worth studying, and whom Wolfgang must have heard
and studied with interest and profit each time he was in Vienna: Florian
Leopold Gassmann (1729-1774). Born in Bohemia, Gassmann had
gone as a youth to study for two years with Padre Martini after which
he settled in Venice and enjoyed much success writing for the theatre.
Then in 1763 he moved to Vienna where not only was he court
composer but where he reorganized the court chapel and founded the
city's first series of public concerts in 1771. In his serious operas Gassmann shared affinity with Gluck; and in his comic operas he managed
to adapt Venetian characteristics for the German taste and thus aided
development of the comic Singspiel. Wolfgang would have realized

immediately, when he went to Vienna at the time of *La finta semplice* and again in the summer of 1773, that Gassmann's music was worlds away from *opera seria*, with which up to *La finta semplice* the boy had had most personal experience. First, he would have noticed that the vocal writing was predominantly syllabic, in sharp contrast to the abundant use of *fioriture* in *opera seria*. But even more noteworthy to one whose music, of whatever genre, reveals such enormous interest in rhythm, was the use made of that element to achieve spontaneity: in Gassmann's comic operas one finds phrases which are shorter than the usual *opera seria* phrase, some built around motives of only two *staccato* notes, which helps to lighten the music; and others which are interspersed with rests, again the interrupted line being in contrast with the continuous and ever-cantabile style of serious opera; one finds, too, various rhythmic patterns employed within a phrase, allowing the music to have a more conversational, 'prose' style rather than the 'poetic' effect achieved by the repetition of a single motive typical of *opera seria*. The stress on music which is conversational and which allows the text to come through (a text which necessarily because of its genre was in itself not poetically stylized) is seen in Gassmann's recitatives which are not as melodic as those of Hasse but, rather, are full of repeated notes. Besides the usual ensembles typical of comedies, Gassmann's *opere buffe* offer excellent finales wherein, with ever more characters on stage, the music changes continually to reflect each new development in the drama, and where tension is increased by speeding up the tempo as the act proceeds to its conclusion.

Wolfgang was certainly familiar as well with the comic opera style of Nicola Piccinni (1728–1800), about whose *La Pescatrice* Burney wrote that it was 'full of that fire and fancy which characterize all productions of that ingenious and original composer'.[45] But the Englishman continued that, since comic opera 'usually abounds with brawls and *squabbles*' and since Piccinni usually had only bad singers (a point which would agree with Algarotti's observation on the state of *opera buffa* cited earlier), he used instruments a great deal both to reinforce the action and to replace the voices. 'Indeed Piccinni is accused of employing instruments to such excess, that in Italy no copyist will transcribe one of his operas without being paid a zechin more than for one by any other composer.'[46] Arteaga, too, was complimentary to Piccinni, finding his music to be 'of great fire, of great genius, of brilliant and florid style.'[47] Wolfgang also knew the music of that other acknowledged master of *opera buffa*, Giovanni Paisiello (1740–1816), another object of Arteaga's praise: Paisiello's music in general, according to him, exhibited 'singular genius, and a marvellous richness of musical ideas, and was magnificent due to a very ornate style and a new type of beauty'.[48]

La finta giardiniera was not, then, a work in a new or unique genre either for Wolfgang or for the opera theatre. It was, on the contrary, one of many such works presented and applauded all over Europe. The noteworthy aspect of it as far as Wolfgang's musical growth was concerned is that it reflects the several comic operas by other composers he must have seen and studied as well as his own experience with *La finta semplice;* it also revealed him to be a competent and mature opera composer.

On 1 January 1775, as Leopold had planned, his and Wolfgang's Litanies were performed, probably at the Frauenkirche;[49] on 4 January, to the delight of all, Nannerl arrived, and they decided upon the festivities to be attended in the coming days.[50] On 5 January, though, contrary to earlier arrangements, Wolfgang's opera was not given but was postponed instead to the 13th.[51] In the same days Leopold heard that Colloredo was to come to Munich and it was hoped that he would see Wolfgang's comedy. In the meantime, the three Mozarts went to a masquerade ball on 10 January, with Nannerl 'disguised' probably as a Salzburg maiden since that was what her father had wanted.[52] The day after, perhaps still sleepy from the party, Wolfgang wrote to his mother of the rush of events he was now involved in: 'I cannot write much as I must rehearse in a moment. Tomorrow is my dress rehearsal, and on Friday the 13th it [the opera] is performed. Mama must not worry, everything will be all right.'[53]

Prospects for success were thus far good. The performance was unfortunately not held in the Residenz Theatre but at least not in the Redoutensaal either. Instead, Wolfgang's *La finta giardiniera* was first heard in Munich's Salvator Theatre, actually Germany's first building conceived as a theatre. Modelled on the Teatro Olimpico in Vicenza, it had offered operas by many distinguished composers with sets designed by artists such as Giuseppe Galli-Bibiena. However in 1745, when Maximillian III came to the throne, expenses were cut and the Salvator Theatre suffered as a consequence. Two years after *La finta giardiniera*, though, Bavaria would come under the control of Karl Theodor of the Palatinate and music would enjoy an enormous revival in Munich because the Mannheim orchestra would play there, all to the benefit of Wolfgang's *Idomeneo*. In any event, at the time of his first Munich opera the Mozarts were not displeased with the results.

Leopold had already written to his wife on 30 December, moreover, that 'the whole orchestra and all who heard the rehearsals say that they have heard no other more beautiful music, where all the arias are beautiful'.[54] He repeated the same sentiments on 11 January: 'Up to now it seems that Wolfgang may have written the biggest opera of the year here.'[55] The dress rehearsal was held the next day, 12 January, in the Salvator Theatre and this, too, must have gone well.[56] Then came word of the only valid proof, that of the performance itself, and about this it was Wolfgang who wrote his mother the day after the opening:

> God be praised! Yesterday, the 13th, my opera was given and it went so well that it is impossible to describe the noise to Mama. First of all the theatre was so full that many people had to be turned away. After every aria there was a terrible din of clapping and of shouting 'Viva Maestro'. Even her Highness, the Palatine Princess and the Widow (who were vis-a-vis to me) said bravo to me. At the end of the opera, until the moment the ballet began, there was only clapping, and shouting of bravo, that now stopped, then began again, and so on. Afterwards I went with my Papa to the room where the Palatine Prince and all the court had to pass and I kissed the hand of the Prince, the Princess, and Their Highnesses who were all most gracious. Very early today His Eminence, the Prince Bishop of Chiemsee sent me his congratulations that the opera was so incomparable in every way.[57]

Wolfgang continued that they wouldn't be leaving for home immediately:

> One good and important reason is because next Friday the opera will be given again, and it is very important that I be at the performance – otherwise one wouldn't recognize it – as things are very strange here.[58]

Leopold also reported home that the opera had been 'a complete success', that all the court liked it, and that His Highness had only compliments for the music. There were just two problems: one was that Colloredo (who had arrived in Munich) 'does not want to hear Wolfgang's opera buffa', and didn't, a clear indication of the Archbishop's growing displeasure with his Vice-Kapellmeister and Third Konzertmeister and their travelling and successes abroad; the other problem was that one of the singers was ill and so it wasn't certain when the opera could be put on a second time.[59] On 21 January he was still concerned about her as she was very sick, 'had a pain in her stomach and a high fever'.[60] If she got better in time, the opera would be performed on Wolfgang's birthday, Friday 27 January.[61]

However the second presentation of La finta giardiniera did not take place until 2 February when, with Elector Karl Theodor present,[62] the opera was not given a completely favourable hearing due to circumstances beyond Wolfgang's control. First of all, the theatre was the noisy Redoutensaal described by Leopold as the scene of gambling and jolly carnival masqueraders where 'no one would pay attention'.[63] Then the opera had to be shortened as the singer was still sick: as Leopold wrote, 'she was miserable'.[64] Regretfully for us, he promised that, although 'there would be lots to write', he would give his wife the details in person once he was home. More than a month was to pass before the family returned to Salzburg, however, giving opportunity for Wolfgang to perform other music.

For example, on 15 February Leopold wrote to his wife that 'on Sunday [12 February] a short Mass by Wolfgang was performed in the Hofkapelle and I conducted. On Saturday it is to be repeated.'[65] On 5 March Wolfgang's Offertory *Misericordias Dominus* (K. 205a/222) was heard in the Palace Chapel.[66] He later wrote to Padre Martini that 'a few days before my departure the Elector desired to hear some of my contrapuntal music: I was then obliged to write this motet in a hurry, to give time for it to be copied for His Highness and to have the parts written out in order to be able to perform it during the Offertory at High Mass on the following Sunday'.[67] His old teacher liked the piece and wrote of it: 'With pleasure I examined it from beginning to end, and I tell you in all sincerity that I liked it singularly, finding in it especially all that modern music requires, good harmony, mature modulation, moderate movement of the violins, natural and well-directed modulation of all the parts.' What was more, Martini felt Wolfgang had progressed in his ability: 'I am happy about it, and pleased that since I had the pleasure of hearing you on the harpsichord in Bologna [one of the few concerts the Maestro deigned to attend] you are now so advanced in composition.' He ended his letter with a bit of fatherly advice to which the diligent Wolfgang needed no prompting to heed: 'You must continue to compose ever more, because music is of such nature that it requires practice and great study as long as one lives.'[68]

Their extended stay in Munich also allowed Leopold, Wolfgang and Nannerl to go to another masked ball, this one in the Redoutensaal on 14 February.[69] Finally Leopold wrote home on Ash Wednesday, 1 March: 'God be praised, Carnival is over'[70] which meant *La finta giardiniera* could be heard again, now back in the Salvator Theatre, the next day Thursday, 2 March.[71] This was the opera's last performance as an *opera buffa* although, with Wolfgang's approval,[72] it was translated into German by the actor and comic bass Franz Xavier Stierle (1741– c. 1800) and given several times by the Johann Heinrich Böhm Theatre Troupe as a Singspiel with spoken recitatives,[73] perhaps even as early as 1779–1780 in Salzburg. It is certain that, entitled *Die verstellte Gärtnerin*, it was performed by Böhm's group on 1 May 1780 in Augsburg and again on 17 or 18 May; and as *Sandrina oder Die verstellte Gräfin* on 2 April 1782 in Frankfurt am Main.[74] After another presentation in this form on 30 April 1789 in the same city, the critic of the *Drammaturgischen Blättern*, evidently not a fan of Italian opera, wrote that *Die verstellte Gärtnerin* had not been well received as was the case with 'most operettas of the Italian stage'. Wolfgang's music, too, had little success, according to the same writer who implied it was too difficult to follow: 'It is more for the connoisseur who knows how to develop its fine points, rather than for the dilettante who follows only natural sentiments and decides only on immediate impressions.'[75] Since the same journal did not approve of *Don Giovanni* either, perhaps one can regard its opinion as not typical of the way audiences felt about *La finta giardiniera* in either its Italian or German version.[76] The clamorous success the opera enjoyed in Munich and the fact that it kept being performed makes it quite clear, in fact, that he was wrong. Further proof of its favourable reception may be found in the commission for *Idomeneo* which was also to come from Munich.

As has been noted, *La finta giardiniera* offers a consummate summary of Wolfgang's experience and training to date. Although it is not known if Wolfgang's opera had the same complement of 23 instrumentalists that an earlier performance of 1774 employed,[77] one can say that in any event his scoring for orchestra is able throughout and is reminiscent of the style he first demonstrated in *La finta semplice* and continued in *Lucio Silla*. The orchestra does not serve simply as a homophonic block to support the voices in *La finta giardiniera* but, rather, it is treated as an ensemble wherein certain instruments are given principal melodies, others intervene with answering or echo phrases, and still others accompany. Most importantly for the drama, the instruments now occasionally present melodic material which is independent of the voice and which, even when employed in a subordinate manner, maintains a separate musical and dramatic function.

A good example of this essentially contrapuntal, if not symphonic, style is the opening vocal piece, the quartet No. 1 'Che lieto giorno' (What a happy day) in which Wolfgang treats every instrumental and vocal part as an element which behaves independently. In aria No. 11 'Geme la tortorella lungi dalla compagna' (Far from its friend the turtledove sighs), the vocal theme and that of the first violins are distinct but their phrases overlap; together they evoke the lovely pastoral atmosphere requested for Sandrina's lament. The voice is sometimes the only part with the melody in No. 15 'Care pupille, pupille belle, volgete un sguardo a me' (Dear eyes, beautiful eyes, look at me), although the varied orchestral accompaniment also underlines the tender singularity of Belfiore's love. The *Larghetto* aria No. 18 'Dolce d'amor compagna' (Love's sweet companion) occasionally employs the orchestra to answer the vocal melody, as though to comment on Ramiro's trust in hope.

A restless orchestral part independent of the voice in No. 21 'Crudeli fermate' depicts the obscure and deserted setting where Sandrina 'afraid and trembling, as she sees various people suddenly flee, leaving her there' cries out 'Cruel ones, stop' to her abductors (example 1); in the

Example 1

second section the orchestra is silent as she, now in recitative, invokes
help, but it soon betrays her inner uncertain sentiments by playing,
between her words, unsettled phrases created by diminished intervals
and strong accents. Sandrina in the following cavatina, 'Ah, dal pianto,
dal singhiozzo respirar io posso appena' (Ah, I am hardly able to refrain
from crying, from sobbing) must interrupt her unsteady and crying
discourse with numerous pauses, and the lyrical intervention of the solo
oboe and bassoon, which accompany her but are independent of her,
underline in a telling manner her solitude and sadness. In No. 27 the
love duet 'Tu mi lasci?' (Do you leave me?) for Sandrina and Belfiore,
their growing ardour is made evident by the ever more flowing accompaniment of the orchestra. Elsewhere in the opera, Wolfgang manages
to intensify an emotion enormously with only a simple tremolo: he
employs this effect, for example, in No. 26 to manifest Ramiro's
agitation while he scolds Arminda saying 'Va pure ad altri in braccio'
(Go to other arms) and calling her a 'donna ingrata' (ungrateful
woman).

A most delightful use of the orchestra is in No. 3, the Podestà's aria
'Dentro il mio pietto', where he sings of his love for Sandrina saying,
'Within my breast I hear a sweet sound of flutes and oboes'. At their
mention, the instruments enter with scalar figures which are designed
not to have them participate thematically but simply to allow them to
state their presence (example 2). Don Anchise goes on to speak of the
changes he feels, which he says are like a viola coming in, and here the
violas have principal melodic material. In the next *Presto* section he

Example 2

speaks of the 'timpani, trumpets, bassoons and contrabass', and now these instruments join the orchestra to illustrate how desperate he is over his love (example 3). The aria, which makes fun of the Podestà by having musical fun with the orchestra, must have been especially popular in Wolfgang's day, since several copies of it exist separately from the rest of the score.[78]

In each of these examples the instruments, which formerly were generally used merely as a vocal support, have added another dimension to the text by commenting on a situation, establishing an atmosphere, expressing a feeling. The orchestra has assumed, in effect, not only the role of listener but of emotional commentator and scenic environment as well; it has become personified and now participates in the dramatic situation. Wolfgang has acquired one of his most potent forces: a contrapuntal orchestra of multiple facets. It must be insisted that his competence was due not just to his exposure to opera, but also to his familiarity with purely instrumental writing (especially by Franz Joseph Haydn and the Viennese school heard during summer 1773). He had begun to consider the symphony an organic whole, wherein each musical line was essential and co-operated in achieving the desired musical expression; it was this same thinking that he was applying now to opera.

As he did in *Mitridate* too, Wolfgang decides upon each aria form in *La finta giardiniera* in consequence of the needs of the drama.[79] Given the fact that one is dealing with an *opera buffa*, one expects to find most use made of the usual structure employed in these operas, the ABA'B' form where A is the tonic, B begins in the dominant but returns to the tonic, A' is a modulating section and B' reaffirms the tonic. However, even if there are examples of it (No. 8 for Contino, 'Da Scirocco a Tramontana', From east to west; and No. 17 for Don Anchise, 'Una damina, una nipote', A girl, a niece) it is not used fixedly by Wolfgang. Instead, and clearly as a means of furthering the drama, one finds the non-repeated binary AB structure in a great number of cases. Sometimes the form is adopted in purely comic moments (as in No. 3, the Podestà's 'Dentro il mio petto', Within my breast); and sometimes in love scenes (as in No. 15, Belfiore's aria to Sandrina 'Care pupille, pupille belle', Dear eyes, beautiful eyes): but in all cases it allows for dramatic continuity.

The clearest indication that this is Wolfgang's principal intent in *La finta giardiniera* is to be found in the two other forms which he employed in the opera, that written either in a single repeated section (as for example No. 6 'Che beltà, che leggiadria'; What beauty, what loveliness) or, demonstrating still greater continuity, *durchkomponiert* (such as No. 21 'Crudeli fermate', Cruel ones, stop, for Sandrina, a marvellous piece of *Sturm und Drang* writing which leads in to her accompanied recitative

Example 3

and then goes on immediately to the following cavatina, No. 22 'Ah, dal pianto', Ah, from crying, also continuous and ending in accompanied recitative). In fact, the only examples of the da capo form (and this in its single-section variety), which at first might seem to be out of place in a comedy, are to be found in the more 'serious' moments of the opera when the drama itself reminds one of an *opera seria*, and when the more stylized upper-class characters are involved, such as Ramiro (No. 2 'Se l'augellin s'en fugge', If the little bird flies away; No. 18 'Dolce d'amore compagna', and No. 26 'Va pure ad altri in braccio', mentioned above) and Arminda (No. 13 'Vorrei punirti indegno', I would like to punish you, unworthy one). These arias offer, as well, almost the only examples of *fioriture* in the opera, again another device employed by Wolfgang to describe more particularly the characters in question. It was probably to insist upon Ramiro's class and to make fun of his aristocratic exaggerated passions that the part was given to a castrato (besides the practical fact that Consoli was a good singer and available!).

Another feature of *La finta giardiniera* which will become typical of Wolfgang's mature writing, is his manipulation of rhythm to create a climax. His early experiments with the technique in *Lucio Silla* are repeated here where the entire score manifests his continued interest in rhythm. For example, syncopation, *forte-piano* accents, and a vocal line characterized by dotted-rhythms combine in No. 13, the above-mentioned 'Vorrei punirti indegno', to create Arminda's fiery explosion as she firmly opposes inconstancy. Wolfgang also varies rhythmic motives in the opera in order to allow each phrase to flow smoothly from the preceding one. Ligatures and *staccato* markings are carefully notated to articulate the rhythm better: how different is a bar of ternary meter such as

which has no specific connotation, and Wolfgang's

which suggests, through its lovely grace, the femininity of Sandrina in No. 16 'Una voce sento al core' (I hear a voice in my heart).

Due to such musical means, the personalities of the various characters are generally well defined: Serpetta and Nardo, through simple, almost folk-like *ariette*, are convincingly presented as servants; Belfiore is shown to be the lover, and believably beloved, through a lyric tenor part; with music which is the most dramatic in the opera, Violante is depicted as a future Donna Elvira, in love but decidedly jealous and virtuous; Wolfgang manages to create a weak and yet comic Podestà by composing for him a rather static vocal part of small range which generally proceeds either in short phrases to demonstrate his impetuosity (as in No. 17 'Una damina') or in longer but repetitive phrases to indicate his insistence of banality; through form and style, as has already been indicated, Ramiro and Arminda are indicated as the most (make-believe) 'serious' characters in the opera.

The finales which end the first and second acts, called 'masterpieces' by Jahn,[80] are excellent septets which present frequent changes of tempo and of re-grouping of characters according to the demands of the libretto..The sections become progressively longer as the finales proceed, while polyphony and homophony serve to communicate opposition or agreement. Other ensembles, such as the aria and duet No. 24 'Mirate, che contrasto' (See what contrast) and the recitative and duet No. 27 'Dove mai son!' (Wherever am I), are also continuous pieces. The opera concludes with a simple four-part chorus for all, a happy shout of 'Viva pur la Giardiniera ... viva il Conte' (Long-live the Gardener ... long-live the Count).

La finta giardiniera is the result of Wolfgang's preceding experiences; it presents no compositional aspects which are completely new. Its most striking feature is an orchestra handled contrapuntally; but this had its origin in *La finta semplice*, where Wolfgang's awareness of the dramatic power of the orchestra became evident for the first time in an opera, and continued to play a role in *Lucio Silla*, where his new employment of instrumental motives was first observed. Less rigid attention to traditional operatic forms – no doubt encouraged as a result of his ever more mature awareness of drama and desire to translate it into adequate musical terms – was first noticed in *Bastien und Bastienne* where Wolfgang had applied the idea of the finale to other ensembles, and then in *Mitridate* where he had employed various forms, even from *opera buffa*, in his *opera seria*. His manipulation of rhythm as a subtle factor in conveying drama was to be seen as well in *Lucio Silla*. However, it is in *La finta giardiniera* that Wolfgang, without doubt enriched through contact with the sonata in its several manifestations, and its text-less expression of drama through development and variation, employs all of these means together, and with decided conviction and assurance.

Wolfgang's subordinate position with regard to eighteenth-century opera may be said to have ended as he is now in possession, at least in embryo, of all the techniques which he will employ in his most mature theatrical efforts. There will still be experiments which will prove him in error and which will convince him that he is applying his talents in unfruitful areas, since the young man needs further opportunity to examine his resources and to learn more surely what can and cannot be communicated through music. Nevertheless, his equipment is complete and needs only adequate opportunity to be put to good use.[81]

Chapter Ten: Notes

1. K. 196 in *WAM*, Serie V, 9, and *NMA*, Serie II, 5, bd. 8.
2. *Dokumente*, p. 130.
3. *Idem*.
4. *Idem* and Leopold's letter to his wife of 21 July: *Briefe*, I, pp. 484-485.
5. See for example the Mozarts' letters of 21 July and 12 August: *ibid.*, I, pp. 484 and 486 respectively.
6. Leopold to his wife on 21 July, *op. cit*. The surprised tone of his letter is further proof that Mesmer's garden theatre was new to him and that *Bastien und Bastienne* had not been performed there.
7. His letter of 12 August, *op. cit.*, p. 485.
8. On his activities in Vienna that summer see Alfred Orel's account gleaned from various sources including the diary of Prince Khevenhüller and reported in 'Zu Mozarts Sommerreise nach Wien im Jahre 1773', *Mozarts-Jahrbuch 1951* (Salzburg, 1953), p. 34 ff.
9. Letter from Leopold to his wife of 12 August, *op. cit.*, p. 486.
10. *Dokumente*, p. 130. He arrived in Vienna on 31 July and left on 2 August.
11. Leopold was anxious for Colloredo to stay away as this meant more freedom for him and Wolfgang: see his letters of 12 and 21 August in *Briefe*, I, pp. 485 and 489 respectively; and Orel, p. 44. The Mozarts had an audience with the Archbishop on his return (12 August), at which time he must have given them permission to stay on a bit longer. He himself was back in Salzburg on 17 August according to Orel, p. 35.
12. See Chapter XII on *Thamos, König in Aegypten*.
13. They met on 29 August as Leopold reported to his wife on 28 August: *Briefe*, I, p. 493. At the same meal the flautist Becke was also present.
14. *Briefe*, I, p. 496.
15. The following list of operas performed in Vienna during Wolfgang's stay is taken from Orel, p. 43: Galuppi, *Puntiglioso amoroso* (15 performances); Salieri, *Locandiera* (11 performances); Anfossi, *Matilda ritrovata* (6); Felici, *Amore soldato* (4); Piccinni, *Finto pazzo per amore* (3).
16. *Briefe*, I, p. 420.
17. The present Markt Platz.
18. Wolfgang was to live here from age 17 to 25 and his father died there in 1787.
19. Otto Deutsch, 'Aus Schiedenhofens Tagebuch', *Mozarts-Jahrbuch 1957* (Salzburg, 1958), p. 18; and *Dokumente*, p. 134.
20. Jahn, I, p. 147. For a brief account of Wolfgang's continued relations with Munich as well as for the period of *La finta giardiniera* see Klaus Gurr, 'Mozart in München', *Mozart und München* (Munich, 1941), pp. 29-70.
21. Letter of 14 December 1774: *Briefe*, I, p. 505.
22. *Idem*.

23. *Idem.*

24. *Idem.*

25. *Idem.*

26. *Germany*, I, p. 143. For a brief history of the theatre and Wolfgang's connections with it see Otto Hödel, 'Das Münchener Residenztheatre: Die Schönste Mozartbühne der Welt', *Mozart und München op. cit.*, pp. 99–109, although he mistakenly believes *La finta giardiniera* was performed there (p. 106).

27. *Ibid.*, I, p. 121. Actually a favourable situation for music prevailed in many parts of Germany at the time; Burney, in fact, said he often heard poor students singing, and well, on street corners and was told 'that in all towns throughout the empire, where the Jesuits have a church or college, young persons are taught to play upon a musical instrument, and to sing' (*ibid.*, p. 145).

28. *Briefe, idem.*

29. Leopold's letters to his wife of 17, 21 and 28 December: *Briefe*, I, pp. 507, 509 and 511 respectively.

30. *Briefe*, I, p. 510.

31. See Burney, *ibid.*, I, p. 126, and Chapter IX here.

32. II, p. 283. Arteaga, III, pp. 138–139, says the same thing.

33. Algarotti, *ibid.*, pp. 283–284.

34. *Ibid.*, p. 284.

35. *Idem.*

36. *Germany*, I, p. 147.

37. Franz Michael Rudhart, *Geschichte der Oper am Hofe zu München* (Freising, 1865), I, p. 161 ff is on *La finta giardiniera*.

38. *Ibid.*, p. 148.

39. *Dokumente*, p. 135, and *Addenda*, p. 24 give as certain only the singers who took the roles of Sandrina and Ramiro; the others I based on Burney, Rudhart, and the possibilities listed in Rudolf Angermüller and Dietrich Berk's introduction to their critical edition of *La finta giardiniera* in *NMA*, pp. xi–xii. However they remain only 'possibilities'.

40. It was repeated in Würzburg on 26 August 1774 and it could be that the libretto made its way to Munich after this performance.

41. See Rudolf Angermüller, 'Wer war der Librettist von *La finta giardiniera?*', *Mozart-Jahrbuch 1976–77* (Kassel, 1978), pp. 1–8, and the introduction to *NMA*, pp. viii–ix. See also Werner Bollert, 'Giuseppe Petrosellini quale librettista di opere', *Rivista musicale italiana* 43 (1939), pp. 531–538, for a brief summary of the poet's other libretti.

42. II, p. 327.

43. *Dokumente*, p. 192.

44. Letters of 21 June (*Briefe*, III, p. 275) and 2 July (*ibid.*, p. 276). See as well *Dokumente*, p. 193.

45. *Italy*, p. 233.

46. *Ibid.*, p. 306.

47. II, p. 327.

48. *Idem.*

49. *Dokumente*, p. 135.

50. *Idem.*

51. Leopold's letter to his wife of 5 January: *Briefe*, I, p. 515.

52. *Dokumente*, p. 135; *Briefe*, I, p. 512, letter of 30 December 1774.
53. *Briefe*, I, p. 515.
54. *Op. cit.*, p. 513.
55. As a postscript to Wolfgang's letter, *op. cit.*, p. 516.
56. See Angermüller, *NMA*, p. xi.
57. *Briefe*, I, p. 516.
58. *Ibid.*, pp. 516–517. This may have been because Wolfgang probably did not conduct and he did not trust what would be done to his music if he were not even in the theatre: see Angermüller and Berke, p. xi.
59. Letter of 18 January: *Briefe*, I, pp. 517–518.
60. Letter to his wife: *Briefe*, I, p. 519.
61. *Idem.*
62. *Dokumente*, p. 135.
63. *Addenda*, p. 24.
64. Undated letter but written between 21 January and 21 February: *Briefe*, I, p. 520.
65. *Briefe*, I, p. 522; see also *Dokumente*, p. 136. It was probably his *Missa Brevis* K. 192.
66. *Dokumente, idem.*
67. Letter of 4 September 1776: *Briefe*, I, p. 532.
68. Letter of 18 December 1776: *Briefe*, I, p. 534.
69. *Dokumente, idem.*
70. *Briefe*, I, p. 524.
71. *Ibid.*, p. 525, and *Addenda*, p. 24.
72. Part of the German score is in Wolfgang's hand and some of the German text is in Leopold's hand.
73. Wolfgang rewrote the accompanied recitatives to adapt them to the German language: See Angermüller and Berke, p. xiv.
74. For the cast at this performance see Angermüller and Berke, p. xv.
75. *Dokumente*, pp. 298–299.
76. Wolfgang's autograph of Act I was probably already lost during the composer's lifetime and has still not come to light; Acts II and III, which were available for *WAM*, disappeared during the Second World War. Recently a late eighteenth-century copy of the score from Náměšťer (entitled *La finta Giardiniera per Amore*), with both Italian and German texts and including the original Italian *secco* recitatives, has been discovered in the Mährischen Museum in Brünn: see Angermüller and Berke, p. xv ff on this and all the sources of the *NMA* edition.
77. *Ibid.*, p. xi.
78. *Ibid.*, p. xiii.
79. As Jahn, I, p. 222 wrote: 'The form and style of opera buffa are maintained in all essential points, but with great freedom of treatment.'
80. I, p. 221.
81. Shortly after, Wolfgang composed a finale to be added to the overture of *La finta giardiniera* so that it could be performed as a proper symphony (K. 207a/121).

Il Re pastore[1]

SOON AFTER Leopold and Wolfgang were home again in Salzburg, where they arrived on 7 March 1775 after only a day's journey from Munich,[2] they were visited on 19 April by the 'Ramiro' of La finta giardiniera, Tommaso Consoli, and the flautist Johann Baptist Becke.[3] The musicians had come from Munich to take part in festivities arranged by the Salzburg court to honour the stay of Archduke Maximillian, Maria Theresa's youngest son who later became the Archbishop of Cologne. He was to come from Vienna and stop over in Salzburg on his way to Italy.[4] Along with other festivities arranged to entertain the Archduke, Wolfgang had been commissioned to do an opera for the occasion, and in the month after his return from Vienna he had to work quickly and choose a libretto. He selected Metastasio's Il Re pastore, which, however, he felt required changes before it could be set to music. Even in what one assumes to have been a hectic situation, Wolfgang's facility allowed him to compose other works at the same time, and the concerto for cello K. 206a and the concerto for violin K. 207 are both from this period.[5]

On the day after Consoli and Becke arrived, 20 April, Joachim Ferdinand von Schiedenhofen, Consistory Counsellor and later Provincial Chancellor, noted in his diary that he was going to the Palace 'where Mozart's serenada [sic] will be rehearsed'.[6] One does not know how many rehearsals had been possible for the rest of the cast, but for Consoli, who was doing the leading role in Il Re pastore, it certainly had to be a quick study as this was perhaps his only opportunity to go through the opera with the other characters, since Maximillian arrived the very next day and all had to be ready.[7] On 22 April von Schiedenhofen noted that there was to be a 'serenada' in which Consoli and Becke would take part.[8] This was not Wolfgang's work, however, but Gli Orti Esperidi, another Metastasian text set to music by Domenico Fischietti (1720-1810), the Salzburg Kapellmeister under whose direction Leopold and Wolfgang both played when at court.[9] For 23 April, a Sunday, Maximillian's Travel Journal is the more complete source of information. His courtier wrote there after the evening's entertainments:

Moreover, as on the previous day, the evening concluded again with a music concert and supper in the palace; and with regard to the concert an alteration was made for a change, that whereas for the previous day the well-known Kapellmeister Fischietti had written the music, for the sung cantata [sic] of this evening the music was by the not less renowned Mozart.[10]

The libretto Wolfgang had hurriedly chosen for Maximillian's *fête* was one the Archduke no doubt already knew, since Metastasio had written it for Maria Theresa's birthday in 1751 when the Austrian composer Giuseppe Giovanni Battista Bonno (1710–1788) set it to music for performance 'in the theatre of the Imperial Garden of Schönbrunn'.[11] Since then it had been set to music 13 times before Wolfgang attempted it, by composers such as Hasse, Gluck, Jommelli, and Piccinni, and would continue to be used for musical settings till the end of the century. It was, as were almost all of the poet's works, extremely successful.[12] For his plot Metastasio cited as his classical sources Justinian (XI, 10) and Curtius (IV, 3) who tell of Alexander the Great setting Abdalonymus on the throne of Sidon. Although a distant descendant of the royal house, Abdalonymus was poor and earned his living as a gardener. He was, however, worthy of the honour for he was supposedly beautiful and noble.

At the same time, his name proved to be a literary problem since Metastasio said it suggested a hypochondriac, possibly associating it with some malady of the abdomen. He wrote to his friend Filipponi on 10 June 1751 that the name 'would have dirtied my frontispiece,' and he rhetorically asked, 'Who would have tolerated an opera entitled *Abdolonimo*?' Besides making the hero a shepherd instead of a gardener and calling the opera *Il Re pastore*, he gave Abdolonymus the assumed name of Aminta. As he confessed, he also avoided the Shepherd King's real name in the course of the drama: 'I tried to name him as little as possible, so that of its many defects my work would not also have this one.'[13] Although finished by May 1751, *Il Re pastore* was not performed until October as the court was away in Hungary.[14] Finally on 1 November Mestastasio was able to write to his banker in Rome, Francesco d'Argenvillieres: 'My *Re pastore* was presented last Wednesday and was repeated on Saturday with a favourable vote for the whole spectacle, which greatly surpassed my expectation.' As he had already noted, the opera was performed by the gentlemen and ladies, 'Cavalieri e Dame', of the court[15] and he wrote: 'The lady performers enrapture by their figures, and voices, and by the incredible expression of their roles. Their Most August Masters are enraptured, and continue to repeat their compliments.'[16] Since Metastasio had to be present for rehearsals he got a cold due to working conditions very similar to those of today: 'The frequent trips to the court [at Schönbrunn] which lies a half an hour away from the city, the inevitable long periods in the empty and cold theatre at rehearsals, the unpredictable behaviour of the season, and of my misbehaving carriage have all made me worse than before.'[17] Nevertheless when due to the success of the opera, his Most August Masters 'threatened with a new request', Metastasio responded immediately saying, 'I already hear it sounding in my ears'.[18]

While the several settings of *Il Re pastore* attest to its popularity with composers as well, literary critics were not all overwhelmingly enthusiastic. After seeing a 1768 performance of Renard de Plainchesne's *Le jardinier de Sidon* based on the same subject (and set to music by François-André Philidor), Friederich Melchior Grimm, whom Wolfgang was later to know in Paris, wrote:

Metastasio dealt with the same subject in his work entitled *Il Re pastore*. One does not need to come from the deserted prairies of Mr de Pleinchesne, full of rocks and bushes, to feel the full charm of a walk over the delightful greens of the divine Metastasio. What lovely and graceful feeling! What an enchanted and sweet colour! This great poet has kept the part of Alexander because he wanted to deal with his topic in the most noble of genres. In any event, and one must say it, when one reads at the beginning of the piece 'The Shepherd King', one expects different things than to see a shepherd, raised by Alexander to the throne of Sidon because of his birth rights, taken only by his passion for his shepherdess and putting all his efforts into renouncing the throne rather than in his love. This pretence of generosity is imitated by another couple of lovers who, following the custom in Italian opera, form a second plot with respect to the main story. Alexander the Great is glad to find so much love and faithfulness in the shepherd king and concludes that he will certainly be an excellent king. I would not have reasoned like Alexander the Great. I may add that this plot is very weakly organized, and that the misfortunes which the characters find themselves bestowing on each other, and the feelings that they give vent to as a consequence, exist only because they do not seem to want to explain things to one another, not to say what they would certainly have said in similar situations. All of that is childish, frivolous, and false; is it, however, Metastasio's fault? Certainly not since, when staged works are destined to relieve the boredom of an assembly of lazy people, they are necessarily affected by the superficiality of their creating institutions. The Shepherd King! What a title! What a subject! And what a piece of work if the dramatic art were to be called upon to make of the European stages a school of public morality, instead of being simply used for the amusement of a group of funny old boys who tried to pose as experts and discuss good taste.[19]

Obviously, when Grimm criticized *Il Re pastore* but yet affirmed that Metastasio was not to be blamed, he was finding fault with the taste of the period which extolled elegant language even when it expressed unbelievable passions and situations. Algarotti and Arteaga noted that the more immediate and direct genre of *opera buffa* was gaining in popularity, attesting, in fact, to a change in the public's preference which Wolfgang himself would later respond to with his famous comedies. At the moment, however, and for the occasion at hand, Metastasio's libretto was considered by all at Salzburg to be most suitable.

The version of *Il Re pastore* employed by Wolfgang, though, was not Metastasio's complete text. It was instead somewhat shortened by Colloredo's chaplain, Gianbattista Varesco, who would collaborate again with Wolfgang on *Idomeneo*. In regard to the later opera, it has been said of Varesco that he 'seems to have been unskilled as a dramatic poet, verbose and with little natural flair for drama though his principal characters are intelligently projected and diversified'.[20] His work in *Il Re pastore* was not very demanding, though, as he was asked mainly to compress Acts II and III into a single act, thus eliminating much dialogue and several arias. Other alterations and additions were made to Metastasio's original text but nothing which radically disturbed the frame: for example, Aminta was given a new first aria and was also provided with an accompanied recitative; this was balanced by eliminating an accompanied recitative before the ending duet of Act I; the short closing chorus was also elaborated, turning it into a sort of finale with alternating *soli* and *tutti* sections.

The drama which eventually emerged begins with Aminta, a shepherd, looking for his beloved Elisa. When she appears he warns her to be careful since Alessandro (Alexander the Great) and his army are encamped nearby. She is not worried as she has eyes only for Aminta; moreover, she believes Alessandro to be honourable since he has liberated Sidon from the tyrant Stratone. They wonder who their new king will be. Elisa, although she is of royal blood and Aminta only an ignoble shepherd, loves him anyway and is ready to give up everything so that they may tend the flock together. When Elisa leaves, Alessandro arrives with Aegenore, a nobleman of Sidon. Aminta does not realize who Alessandro is and responds naively to the warrior's questions, telling him he is contented in his poverty. When the unknown soldier offers to lead Aminta to Alessandro and have his fate changed, the shepherd refuses saying he could not be happier. Left alone, Aegenore and Alessandro comment on the secret that Aminta is the true heir to the throne and marvel at his noble heart; Alessandro is convinced that to aid the oppressed is better than winning battles. The leader then departs and Tamiri, the daughter of Stratone and beloved of Aegenore, appears disguised as a shepherdess, and she and Aegenore lament her harsh fate. She is staying with Elisa but fears what Alessandro will do to her. Aegenore counsels her to beg Alessandro for mercy but she is afraid. The scene changes to Elisa's house where, as she and Aminta are about to look for her mother who is in the fields, Aegenore enters and greets Aminta as though he were a king calling him Abdalonimo (Abdalonymus), 'the sole heir of the Kindom of Sidon'. He then explains how, when Stratone forced his way to power, Aminta's father gave his baby to Aegenore who in turn gave him to a shepherd to raise. Aminta and Elisa, although happy, fear that if he becomes king they will have to part and try to be brave in the face of responsibility.

Act II begins with Elisa wanting to see Aminta but being told by Aegenore that now, as King, Aminta cannot see her nor can he come to her. Aegenore will try to tell him she has come by. Elisa then accuses Aegenore of forgetting Tamiri but he assures her that he is trying to speak to Alessandro about his beloved. When she leaves Aminta appears but, running off to see Elisa, he is also stopped by Aegenore, who says that, as King, he may not. Aminta argues that he had had more freedom as a shepherd. Alessandro comes onto the scene now and, after reassuring the worried Aminta that he will be fit to reign, with the help of Heaven of course, sends him off to don royal garments. Left alone with Aegenore, Alessandro begins to wonder why Tamiri has not presented herself. When Aegenore hears he wishes his beloved no harm, he tells Alessandro she is nearby. As he is about to leave to get Tamiri, Alessandro tells him to convey to her that she will reign anyway, but now as Aminta's wife. Aegenore departs crestfallen, but Alessandro is delighted believing he is making everyone happy. Aminta now sings of how he will love his wife, meaning Elisa. But Elisa has heard the rumour that he is to marry Tamiri and she is desperate; Aegenore hears Aminta singing and, without knowing the truth, tells Elisa Aminta has declared his trust to Tamiri. She is determined to confront Aminta. Tamiri now comes to accuse Aegenore of casting her off and declares she will have her revenge. Alessandro next comes on the scene, and Elisa throws herself at his feet begging mercy. Aminta seconds her account of their love and says that while Tamiri is worthy of a king, Elisa does not deserve being abandoned. He prefers to return to his flock and Elisa and to give up the throne. Alessandro solves the dilemma by joining the couples as they wish: Aminta and Elisa will rule over Sidon; Aegenore and Tamiri shall have the next kingdom Alessandro conquers. All sing the joys of love.

The cast of Wolfgang's *Il Re pastore*, with the exception of the role of Aminta taken by Consoli, is not certain. One knows only that the singers were from the Salzburg court and were probably those who figured in Wolfgang's *Die Schuldigkeit des ersten Gebotes, La finta semplice* and *Il sogno di Scipione* since, as in these cases, the score calls for only sopranos and tenors. The roles and their voice parts were the following:

ALESSANDRO, King of Macedonia (tenor)

AMINTA, shepherd, in love with Elisa, who, unknown even to himself, is discovered to be the sole legitimate heir to the Kingdom of Sidon (soprano, Tommaso Consoli)

ELISA, noble nymph of Phoenicia, of the ancient race of Cadmus, in love with Aminta (soprano)

TAMIRI, refugee princess, daughter of the tyrant Stratone, dressed as a shepherdess, in love with Aegenore (soprano)

AEGENORE, nobleman of Sidon, friend of Alessandro, in love with Tamiri (tenor)

Wolfgang's realization of the libretto is an attempt at mixing serious and comic opera, with pastoral overtones added. He vacillates between the various styles, utilizing whatever he thinks necessary to depict a character or situation. By indicating pertinent examples, his compositional approach will be made clear. The opening aria, Aminta's 'Intendo, amico rio, quel basso mormorio' (I mean, naughty friend, that low murmur) accompanied by the pastoral instruments flutes and horns besides the usual strings, outlines a simple melodic part and exudes all the rustic charm that will be found later in *Don Giovanni;* keeping to the natural accents and inflections of speech, the number is also well suited to the stage. In the first aria for Elisa, No. 2 'Alla selva, al prato, al fonte' (To the woods, to the field, to the spring), a pastoral quality is again evident; however with the help of some splendid *fioriture* a bit of bravura is added (example 1) as the girl expresses her enthusiasm for her rustic life. Aria No. 3 'Aer tranquillo e dì sereni' (Tranquil breeze and sereni day) for Aminta also has an occasional phrase of *fioritura* and is again in the shorter ABA' tripartite form (as are most of the arias in *Il Re pastore*). The next aria, No. 4 'Si spande al sole in faccia' (The face opens to the sun), however, opens with an orchestral introduction appropriately majestic and including 'royal' trumpets for King Alessandro's entrance, and it is more of an *opera seria* piece; his vocal part comprised of calm minims combined with a moving orchestral accompaniment of semiquavers suggests his dignity in the midst of splendour. The aria also follows the usual ABA' structure and has an orchestral postlude suitable to underline Alessandro's royal position. The situation in No. 8 'Barbaro, o Dio! mi vedi divisa dal mio ben' (Barbarous one, oh God! you see me divided from my beloved) presents Elisa angered by Aegenore, and Wolfgang writes an effective rage aria in the pure style of *opera seria* (example 2), although it follows an untypical

Example 1

ABA'B' Coda structure (if anything, more closely associated with *opera buffa*). Aria No. 10, on the other hand, is indicated 'Rondo' and is not representative of any particular style (as John Brown's description of the form implied); the theme which carries Aminta's principal thought, 'L'amerò, sarò, costante' (I will love her, I will be faithful) recurs four times, the last an abbreviated presentation.

Two arias, both for Alessandro, the most regal and important personage in the opera, are set to truncated forms. More clearly, No. 9 'Se

Example 2

vincendo vi rendo felici' (If by winning I make you happy) and No. 13
'Voi che fausti ognor donate' (You who always happily give) begin
with four presentations of a single stanza of text, as did most of the arias
of Wolfgang's *Mitridate* for example, and outline an A(*ab*) A'(*a'b'*)
structure. The initially grand setting for King Alessandro is not completed however, as the expected B and A' sections (which would have
therefore concluded the *dal segno* form) are omitted. Obviously, the
grandeur but not the length of the structure was what interested

Wolfgang and so he took from it only what he wanted. Again to serve
his purpose, a finale, typical instead of *opera buffa*, brings the opera to its
end: a homophonic five-part ensemble in praise of Alessandro which
returns in the manner of a rondo alternates with smaller ensembles
where the solo voices proceed occasionally in imitation. In short, a
variety of forms and styles and treatments are to be found in *Il Re
pastore*.

Example 3

Hasse's 1755 setting of *Il Re pastore*, as one would expect, was of a
very different sort and unquestionably an *opera seria*. While Wolfgang's
revisions to Metastasio's text do not allow for comparison between the
two scores throughout, it is interesting to see what the composers did
when their texts do coincide. On the whole one must admit that Hasse
is the more ornate in style. In Elisa's aria No. 2 'Alla selva' mentioned
earlier, one might think Wolfgang not so simple since to Hasse's string
orchestra he added oboes and horns: however, these particular instruments serve to set the wooded scene better. Then both composers' arias
are tripartite, traditionally a form associated with *opera seria*. But it is in
the lines themselves, especially the vocal lines, that Hasse reveals himself
to be more taken with writing ornate music than melodies suitable for a
shepherdess (example 3).

Five years later, in 1760, Piccinni too set *Il Re pastore*, but here there
are more similarities with Wolfgang's setting. This is true not only in
the general overall style but, in certain aspects of their writing, one
wonders if Wolfgang was familiar with Piccinni's score. For example,
the duet which closes Act I, 'Vanne, vanne a regnar' (Go, go to reign),
No. 7 for Elisa and Aminta who are sopranos in both operas, begins in
each case with a descending line (example 4). Both composers chose to
have the second voice enter after the first had completed an entire
phrase, and both had the second voice repeat the same music but with
new words. Now both Piccinni and Wolfgang used an ascending line for

Example 4

Example 5

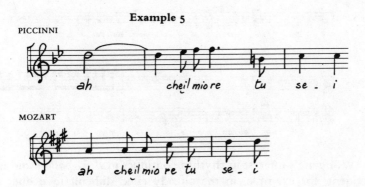

the next text (example 5). Later on they both repeated the opening text
but now to new although similar music. Although Wolfgang's setting
is the more graceful and varied, it does agree with much of Piccinni's
general format. Naturally such procedures were part of a common
musical language in eighteenth-century music and one cannot assert
that Wolfgang did without doubt imitate Piccinni. It is clear, though,
that composers of Piccinni's generation rather than Hasse's were his
models.

As has been seen, Wolfgang's *Il Re pastore* exhibits a middle-of-the-
road style; rather than obtain a true mixture or compromise of styles,
however, the score demonstrates distinct traits of both *opera seria* and
opera buffa. Wolfgang obviously wanted a less conventional setting than
an *opera seria* libretto traditionally suggested and so let the protagonists
sing music which was often florid but occasionally in a lighter, almost
opera buffa style.[21] Unfortunately, he managed only to prove that, at
least in this case, the two styles were incompatible, for one is aware of
him shifting gears (and looking for suitable structures) as the opera
progresses.

The orchestral writing in *Il Re pastore* is simple but contrapuntal, the instruments responding and imitating one another with a great interweaving of vocal and instrumental lines. Aria No. 9 'Se vincendo vi rendo felici' for Alessandro (mentioned above) contains an interesting example of independent treatment of the flutes, which are employed as *obbligato* instruments and as an echo of the voice (example 6); No. 10 'L'amerò, sarò costante' (also mentioned above) uses the entire orchestra but has a single violin, horns and woodwinds (flutes, English horns, bassoons) play independently.

Example 6

Wolfgang's interest in rhythm continues in *Il Re pastore* and is quite evident, for example, in the already cited difficult love duet No. 7 'Vanne, vanne a regnar' where harmonic rhythm, rhythmic motives, and varying phrase lengths combine to create a part which, through its spirited and effervescent fluidity, expresses the raptures of love extolled in the text (example 7).

In short, his interest in an orchestra handled contrapuntally, in rhythm, and in form as musical means for interpreting drama, although demonstrated more completely in *Lucio Silla* and in *La finta giardiniera*, all continue to be evident in *Il Re pastore*. Wolfgang remains convinced of their power. However, every artist needs to work in the genre most compatible with his talent, and, unfortunately, the conventions of a libretto for a courtly celebration frustrated every attempt to create a realistic music drama. Wolfgang employed all his musical resources in interpreting the text, but *Il Re pastore*, in spite of its many beautiful moments, is artificial and heterogeneous.

On 24 April, the day after Wolfgang's opera, the Archduke's Travel Journal continues:

As on the preceding days a musical entertainment was arranged, in such a way however, that this evening Countess Lüzau, a niece of the

Example 7

ELISA
(plus
orchestra)

AMINTA

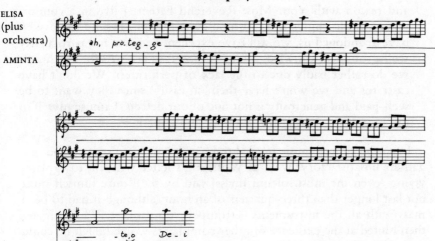

Archbishop, together with another lady, played the clavier, and together with the Archduke, the Counts Ugarte, Czernin, and Hardegg were accompanied by the Archbishop.[22]

The diary of Abbot Beda Seeauer affirms the account adding that the Archduke played second violin and that the 'group of both sexes of the aristocracy was headed by the respected Herr [Colloredo] himself'.[23] Burney is able to confirm the Archbishop's skill, for he stated that 'the prince [Colloredo] is himself a *dilettante*, and a good performer on the violin'.[24] After their own music the Travel Journal reported that the court asked 'the renowned young Mozart' to give them some music and that 'he played several things out of his head with as much art as charm'.[25] One hopes that the amateur violinist also appreciated his talented 19-year-old third Konzertmeister.

As the Archduke left the next day, *Il Re pastore* was to have no further performances, and Wolfgang settled down to life in Salzburg and the routine work asked of him by his unimportant court position. Luckily he was able to busy himself with the more interesting activity of composing and worked on, among other music, various concertos for violin and *Klavier* (K. 211, 216, 218, 219, 238, 242, 246) and, for Nannerl's 24th birthday on 30 July 1776, a Divertimento (K. 251), the 'Nannerl Septet'.[26] However, on the whole, it was not an especially satisfying period for him and he took the occasion of sending his Munich motet, 'Misericordias Domini', mentioned earlier,[27] to Padre Martini as an opportunity to vent his discontent. On 4 September 1776 after discussing the motet he wrote:

Oh, how many times have I wanted to be nearer to be able to speak and reason with Your Most Reverend Father. I live in a country where music enjoys little fortune even though, besides those who have abandoned us, we still have excellent teachers and particularly well-grounded, knowledgeable composers of taste. As for the theatre we do rather badly due to the lack of performers. We don't have castratos and we won't have them so easily, since they want to be well-paid and generosity is not one of our defects. I amuse myself in the meantime writing for chamber and church.[28]

Even the church music needed to be composed in a special, and one gathers unsatisfactory, way, as Wolfgang's letter went on to explain, saying 'even the most solemn [mass] said by the Prince himself must not last longer than three-quarters of an hour' although it had to be 'a mass with all the instruments – trumpets, timpani, etc.'[29] Wolfgang then hinted at the existence of other complaints which he felt he could not write in a letter: 'Ah! we are so far apart, most dear Signor Padre Maestro, how many things I should have to tell you!'[30] Padre Martini's favourable judgement on his motet no doubt pleased Wolfgang,[31] but it offered little help in putting up with his ungratifying work. Throughout his career personal problems seem to have had little effect on his music, though, and this was true not only of 1776 but also of 1777, much of which was spent in Salzburg composing works such as his first 'important' piano concerto, K. 271. But he was discontented and eventually determined to do something about it.

Chapter Eleven: Notes

1. K. 208 in *WAM* Serie V, 10. Wolfgang's autograph has disappeared since the Second World War.
2. *Dokumente*, p. 136.
3. *Idem.*
4. *Dokumente*, p. 137, and *Addenda*, p. 25.
5. K. 206a was composed in March and K. 207 is dated 14 April 1775.
6. Otto Deutsch, 'Aus Schiedenhofens Tagebuch', p. 18, and *Dokumente*, p. 136.
7. *Dokumente*, p. 137.
8. *Deutsch, idem*, and *Dokumente, idem*.
9. *Addenda*, p. 24.
10. *Dokumente, idem*. According to the *Addenda*, p. 25, the travel journal was kept by Count Johann Franz Hardegg who had accompanied Maximillian on his journey. Schiedenhofen's diary also notes the performance: see Detusch, p. 19.
11. As stated on the libretto.
12. See Chapter VIII on *Il sogno di Scipione* for a contemporary evaluation of Metastasio's skill as a librettist.
13. *Lettere del Signor Abate Pietro Metastasio*, Tomo IV, p. 49.

14. See Metastasio's letters of 10 May, 4 October, 18 October, 1 November, *ibid.*, Tomo III, pp. 48, 51, 52 and 53 respectively; as well as that of 10 June, *op. cit.*

15. According to Metastasio's letter of 10 May, *op. cit.* and not by Maria Theresa's children as claimed by William Mann, *The Operas of Mozart* (London, 1977), p. 211.

16. *Ibid.*, p. 53.

17. *Ibid.*, pp. 53–54.

18. Letter to the same of 6 December 1751: *ibid.*, p. 60.

19. Grimm, Part I/6, pp. 136–137. In 1776 Grimm saw another version of *Il Re pastore*, in French by Collet, but in this poor copy of Metastasio the writer had created 'a king more sheep than shepherd, and his Elisa a strong spoiled child' (*Ibid.*, Part III/1, p. 123).

20. Mann, p. 253.

21. Georges de Saint-Foix in his *Symphonies of Mozart*, p. 51, insists that all of Wolfgang's music of 1775 was of a lighter vein, and that although his style remained the same 'it was now a question of amusement rather than emotion'. Sainte-Foix considers it a *galante* period.

22. *Dokumente*, p. 137.

23. *Ibid.*, p. 138.

24. *Germany*, II, p. 322.

25. *Dokumente*, p. 137.

26. *Ibid.*, p. 139 ff, and *Addenda*, p. 25. In the same period he composed a section to be added to the overture of *Il Re pastore* to make it a proper symphony (K. 213c/102).

27. See chapter X here, notes 67–68 and relevant passages in the text.

28. *Briefe*, I, p. 532.

29. *Ibid.*, pp. 532–533.

30. *Ibid.*, p. 533.

31. *Briefe*, I, p. 534.

CHAPTER TWELVE

Thamos, König in Aegypten[1]

IN 1773 Tobias Philipp von Gebler (1726-1786), Vice-Chancellor of the Bohemian-Austrian court in Vienna and author of *Der Minister* and *Clementine oder das Testament*, wrote another play which was published in Prague and Dresden and performed on 11 December of the same year by the Karl Wahr company of actors in Pressburg.[2] Entitled *Thamos, König in Aegypten*, it had incidental music by an unknown composer. Actually Gebler hoped that Gluck would have written the music; in fact, from a letter he wrote to his friend Christoph Friedrich Nicolai in Berlin on 31 May 1773, one realizes that he was expecting Gluck to do so. Johann Tobias Sattler set two of the choruses which may have been revised by Gluck, but they seem not to have been used.[3]

In this same period the Mozarts were visiting Vienna,[4] once again seeking commissions either from the court or one of the theatres. Wolfgang composed a great deal during his 1773 summer in Vienna but unfortunately received no requests for music from those who could have helped him most. Of course he often saw and made music for Dr Anton Mesmer, patron of his *Bastien und Bastienne;* and it was probably through Mesmer's circle of friends that he made the acquaintance of Gebler,[5] who invited him to set the *Thamos* choruses to music which he did to the poet's satisfaction. As Gebler wrote his Berlin friend in December of 1773: 'It is his [Mozart's] first draft and the first chorus is very lovely.'[6]

While it is not certain if, in fact, the Karl Wahr group had already made use of Wolfgang's music for their December 1773 performance, it is known that when the play was given again, on Easter Monday, 4 April 1774 at the Kärntnertor Theatre, his choruses were included. Although the theatre poet Christian Hieronymous Moll wrote in the *Historisch-Kritischen Theaterchronik von Wien* on 24 March 1774 that the music was to be by Joseph Starzer, the noted violinist and well-known Hoftheatre composer, he corrected the notice in the 13 April issue.[7] At this time he also reviewed the tragedy, saying it had the 'warmth' and 'dignity' one expected of such heroic dramas, and fortunately was not inordinately long as other *Trauerspiele* tended to be. In his preface Gebler tried to excuse the inclusion of music in his work, but the critic felt this was not necessary: 'The apology for the choruses in the first and fifth acts is not less praiseworthy although to my mind not necessary. They served their purpose – as the music by Herr Karl Mozzart [sic] is artistic and beautifully set – and I believe the author could not wish for more.' While one is surprised Wolfgang's name was so little known as to be incorrectly given by the critic, his next remark is to be regretted even more. Continuing on about the choral music he wrote, 'It is only a pity that it is not better sung.'[8] Reflecting the current enthusiasm for ballet, Gasparo Angiolini (who replaced Noverre as Hoftheatre ballet master in Vienna) choreographed *Le roi et son fermier* for presentation on the same programme.[9]

Thamos received another performance with Wolfgang's music on 4 May at the summer court residence of Laxenburg outside Vienna.[10] A second favourable comment on the music is found soon after, in a letter the poet and playwright Christoph Martin Weiland sent to Gebler on 19 May thanking him for his present of 'the beautiful music to Thamos.'[11] Whether Wolfgang had composed more than just the two choruses by this time is not certain.[12] He was, of course, quite busy in 1774 anyway, doing, among other music, two masses, three symphonies, a divertimento, six sonatas, and a serenade; and then *La finta giardiniera* was made ready for the Carnival season of 1774-1775 in Munich. Once back in Salzburg there was *Il Re pastore* to attend to. Various arias (K. 209, 210, 217, 255, 256) are from the same period, such as the splendid soprano recitative and aria 'Ah, lo previdi! ... Ah, t'invola agl'occhi miei!' (K. 272).

Then on 3 January 1776 the Karl Wahr company came to Salzburg with *Thamos*, and for this performance a closing chorus on a text by Johann Andreas Schachtner was added to the play. The reviewer for the *Theaterwochenblatt für Salzburg* noted on 17 January that Gebler had apparently wanted, in the manner of Klopstock, to 'bring the choruses of the ancient dramatists into heroic tragedy, and to link them up with the scenes in such a way as not to lessen the interest of the action'. He felt the composer had lengthened the fifth act unnecessarily by having too many repetitions and that, instead, 'the choruses should be sung straight through, and would be better interchanged'. Referring to performances of Gebler's play done without music, he added: 'They [the choruses] could also be entirely omitted without hurting the play, as was done in Vienna.'[13]

As mentioned earlier, the period 1775-1777 in Salzburg was not a gratifying one for Wolfgang as his letter of September 1776 to Padre

Martini clearly showed.[14] Not only was Salzburg without the castratos so necessary to serious opera, and without the comic singers essential to *opera buffa*, but, worse, the Archbishop was not well disposed towards the Mozarts. As one reads in Wolfgang's letter written to him in August 1777, on 14 March Leopold had asked permission to travel but had been refused.[15] In June the father again wanted to leave, but Colloredo had given orders that music was to be prepared for a visit of Emperor Joseph II. A later petition was also refused, but now the Archbishop suggested Wolfgang could travel alone, thus implying he was dispensable. The young man's letter, which insisted upon the necessity of his travelling in order to provide for his family which had given him so much, was clearly designed to stir the churchman's moral conscience, but it fared no better and Colloredo now suggested (on 28 August) that both Leopold and Wolfgang leave Salzburg for good.[16] Concerned for his future, Leopold quickly pledged his desire to remain in the Archbishop's employ; but Wolfgang, accompanied this time by his mother, left Salzburg on 23 September 1777 to try his fortune elsewhere.

Their first important stop was Munich, where he tried to obtain a commission through the good offices of Count Joseph Anton Seeau, Superintendent of Court Entertainments, and his enthusiastic supporter, the Bishop of Chiemsee. Prospects at first seemed good, and he wrote a hopeful letter home of his operatic plans on 2 October:

> I should draw up a contract with Count Seeau (all on the advice of my good friends) on the following lines: to compose every year 4 German operas, some buffe, some serie; of which I would have one *sera* or benefit performance of each for myself, as is the custom.[17]

As always when a new prospect for composing presented itself, Wolfgang threw himself into it: 'And how much more popular I should be if I could further the German national theatre! – And through me that would happen.'[18] In the same letter he related that he had gone to hear Piccinni's *La Pescatrice* but, as was usual, in translation. 'They still have no original works. They would also like soon to give a German opera seria – and want me to compose it.'[19] Wolfgang desired very much that this possibility be realized, as he wrote on 11 October: 'I have an inexpressible longing to write an opera again.'[20] And if things didn't work out in Munich, '*eh bien*, then I'll have something in Italy'.[21] His optimism led him to write, 'When I have once written for Naples, everyone will want me.'[22] He confessed, 'I am happier when I have to compose, which is my sole joy and passion'; but also added that composing an opera seemed to him best of all: 'I have only to hear an opera discussed, I have only to be in a theatre, to hear voices – oh, then I am completely beside myself.'[23]

As so often seemed to happen, however, Wolfgang's dreams came to

nothing, and he and his mother left Munich on 10 October for Augsburg to visit friends and relatives of his father.[24] It was not an especially
pleasant stay as he was often poked fun at by the provincial inhabitants.
One happy meeting was with his cousin Maria Anna Thekla, the 'Bäsle'
to whom he later directed his most uninhibited humorous correspondence. The Mozarts soon moved on and were in Mannheim by 30
October where once again they hoped for some position for Wolfgang.
Burney also visited the city and remarked on the 'expense and magnifi-
cence of the court', whose 'palace and offices extend over almost half
the town'.[25] He commented on the orchestra, too, which was 'so
deservedly celebrated throughout Europe':

> I found it to be indeed all that its fame had made me expect: power
> will naturally arise from a great number of hands; but the judicious
> use of this power, on all occasions, must be the consequence of good
> discipline; indeed there are more solo players, and good composers in
> this, than perhaps in any other orchestra in Europe; it is an army of
> generals, equally fit to plan a battle, as to fight it.[26]

Wolfgang could not help but be impressed with the musicians he
found and heard there.[27] Moreover Cannabich was especially friendly
towards him, and the young man felt he had an ally in him. The Elector,
too, seemed to offer hope for his future in Mannheim. Wolfgang wrote
home on 8 November that when he told the Elector 'my greatest desire
is to write an opera here', he was answered, 'that can easily be arranged'.[28] However the plan fell through and Wolfgang thought once
more of Vienna. He wrote his father on 11 January 1778:

> I know for a fact that the Emperor has in mind to establish German
> opera in Vienna and that he is trying hard to find a young Kapell-
> meister, who understands the German language, is talented and able
> to do something new.[29]

But this idea, too, came to nothing and on the repeated urgings of his
father, Wolfgang and his mother, after four and a half months, moved
on to Paris leaving behind, among other attractions of Mannheim,
Aloysia Weber, the young man's first serious love.

On 23 March mother and son arrived in the French capital, home of
the important *Concert spirituel* where Wolfgang heard more music of
the fine quality he had encountered in Mannheim. The director, Jean
Le Gros, was also quite kind to him as were several other acquaintances
(including Baron Friedrich Melchior Grimm, Minister-plenipotentiary
of Saxe-Gothe; Noverre; François Joseph Gossec); however, after an
initial burst of activity which included his 'Paris' Symphony K. 300a/
297 and the ballet *Les Petits Riens* for Noverre, Paris, too, offered little

that was permanent to Wolfgang. His stay there was made especially sad by the loss of his mother on 3 July 1778 whose unexpected death was difficult to explain to his father and sister at home. With no positive prospects for a future elsewhere and after a short stay in Munich, Wolfgang eventually returned to Salzburg on 15 January 1779, where he asked for and received the position of Court Organist, left vacant by the death of Adlgasser,[30] and more or less settled down to life in the provinces and composed some excellent music.

The following December Johann Böhm's company of players came to Salzburg, and Wolfgang showed them Gebler's *Thamos, König in Aegypten* and his music for it. Under Böhm's encouragement, he then rewrote his earlier first chorus for the play which, with his second chorus, was added to four of five instrumental movements intended to be played between the acts of the play – and which Wolfgang may already have composed – and to Schachtner's chorus (which had substituted the fifth and earlier closing instrumental piece in the 1776 Wahr company performance). In this form *Thamos, König in Aegypten* was performed by Böhm during the 1779–1780 Winter season in Salzburg.[31]

Although not common, it was not a completely new idea to have instrumental music accompany a spoken play. Johann Adolf Scheibe (1708–1776) published an article on the subject in the Hamburg weekly *Kritischen Musicus* after having written music for *Polyeucte* and *Mitridate* in 1738, insisting that part of the *entr'acte* music was to be connected with what had just transpired in the play, and part was to deal with the following events. In other words these 'symphonies' in two sections were to lead the audience from one act to another. Next Johann Wilhelm Hertel (1727–1780) composed music to Cronegk's *Olint und Sophronia*, and Johann Friedrich Agricola (1720–1774) to a version of Voltaire's *Semiramis*. Michael Haydn's music for Voltaire's *Zaïre* was heard in Salzburg and Abt Vogler's overture and *entr'actes* to *Hamlet* were presented in Mannheim in 1779. Therefore it was a fashionable trend that Böhm and Wolfgang were interested in following with their *Thamos*. Rather than adhering exclusively to Scheibe's thought on the music, though, they seemed to have also honoured theatre critic Lessing's views of 1767 that the *entr'actes* could also be in one section and related only to what had happened thus far in the play. In any event the instrumentation, he said, as well as the style of the music, was to be decided upon with concern for dramatic relevance.[32]

Gebler, a Freemason, based his *Thamos, König von Aegypten* on an ancient Egyptian tale and made various allusions to the ideals of the new illuministic religion which was spreading everywhere in Germany. The stage settings alone reveal the Eastern atmosphere. As one reads on the score:

The action takes place in the City of the Sun. In Acts I, III, IV and V
the scene represents the Temple of the Sun; and in Act II, a gallery of
the house of the Sun Virgins. The poet has the Temple of the Sun in
the middle of the set; behind it there are the dwellings of the High
Priests; to one side is the house of the Sun Virgins, and to the other
the Royal Castle, and these two buildings are attached to the Temple
of the Sun. The action takes place [in a single day] from morning to
evening.

The plot itself of the *heroisches Drama* continues the impression that
one is dealing with a forerunner of *Die Zauberflöte*. Menes, King of
Egypt, has been deposed by Rameses and, while believed to be dead, is
actually now a High Priest of the Temple of the Sun under the name of
Sethos. Thamos, son of Rameses, is heir to his father's throne and on
attaining majority is in vain urged by Menes' friends to refuse the
position. Pheron, supposedly a friend of Thamos, and Mirza, chief of
the Sun Virgins, conspire to overthrow Thamos. Tharsis, daughter of
Menes whom he believes dead, has been brought up by Mirza under
the name of Sais, and they want to proclaim her queen and marry her
to Pheron. However, Sais loves Thamos and he her. Upon discovering this, Mirza leads Sais to believe Thamos actually prefers another
maiden, Myris, and Sais generously sacrifices her love, and the throne,
to the friend. Thamos, too, refuses to suspect Pheron and gives him
command of the army. But Pheron discloses his plan to Sethos who
will not oppose his young friend Thamos but decides to reveal all to
him. Sais is also sworn to secrecy and told she must choose Pheron; but
she refuses to decide, whereupon Pheron is determined to take the
throne by force. Sais, believing herself unloved, will not stand in
Thamos' way and takes the solemn and irrevocable oath of Sun Virgin.
She and Thamos discover their reciprocated love too late. When Thamos is about to be declared King, Mirza announces that Sais is Tharsis
and the true heir to the throne. Although Thamos is ready to step
down, Sais reveals her oath and chooses Thamos over Pheron to replace
her. When the latter calls his followers to arms, Sethos finally discloses
his identity to everyone's joy. Pheron is led away, Mirza stabs herself,
Menes (as supreme ruler) releases Sais from her vow and joining her to
Thamos puts them both on the throne. Word arrives that Divine
Judgment in the form of lightning has struck Pheron.[33]

In order to study Wolfgang's score, one must know the particular
situations, the scenes, and the people he tried to describe. As he took a
dramatic idea from every act and used it as the basis for his composing,
the instrumental music which follows each act of the spoken drama
therefore contains a 'programme'. To communicate specific emotions
through music is difficult even when there is a text which is able to

clarify any ambiguity of intention, but music without text can only suggest vast areas of emotion, such as tension or serenity, it cannot convey precise sentiments. As Daniel Webb had noted some years earlier in his *Observations on the Correspondence between Poetry and Music*:

> On hearing an overture by Iomelli [sic], or a concerto by Geminiani, we are, in turn, transported, exalted, delighted; the impetuous, the sublime, the tender, take possession of the sense at the will of the composer. In these moments, it must be confessed, we have no determinate idea of any agreement or imitation; and the reason of this is, that we have no fixed idea of the passion to which this agreement is to be referred.[34]

He had already insisted in Remarks on the Beauties of Poetry:

> For as Music has no means of explaining the motives of its various impressions, its imitations of the Manners and Passions must be extremely vague and undecisive: for instance, the tender and melting tones which may be expressive of the Passion of Love, will be equally in unison with the collateral feelings of Benevolence, Friendship, Pity, and the like. Again, how are we to distinguish the rapid movements of Anger, from those of Terror, Distraction, and all the violent agitations of the Soul?[35]

What 23-year-old Wolfgang's attitude on the subject was is impossible to determine, although one may suppose, noting the subjects chosen as themes for representation, that he believed fervently in the descriptive powers of instrumental music; examining the score itself one can see which musical means he felt were capable of executing his intentions. For these reasons the study of *Thamos* is valuable for an understanding of Wolfgang's theory and philosophy of music in a way which an analysis of a true opera cannot be; it also offers us an example of pre-Romantic orchestral programme music.

Written over the *entr'acte* which follows Act I of Thamos (No. 2) one finds Wolfgang's first subject for orchestral depiction:[36] 'The first act finishes with the determination of Mirza and Pheron to place the latter on the throne'. He began by scoring three loud chords separated by rests (a masonic figure of three chords in a key of three flats which foreshadows that used with such good effect in *Die Zauberflöte*) to be played after Mirza's last words, 'Mirza, a woman, does not tremble. You are a man; conquer or die!', and then followed them with an excited *Allegro* in a minor tonality. The three chords, scored for oboes, bassoons, horns, trumpets, strings, and timpani, apparently serve (for the uninitiated) to depict the force of Mirza's 'determination', while the *Allegro* section illustrates the violent emotion caused by her energetic resolution (example 1).

Example 1

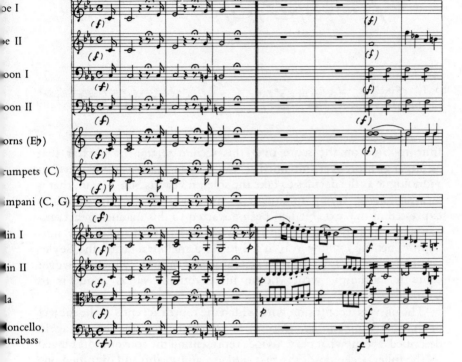

Written after the second act is: 'The noble nature of Thamos is shown at the end of the second act; the third act opens with Thamos and the traitor Pheron.' Here, with a slightly reduced orchestra (no trumpets or timpani) and closer to the manner advocated by Scheibe, the second and third acts are joined through the presentation of two musical ideas which are to represent the 'hypocrisy of Pheron' and the 'honesty of Thamos' (No. 3). The two themes are quite different (a restless chordal idea for Pheron and a lovely oboe solo for Thamos) and, since their significance has been clearly defined, it is easy to identify them with good and evil as Wolfgang passes from one to the other insisting on their diversity (example 2).

'The third act closes with the perfidious dialogue between Mirza and Pheron.' To describe this subject Wolfgang scored for the same orchestra as the Act II *entr'acte* and wrote a brief and agitated *Allegro* (No. 4) which leads into the music intended to be performed at the beginning of the fourth act, a rather interesting piece full of unexpected changes of tempo, of tonality, and of sentiment. Since various lines spoken by Sais ('who exits alone from the house of the Sun Virgins') appear from

Example 2

Violin I
(Pheron)

Oboe I
(Thamos)

time to time on the score over this second section, it is clear that
Wolfgang, moreover, intended to use it as an accompaniment to her
monologue as she decides to take the solemn vow as Sun Virgin, that is
as a *melodrama*, trying to mirror in his music the various meanings
expressed in the text. He had been attracted to this manner of accompanying a spoken drama since 1777 when he saw such a play in Mannheim. Then in 1778 he was asked to do a melodrama for the Seyler
company and, besides being excited at the project (which however
came to nothing), wrote home his favourable ideas about it to
Leopold.[37]

'The universal confusion with which the fourth act ends' is the subject
of the following *entr'acte* (No. 5) in which the two themes are again
described: a somewhat nervous idea representing the conspirators played
by the fuller orchestra of the first *entr'acte*, and a calm and dignified one
for Thamos outlined by the bassoons and violins. The fifth act presents
'The desperation of Pheron, his evil nature, and his death', and, since
the act finishes with a lightning storm, Wolfgang here initially composed an instrumental piece with several rapid scale flourishes to describe
it (No. 7a).

Taking note of the pertinent ideas Wolfgang chose for musical depiction, one is led to believe that he embraced the doctrine of the
affections (discussed in the 'Introduction') whole-heartedly: it would
seem that he was convinced that his music could describe 'hypocrisy', 'a
noble nature', the atmosphere of heated argument; that it could, in
other words, communicate a moral, or emotions, or complex scenes.

For a public who attended a performance of *Thamos*, Wolfgang's
music should have helped to underline the dramatic sense and emotion
of each act. As Webb had written:

But, let Poetry cooperate with Music, and specify the motive of each
particular impression and we are no longer at a loss; we acknowledge
the agreement of the sound with the idea, and general impressions
become specific indications of the Manners and the Passions.[38]

For those who might listen to the music without the recited text, however, it does not seem likely that it could offer any summary of the plot, or any explicit representation of character, situation, or scene. Arteaga, Algarotti, and Webb, to name only three of Wolfgang's contemporaries, felt that instrumental music was not specifically descriptive and, even if its elements were precise, its association with particular sentiments or situations was not. The subtle distinctions between human emotions were agreed to be difficult to express in words, but impossible without them.

One must conclude then that, while Wolfgang was convinced of the power of orchestral music and of the essential role instruments played in increasing or diminishing tension and in aiding the listener to envisage a described scene or to participate in an emotional situation, he would not have held it possible that the interludes of *Thamos, König in Aegypten* could have substituted for the spoken dialogue or that they could have presented exactly what transpired in the course of each act without the dialogue. In an opera both words and music are necessary to communicate the drama, neither of the elements may be eliminated nor should it be considered merely a pleasant 'extra'; but here Wolfgang's music is just that: an addition to *Thamos* which, although not essential to it, is capable of intensifying it. Certainly Wolfgang never intended his music to replace the play or to be performed apart from it, as one realizes from a letter he wrote to his father from Vienna some years later on 15 February 1783 after the work had been unsuccessfully translated into Italian and French:

> I am truly sorry that I cannot make use of the music to *Thamos*. Having failed here, it is destined never to be performed. If it were, it would be only on account of the music, and that is scarcely likely. It is certainly a pity.[39]

Together with the instrumental pieces, composed as has been noted for an orchestra comprised of oboes, bassoons, horns, trumpets, timpani, and strings, Wolfgang wrote an opening chorus, a closing chorus and a chorus inserted in the course of the play (No. 1, No. 7b, No. 6 respectively) which called for, in addition to the rest of the orchestra, flutes and three trombones (alto, tenor, and bass). These three pieces are Wolfgang's most original theatrical treatment of chorus and orchestra. His earlier two choruses for *Thamos* were quite different. While the first underwent changes mainly of improved instrumental and orchestral writing (reflecting Wolfgang's interim visits to Mannheim and Paris as well as his own experiences with the orchestra in Milan), the second is quite different in all respects. Of this revision of a first draft (which Wolfgang never quite completed), Jahn said it proved Wolfgang a true artist who 'after no matter how many experiments in the process of his work, he seizes in the end on what is best for his purpose'.[40] In fact *Thamos* begins, not with the expected overture, but directly with one of these choruses, a solemn sacrifice in the Temple of the Sun where a four-part ensemble of Virgins and High Priests sing the hymn 'Schon weichet dir, Sonne, des Lichtes Feindin, die Nacht' (Night, the enemy of light, already gives way to you, Sun!). The writing for chorus here is varied: accompanied by the entire orchestra, it begins homophonically (example 3) but introduces a phrase of double counterpoint towards the end of the section; next there is a duet for tenors and basses with an active and rhythmically varied string accompaniment; a return to a

Example 3

(contd. overleaf)

four-part texture for the concerted call to the Sun to 'Hear our wish'; a second duet now features sopranos and contraltos, the 'daughters of Egypt'; after a generally homophonic repeat of the pleas to the Sun, a return to the opening section concludes the number. The spectacular scene is made even more grandiose and magnificent by the exuberant treatment of the chorus and orchestra, which are thematically independent of one another: Wolfgang writes generally for both groups contrapuntally in a way which explores their individuality. None of his preceding operatic choruses had had as forceful a musical and dramatic impact.

Chorus No. 6, 'Gottheit, über alle mächtig!' (Divinity, powerful over all!), is conceived on an equally large multi-sectional scale of four

Example 3 (contd.)

tempo changes with various, and independent, vocal and instrumental interweavings. In place of No. 7a, the above-mentioned purely instrumental piece, Wolfgang set Schachtner's new text as a grandiose number for chorus with an opening section for bass solo, a High Priest (who reminds one naturally of Sarastro in *Die Zauberflöte*) whose authoritarian character is emphasized by timpani rolls heard in the orchestral accompaniment as he exhorts the people, saying 'Ihr Kinder des Staubes, erzittert und bebet, bevor ihr euch wider die Götter erhebet!' (Children of dust, you tremble and quake; praise the Gods!: example 4). Following this is a solemn four-part chorus in common time which leads to a brisk *Allegro* in 3/4 where the whole orchestra but above all the strings intensify the affirmed sense of joyful trust in the almighty

Example 4

'gentle Sun' expressed by the voices. A brilliant ending was the rule in the eighteenth-century theatre, but none the less Wolfgang's music must have pleased his audience especially.

In each of these three numbers Wolfgang combined chorus with orchestra but contrapuntally, maintaining their several lines distinct, as though he could not resist the power which resulted from these multiple forces even when writing simply incidental music. The symphonic treatment of the chorus in *Thamos, König in Aegypten*, new in Wolfgang's manner of composing and to be seen again in *Die Zauberflöte*, is not far distant in concept from Beethoven's handling of the chorus in his *Ninth Symphony*. Moreover, these numbers attest that the young man has awakened to the challenge offered by the new classical symphony, encountered in Mannheim and Paris, and its exciting possibilities for compositional development. Tonality is explored deeper and wider, and the usual musical elements, handled contrapuntally – long a favourite procedure with him – now serve to carry the listener further, and more dramatically, than Wolfgang was heretofore capable of doing. This new breadth to his music, in fact, is the most striking feature of the choral numbers in *Thamos*. As Dent observed, Wolfgang learned to think symphonically, and to conceive of music, of whatever genre, 'as a complex organization in which various players sank their individualities to co-operate in giving life to the most direct expression of the composer's brain.[41]

In spite of Wolfgang's concern that *Thamos* would not be given again after its presentation in Salzburg in the winter of 1779-1780, it may have been heard in Berlin in 1786.[42] From 1785 on Böhm certainly used the music in connection with Karl Martin Plümicke's *Lanassa* and it was in this form that Wolfgang heard it in Frankfurt in 1790 where it was done as part of the coronation festivities.[43] His choruses were also later used separately with new, sacred texts: No. 1 both as 'Splendente te, Deus' and 'Preis dir, Gottheit'; No. 6 as 'Jesu, Jesu, rex tremendae Majestatis', 'Gottheit, dir sey Preis und Ehre', and 'Töne laut durch alle Sphären'; and No. 7b as 'Ob fürchterlich tobend' and 'Ne pulvis et cinis'.[44]

Chapter Twelve: Notes

1. K. 336a/345 in *WAM*, Serie V, 12, and *NMA*, Serie II, 6, bd. 1.
2. Now Bratislava: see *Dokumente*, p. 130. For a facsimile of the opening pages of the first edition, see Harald Heckmann's introduction to his edition of *Thamos* in *NMA*, p. xiv.
3. *Ibid.*, p. viii.
4. See Chapter X.
5. See Orel, 'Mozarts Sommerreise ...', p. 47.
6. *Idem.*
7. *Dokumente*, p. 133, and *Addenda*, p. 23.
8. *Dokumente, idem.*
9. *Idem* and *Addenda, idem.*
10. *Dokumente*, p. 134 and *Addenda, idem.*
11. *Dokumente, idem.*
12. He may already have composed the closing instrumental piece later replaced by a choral setting.
13. *Dokumente*, pp. 130 and 139-140.
14. See Chapter XI, notes 27-29 and the related passages in the text.

15. *Briefe*, II, p. 4 and *Dokumente*, pp. 145-146.

16. *Dokumente*, p. 146.

17. *Briefe*, II, p. 29.

18. *Idem*.

19. *Ibid.*, p. 30.

20. *Ibid.*, p. 45.

21. *Idem*.

22. *Ibid.*, pp. 45-46.

23. *Ibid.*, p. 46.

24. *Dokumente*, p. 147.

25. *Germany*, I, p. 81.

26. *Ibid.*, pp. 92-93.

27. Such as Anton Raaf who would star in his *Idomeneo*. See *Briefe*, II, p. 125 ff.

28. *Ibid.*, p. 110.

29. *Ibid.*, p. 222.

30. *Dokumente*, p. 163.

31. *Dokumente*, p. 130. See note 12 here.

32. The information presented here on earlier attempts at incidental theatre music is taken from Gotthold Ephraim Lessing, *Werke*, Part V, 'Hamburgische Dramaturgie' (Berlin, 1925; facs. ed. Hildesheim, 1970): the earlier history including long quotations from Scheibe are on pp. 122-125, and an analysis of Agricola's *Semiramis* (which includes Lessing's own views) appears on p. 125 ff.

33. The complete text is included in *NMA*. Like most Freemasons, Gebler was familiar with Abbé Jean Terrasson's romance *Sethos, histoire ou vie tirée des monumens anecdotes de l'ancienne Egypte*, which may have encouraged him to choose an Egyptian subject. Certainly *Die Zauberflöte* owes much to *Sethos*.

34. (London, 1769), p. 11.

35. (London, 1762), pp. 102-103.

36. As one often finds in Wolfgang's autographs, the verbal indications are in Leopold's hand. The original score is now in the West Berlin Staatsbibliothek Preussischer Kulturbesitz.

37. See his letter of 12 November 1778 in *Briefe*, II, pp. 505-506; it is translated here in Chapter XIII. Mann, p. 248, believes the orchestral music was not intended to be played during the spoken recitation. I think he is mistaken that the actress could not have had pauses in her lines to allow the orchestra to 'catch up': at the moment she is supposed to be reflecting, and pauses, especially ones filled with music, would be most suitable.

38. *Ibid.*, p. 103.

39. *Briefe*, III, p. 256.

40. II, p. 114.

41. P. 18.

42. John, II, p. 104.

43. Heckmann, *idem*.

44. *Ibid.*, p. viii and Köchel 6, p. 778.

CHAPTER THIRTEEN

Zaide[1]

IN THE SAME 1779-1780 period of *König Thamos*, and when Wolfgang was composing much sacred music as required by his position of Court and Cathedral organist, he also began work on another Singspiel. Since setting the delightful *Bastien und Bastienne* in 1768 when he was 12, he had had no further opportunity to consider the genre. True, there had been some talk in Munich and Vienna in 1777 and 1778 of his composing German operas,[2] and this would surely have meant of the Singspiel type as well; however, nothing had come of these rumours. His operatic experience since *Bastien* had been, rather, with Italian serious and comic opera, and then the incidental music for the German play *Thamos, König in Aegypten*. Now, however, partly no doubt because there was hope of its possible performance by the Böhm Truppe which was visiting Salzburg, he was encouraged to write such a work. It also meant collaborating with an old family friend, the court trumpeter Johann Andreas Schachtner, and Wolfgang understandably enjoyed being able to compose for those who appreciated his talents.

Besides being a musician, and playing violin and cello as well as trumpet (a normal combination for wind players at Salzburg), Schachtner (1731-1795) was a writer; in fact he had already collaborated on Wolfgang's operas and would continue to do so: he had written recitatives for *Bastien und Bastienne*, provided a chorus for *Thamos*, and would translate *Idomeneo* into German. In 1777 Voltaire's *Zaïre* was given in Salzburg and this may have given Schachtner the idea for a new play; or perhaps he was familiar with Franz Joseph Sebastiani's Singspiel, *Das Serail, oder Die unvermuthete Zusammenkunft in der Sclaverey zwischen Vater, Tochter und Sohn* set to music in 1779 by Joseph von Friebert and performed by Felix Berner's company in Bozen (or Bolzano). Since only this libretto exists, it is not possible to decide which was Schachtner's direct source of inspiration, and both might even have influenced him.[3] In any event, he provided Wolfgang with a new libretto, perhaps not in the end what the young composer would ideally have preferred (or simply had opportunity to utilize), since he never finished the music, writing only 15 vocal numbers (two of probably three acts);[4] but certainly it was at least that longed-for occasion to write again for the theatre that Wolfgang so desired in Salzburg.

Although initially the Singspiel was any seventeenth-century opera, serious or comic, in the German language, by Wolfgang's time it was quite a distinct genre. Not surprisingly, it was the result of various influences: medieval mystery and passion plays; school dramas; 'jiggs' (song and dance finales to theatrical entertainments); Stegreifkomödie (improvised comedies); and, of course, opera.[5] Apart from the simple efforts of travelling companies, German opera was to be heard only in the Free Cities, such as Hamburg where Reinhard Keiser and Georg Philipp Telemann were its principal exponents. However, due to the hotchpotch often made of such works (pasticcios by several composers which reflected every current foreign musical fashion), German opera came to an end in Hamburg in 1738 as it had already done elsewhere.

Then in the early 1740s, the newer comic genres, the English ballad opera and the French opéra-comique, began to be translated in northern Germany; soon Johann Adam Hiller (1728-1804) composed similar works of German origin which catered to national preferences. With him Leipzig, already the seat of a rich theatrical and musical tradition, became the centre of the new genre. What is probably his best work, Die Jagd of 1770, exhibits the musical characteristics generally associated with the Singspiel: folk-like songs in the main, great use of strophic and dance forms, occasional serious numbers, ensembles, choruses, and a final vaudeville-rondo where each character sings a verse in turn and all join in the chorus.

Hiller and his librettist Weisse had many imitators, as well as other followers who were also innovators. One of the latter was Georg Anton (Jiří) Benda (1722-1795) in Berlin, who introduced accompanied recitatives and melodramas (perhaps originally a French practice) into the Singspiel. His best-known work was Ariadne of 1775.[6] While Emperor Joseph II tried to encourage German opera, and even opened a National Theatre in 1778 with Umlauf's Bergknappen, the Viennese did not fully appreciate the northern style, probably having lived with the more sophisticated style of Italian opera for too long, and so the Singspiel, which was by now a play with incidental if not often irrelevant music, changed in character, librettists making plots more sentimental and composers giving more importance to the music. In short, it tended to become German opera with spoken dialogue. Bastien und Bastienne, based on Favart's French comedy, had been of the earlier type, whereas Wolfgang's new effort reflected later developments.

Found among his manuscripts after his death, Wolfgang's Singspiel was not only incomplete but untitled as well. The composer's widow then sold it, together with all her husband's music in her possession, to Johann Anton André who published it in 1838 as Zaide, giving it as its

title the name of its principal female character, and Wolfgang's work
has been known in this way ever since.[7]

The plot of *Zaide* shows similarity with Wolfgang's later Singspiel
Die Entführung aus dem Serail, as it too deals with Turks, a popular
eighteenth-century subject, and a young girl in love who escapes from
a Sultan's harem.[8] Gomatz (tenor) is forced to serve the Sultan Soliman
(tenor), but in doing so he falls in love with Zaide (soprano), a maiden
of the harem. She returns his affection, and together they manage to
convince the Sultan's guardian Allazim (bass) to help them escape.
Unfortunately, the Sultan discovers their plan and has them brought
back. Wolfgang's manuscript leaves off with the three fugitives begging the Sultan's forgiveness. Other characters are the slow and suspi-
cious Osmin (bass), four slaves (tenors) and Zaram, Head of the Guards
(a speaking role).

The melodies of *Zaide* offer occasional vocal *fioriture* but are, for the
most part, simple and thus conform to the style of the lighter German
Singspiel. But since Wolfgang writes them contrapuntally for voice
and orchestra, they assume an importance, if not a gravity, uncharac-
teristic of the earlier genre, which does not allow the work to be folk-
like or pastoral even though it lacks the 'affections' or pretensions of
Italian opera. While the style of *Ascanio in Alba* was ambiguous due to
the mixing of *opera seria* and *buffa*, the style of *Zaide* is uncertain, an
uncertainty which one notices both in the wide variety of its musical
forms, taken from serious as well as comic opera, and – above all – in its
musical language, which often seems a forced marriage between simple
melodies and a complex texture. With this in mind, one can examine
an aria for Gomatz, for example No. 4 'Rase Schicksal, wüte immer'
(Run, forever raging Fate) where the vocal part, generally syllabic and
rhythmically simple, is inserted into an interesting but too 'important'
and contrapuntal a setting given the genre (example 1).

Example 1

At the same time counterpoint is also used to good effect in *Zaide*, for example, when it serves to affirm simultaneously different ideas expressed by diverse roles. Wolfgang had already taken advantage of the technique in the third-act finale of *La finta semplice* and in the trio of *Lucio Silla*; now in *Zaide* it appears in the first section of the trio 'O selige Wonne' (No. 8, O blessed delight) where each character, when he has a different text, may be given a different musical line; but then when Zaide, Gomatz and Allazim are in agreement that 'Möchten doch einst Ruh' und Friede nach so vieler Qual und Pein unser Treue Preise sein' (If only peace and tranquillity might be, one day after so much grief and pain, the prize for our fidelity) predominant use is made of the technique of 'togetherness', homophony. The independence of the musical parts as a means to indicate independence of thought is seen even more in the quartet 'Freundin, stile deine Thränen' (No. 15, Friend, quiet your tears) which, through counterpoint, permits the Sultan to deal with the different cases of the lovers Zaide and Gomatz, and of their protector Allazim (example 2).

Example 2

(contd. overleaf)

Example 2 (contd.)

In spite of the ambiguity which results from having simple lines set in a contrapuntal texture (definitely a shortcoming in a lighter genre unless one is dealing with an ensemble where the technique may be used to good effect), there are still some noteworthy aspects of the score which must be indicated. First and foremost is Wolfgang's now ever-present intent to characterize the roles. Comparison between two arias, for example No. 10 for Osmin and No. 11 for Soliman, will show his approach to be different in the case of each character. The first aria, 'Wer hungrig bei der Tafel sitz' (Who hungry sits at table), offers music which is not only syllabic but full of repeated notes, both for the voice as well as the strings, and thus insists on the simplistic personality of Osmin. He is so contented (now that he is 'seated famished at the laden table') that he laughs continually and his phrases of 'ha ha ha ...' are accompanied by an orchestra that also tries to 'laugh' in *staccato* notes (example 3). In the following aria, 'Ich bin so bös' als gut' (I am as evil as I am good), the bouncy 6/8 rhythm adopted for Osmin would not be suitable to characterize the contrasting personality of the majestic Sultan Soliman; and, therefore, not only is there a change to common time but also now a fuller orchestra (added woodwinds and horns) is em-

Example 3

ployed in creating a contrapuntal accompaniment, varied and more dramatic than before, to suggest this important and more complex person as he describes himself and reveals his readiness to use any means of punishment necessary to avenge his anger (example 4).

In *Zaide* one also notices that, within the vocal and instrumental contrapuntal texture, there are instruments which, by reinforcing or commenting on the vocal part, aid in interpreting the drama: for example, in No. 3 'Ruhe sanft' (Placid calm) the solo oboe and bassoon melodically second Zaide's gentle urgings to Gomatz to sleep; in No. 9 'Der stolze Löw' lässt sich zwar zähmen' (The proud lion lets himself be dominated), trumpets and timpani give emphasis to the Sultan's anger. In fact, the instrumentation of *Zaide* is in general most interesting. Added to the usual strings are flutes, oboes, bassoons, horns, trumpets, and timpani which are employed in various combinations. Without doubt, Wolfgang's mastery of the orchestra, very evident in this score not only for the instruments used but for the way in which they are employed to achieve a wide vocabulary of timbres and of dynamic effects, is due in great part to his recent visits to Paris and Mannheim, as well as to his earlier experiences with the large orchestral forces of the

Example 4

Milan Opera House and to the symphonic music he heard in Vienna in 1773.

In the manner of Benda, and perhaps imitating a work of his seen in Mannheim, *Medea*, Wolfgang included two *Melodramen* (lines spoken over an orchestral accompaniment) in *Zaide*. Rousseau had treated the recitative of *Pygmalion* (Lyons, 1770; Paris, 1775) in this way; at the same time and independently of the effort in France, Brandes had Schweitzer set Gerstenberg's *Ariadne* as a melodrama for his non-singing actress wife (Weimar, 1772). But Benda's music for the same poem was that which was finally used, and it met with great success, as Jahn asserts, 'mainly due to Benda's expressive music, which all joined in praising, ... [and] none of his successors have been able to produce a similar effect'.[9]

Through a letter Wolfgang wrote to his father from Mannheim on 12 November 1778, we know that this kind of composition attracted him too:

> The Seyler Troupe, that you will already know, is here. Herr von Dalber is the Director. He won't let me leave till I have composed a Duodrama for him and, in fact, I didn't have to consider the question long, because I have always wanted to compose this type of drama. I don't know, but didn't I ever write to you, the first time that I was here, about this type of piece? It then gave me much pleasure to see such a piece presented two times; in fact, nothing ever so surprised me, because I had always thought that something similar should not have had any effect. As you well know, one doesn't sing, but one declaims, and the music is like an obbligato [ie accompanied] recitative; sometimes one also speaks while the music plays and then the effect is magnificent. ... Now you can imagine what joy to do what I have always wanted to do! You know what my idea would be? One ought to treat the major part of the recitatives in opera in this manner and only sometimes, when the words can be well expressed with music, to sing the recitative.[10]

While generally in his operatic accompanied recitatives, Wolfgang used only strings, for the melodramas of *Zaide* he also employed woodwinds in the first and woodwinds and brass in the second. The text, however, was probably declaimed most of the time without the direct accompaniment of the orchestra which, instead, played between one textual phrase and the next, a solution to the problem of covering the voice with the sound of the instruments. Wolfgang is also very attentive to the subtle changes in sentiment expressed by each actor, and the instrumental part continually changes metre, tonality, and spirit to adapt itself to the text. The two sections of melodrama, No. 2 'Unerforchliche Fügung' (Inscrutable submission) for Gomatz and No. 9

Zaide entflohen?' (Zaide run away?) for Soliman, give evidence, more than does almost anything else, of Wolfgang's dedicated interest in drama and his conviction in the capability of music to communicate it.

Having weighed the positive and negative aspects of the score, one must admit that *Zaide* proves that at this stage of his development Wolfgang's approach to composing and his style of composition is too extended and varied for the simple Singspiel, at least for the way the genre is conceived in this case. Or perhaps one must admit that Italian *opera seria* and *opera buffa* were still too much in his veins and that he had not found proper expression for the quite different style of Singspiel. In either case, since at the moment he is apparently reluctant to sacrifice musical interest, or write banal music for banal plays, he must choose libretti which are less naive and allow for greater musical involvement and development than the one he was given on this occasion.

At the end of 1780, when Wolfgang was hard at work in Munich at *Idomeneo*, his next operatic effort, he apparently wrote to his father about *Zaide*, for Leopold answered on 11 December:

> As for Schachtner's play, it is not possible to do anything at the moment as the theatres are closed [due to Maria Theresa's death on 29 November], and there is nothing to be had from the Emperor.

He added that this was probably just as well 'as the music is not finished', implying that Wolfgang should still work on *Zaide*. Leopold's old dream of having Wolfgang compose something for Vienna cropped up again as he continued: 'Besides, who knows, this opera may give you an opportunity later of getting to Vienna.'[11]

When Leopold was planning to travel to Munich for the opening of *Idomeneo*, Wolfgang wrote to him to 'bring Schachtner's operetta. There are some people who come to the Cannabichs who might just as well hear something of this kind.'[12] However on 18 April 1781 he had to admit that 'there is nothing to be done [about *Zaide*]'. In fact, Gottlieb Stephanie had offered him a new libretto, since Wolfgang had told him that 'except for the long dialogue [of Schachtner's play], which could easily be altered, the piece was very good, but not suitable for Vienna where people prefer comic pieces'.[13] Once again Vienna had said No to Wolfgang, this time even managing to discourage him from finishing a work.

The happy ending to *Zaide* was Stephanie's replacement libretto, *Die Entführung aus dem Serail*, which offered Wolfgang a better play to set to music. At least *Zaide* had provided him with some experience in composing a Singspiel and no doubt his thinking about the genre was the better for it. Certainly he seems to have revised his conviction about the effectiveness of melodrama, as he never wrote another.

★   ★   ★

After *Zaide* Wolfgang was to live little more than ten years, but, as is so well known to audiences the world over, the decade would see the creation of his greatest operas. The works discussed here, on the other hand, are not acclaimed in the same manner and have even been called (and not just for the sake of chronology) 'early' works. None the less, they comprise the majority of Mozart's operas; moreover, they provide the necessary background to our understanding both of the genres he later set to music and the way in which he composed them. As has been seen, the 14 years which separated *Die Schuldigkeit des ersten Gebotes* from *Idomeneo* were dedicated to developing Wolfgang's talents by providing him with the most complete musical education possible: he studied score after score, he heard music almost constantly, he applied himself to acquiring special techniques – counterpoint, orchestral writing, ways of extending musical sections ('development') – and so forth. And he tried his hand and proved his new skills in composition after composition. Masterpieces such as *Die Entführung aus dem Serail*, *Le Nozze di Figaro*, and *Don Giovanni* were not, could not have been, his first attempts at *dramma in musica*.

Even the sketchiest biography shows Wolfgang's life to have been filled with opera. True, he wrote other genres, and the orchestral and chamber music repertoires would be sadly depleted without his contributions. But it must also be evident that in the years prior to *Idomeneo* his major efforts were given to opera: this was the exciting world in which he wished to participate and from which he longed for acclaim. It was an all-consuming interest Mozart was not to lose in the next ten years although circumstance did force him to modify it. Wolfgang had considered *opera buffa*, *opera seria*, Singspiel, and their various off-shoots often before *Zaide*, and – as we leave him – he is simply awaiting other opportunities to do so yet again; however, in the future he will be fortified with the maturity which was his as a result of these earlier experiences.

Chapter Thirteen: Notes

1. K. 336b/344 in *WAM*, Serie V, 11, and *NMA*, Serie II, 5, bd. 10.
2. See his letters of 2 October 1777 and 11 January 1778, *op. cit.*
3. Alfred Einstein, 'Die Text-Vorlage zu Mozarts *Zaide*', *Acta Musicologica* 8 (1936), pp. 33–35 gives changes made to the Botzen libretto; see also Friedrich-Heinrich Neumann's introduction to his critical edition of *Zaide* in *NMA*, p. vii; and Osborne, p. 134. Jahn, II, p. 116, also suspected a French source for Schachtner's work.

4. Jahn, *idem*, stated plainly that 'Schachtner's libretto is truly insufferable'. Wolfgang's autograph, now in the West Berlin Staatsbibliothek Preussischer Kulturbesitz, with very few cancellations proceeds in a clear, small and adult hand to the end of the quartet No. 15 and then stops. All parts up to that point are complete (except of course the recitative texts which are missing), and nothing is begun after. It is as though his creativity carried him to that point and he had not a single idea (or encouragement or motive) to go on.

5. For a brief but clear history of the Singspiel, see Thomas Evans' article in *Grove's Dictionary of Music and Musicians*, VII, p. 814 ff which in turn owes much to the Augsburg Kapellmeister Hans Michael Schletterer's study *Das deutsche Singspiel* (Augsburg, 1863; facs. ed. Hildesheim, 1975). See also Anna Amalie Abert's chapter on 'German Opera' in *The New Oxford History of Music* (London, 1973), vol. VII, pp. 65-97, which contains many musical examples.

6. Schletterer includes a list of eighteenth-century *Melodramen* in note 81 on p. 125.

7. André had Schachtner's text altered by Karl Gollmick and added an overture and closing chorus to complete the Singspiel (see Jahn, *idem*, and Neumann, *idem*). In this form *Zaide* had its first performance in Frankfurt on 27 January 1866.

8. For example, both Gluck's *La Rencontre* of 1764 and Haydn's *L'incontro improvviso* of 1775 (actually based on the same tale) dealt with a seraglio.

9. P. 123. See also Zdeňka Pilková, 'Das Melodram Jiří Bendas im Zusammenhang mit der Mozart problematic', *W. A. Mozart* (Prague, 1956), pp. 85-94.

10. *Briefe*, II, pp. 505-506.

11. *Briefe*, III, p. 53.

12. Letter of 18 January 1781: *Briefe*, III, pp. 90-91.

13. *Briefe*, III, pp. 107-108.

Index

Since they are continually referred to, and therefore will need no help to be found, the authors of the following works have not been listed in the Index:

Wilhelm A. Bauer and Otto E. Deutsch, *Mozart, Briefe und Aufzeichnungen*, 7 vols. (Kassel, 1962–75)

Otto Erich Deutsch, *Mozart. Die Dokumente seines Lebens* (Kassel, 1961); and its *Addenda und Corrigenda* (Kassel, 1978) by Joseph Heinz Eibl

Lugwig Ritter von Köchel, *Chronologisch-thematisches Verzeichnis sämtlicher Tonwerke Wolfgang Amadeus Mozarts*, 6th ed. (Wiesbaden, 1964)